RESILIENCE

*Learning from People with Disabilities
and the Turning Points in Their Lives*

Edited by Gillian A. King, Elizabeth G. Brown,
and Linda K. Smith

Foreword by John A. LaPorta

Praeger Series in Health Psychology
Barbara J. Tinsley, Series Editor

Westport, Connecticut
London

Library of Congress Cataloging-in-Publication Data

Resilience : learning from people with disabilities and the turning points in their lives /
   edited by Gillian A. King, Elizabeth G. Brown, and Linda K. Smith ; foreword by John
   A. LaPorta.
      p. cm.—(Praeger series in health psychology, ISSN 1543-2211)
   Includes bibliographical references and index.
   ISBN 0-275-97943-1 (alk. paper)
   1. Resilience (Personality trait) 2. Meaning (Psychology) I. King, Gillian A., 1953–
II. Brown, Elizabeth G. III. Smith, Linda K. IV. Series.
   BF698.35.R47   2003
   155.9'16—dc21   2002044543

British Library Cataloguing in Publication Data is available.

Library of Congress Catalog Card Number: 2002044543
ISBN: 0–275–97943–1
ISSN: 1543-2211

First published in 2003

Praeger Publishers, 88 Post Road West, Westport, CT 06881
An imprint of Greenwood Publishing Group, Inc.
www.praeger.com

Printed in the United States of America

(∞)™

The paper used in this book complies with the
Permanent Paper Standard issued by the National
Information Standards Organization (Z39.48–1984).

10   9   8   7   6   5   4   3   2   1

Copyright Acknowledgments

Grateful acknowledgement is made to the following for permission to reprint published
material:

Love and Understanding © 1988, 1989 by G. Keeler and J. Cuddy. All rights administered by Warner Music Canada Ltd., 3751 Victoria Park Avenue, Scarborough, ON M1W
3Z4. All rights reserved. Used by permission.

Moving Pictures © 1979 Davray Music Ltd. All rights administered by Sony/ATV Music
Publishing, 8 Music Square West, Nashville, TN 37203. All rights reserved. Used by
permission.

CONTENTS

ILLUSTRATIONS

FIGURES

TABLES

FOREWORD

North American society is undergoing rapid and unprecedented change, which creates a heightened need for people to be able to adjust to changing circumstances. This book explores the nature of resilience and how people create a sense of meaning in everyday life. It provides an important and topical message about the benefits of adversity. Challenging experiences can lead to new realizations and clarify the path one wants to take in life.

Our contemporary society accepts the philosophy that life is what we make of it. The process of defining and creating meaning in our lives is not, however, a simple one. Creating a sense of meaning is even more complex when one has a disability. But, as this book clearly indicates, having a disability adds a critical stimulating element to the mix—adversity. Resilience exhibited in the face of challenge is a powerful force that propels individuals on their journey to finding what is truly important in life.

The book speaks to the strengths and capacities of individuals with disabilities, a notion that too often surprises our society. The authors have learned, from their research and interaction with the six women and nine men profiled in this book, that having a disability is not necessarily a tragedy. Rather, in a revolutionary reframing, the authors have come to consider this very personal experience as not only life-changing, but also life-enhancing. Is this an optimistic, new-age twist on century-old thinking? Not at all.

The authors questioned what gave direction to the life journeys of people with disabilities. They found that significant life experiences—or turning points—are key vectors in the search for meaning in life. This book appraises and expands upon the insights gained from a detailed qualitative study that provided the viewpoints of fifteen individuals with disabilities.

The authors were captivated by the simple truths they learned from this exploration. They realized the commonality and application of these helpful aspects for us all. This book was born out of their passion to share this knowledge. This text challenges accepted beliefs about people and their existence, resulting in a new awareness about the diversity and commonality of human experience.

Aimed primarily at the college and university environments, this work will also appeal to people with disabilities and their families. Personally, I think it is a must read for those who plan to or currently provide educational, health, or social services for individuals with disabilities.

John A. LaPorta, Ph.D.
Chief Executive Officer
Thames Valley Children's Centre

SERIES PREFACE

The field of health psychology experienced tremendous growth in the last two decades. This growth reflects an increasing recognition of the many social and psychological factors affecting health and illness, and the realization that physical health can no longer be addressed solely from a biomedical perspective.

The books in this series focus primarily on how social, psychological, and behavioral factors influence physical health. These volumes will serve as important resources for lay readers, as well as students and scholars in psychology, medicine, sociology, nursing, public health, social work, and related areas.

Series Editor, Barbara Tinsley
Professor of Psychology
Chair, Human Development Program,
University of California at Riverside

Editorial Board

Andres Baum
Professor of Psychology and Psychiatry
University of Pittsburgh
Deputy Director,
University of Pittsburgh Cancer Institute

Vicki Helgeson
Associate Professor of Psychology
Carnegie Mellon University

Matthew Burg, Assistant
Clinical Professor, Psychology
Yale University School of Medicine
Chief, Health Psychology Section,
VA Connecticut Healthcare System

Jerry Suls
Professor of Psychology
Coordinator of Graduate Studies
University of Iowa

ACKNOWLEDGMENTS

WE WOULD LIKE TO EXPRESS OUR THANKS TO...

The study participants, who gave their time, energy, and selves to reflect and share their experiences. We thank you for your candor and insight.
The groups providing financial support:

- The St. Mary's Fund of London, Ontario, financially supported the research study that forms the basis of this book. This Fund was a partnership venture between the Long Term Division of the Ontario Ministry of Health, St. Joseph's Health Centre of London, and the community. The aim of the fund was to support projects that develop and enhance services required by elderly people, adults with disabilities, or children who are technologically dependent.
- The Canadian Occupational Therapy Foundation awarded a publication grant that helped us to write this book.
- Thames Valley Children's Centre provided additional funds that allowed us to prepare this book.

The community agencies that assisted us in recruiting study participants:

- Action League of Physically Handicapped Adults (ALPHA)
- Cheshire Homes of London, Inc.

- Employment Training Access Centre
- Independent Living Centre London & Area
- Participation House Support Services
- Persons United for Self Help (PUSH)

Our employers who supported us in this research endeavor and in the writing of this book:

- Thames Valley Children's Centre
- Huron University College
- The University of Western Ontario
- Child and Parent Resource Institute

Our colleagues who assisted us with various aspects of preparing this book—Michelle Servais and Melissa Currie.

Our families, friends, and coworkers for their interest, patience, and encouragement.

INTRODUCTION:
AN INVITATION TO LEARN
FROM THE TURNING POINTS OF
PEOPLE WITH DISABILITIES

Gillian A. King, Elizabeth G. Brown,
and Linda K. Smith

> People with disabilities are just like everyone else.
> —Study participant

Each day we tell stories. We do so when we talk with others at home, work, school, and in our neighborhoods. The stories we tell are not complete life chronicles. They are snippets of our experiences, events, thoughts, and feelings at a particular time and place. They are capsules of the experiences that are most important or meaningful to us—the things that we value. Stories about meaningful experiences also are told in a more formal way in newspapers, on radio and television, and in books.

Stories offer windows through which we can see into each other's lives. If we listen carefully, we will hear both unique and commonly shared experiences. Stories illuminate our attitudes, beliefs, and assumptions. They can teach us new things about our world, each other, and ourselves. Stories reveal our history and our hopes. They bring to life our struggles and triumphs and our hopes and dreams. Through telling stories, we create meaning: we make sense of our world and experiences. We have much to learn from the stories others share with us.

This book is based on a research study in which nine men and six women with disabilities were interviewed about the turning points in their lives and how they dealt with these critical life events and experiences (King et al., 2003; Specht, King, Brown, & Foris, 2002; Specht, Miller Polgar, Willoughby, King, & Brown, 2000). The book explores the nature of resilience and adaptation to change by looking at the turning points of people with the chronic health conditions of cerebral palsy, spina bifida, and attention deficit disorder. Knowing what factors help and hinder people at critical life junctures can show us all how to prepare for both unexpected life events (such as sudden death, divorce, and loss) and the natural life stages most of us face (such as finishing school, leaving home, or retiring).

Using turning points in life as the vehicle, this book explores the ways in which we create or acquire meaning in our lives and the things that help us accomplish this. By weaving the compelling stories and experiences of people with disabilities into what is known about topics as varied as resilience, self-help, mentoring, caregiving, motivation, and social support, the book illustrates how meaning in life is created. The book proposes that we all create meaning in three fundamental ways that reflect how we involve, engage, and commit ourselves in life. These are the processes of belonging, doing, and understanding ourselves and our world.

There is a clear link between being resilient and feeling that everyday life is meaningful. Resilient individuals have purposes. They find challenge and enjoyment in commitment to activities and relationships with others, and thereby create a sense of meaning for themselves and their lives. This making of meaning is a basic building block of resilience and a central aspect of many theories of personal growth and change following challenge or crisis in life (O'Leary, Alday, & Ickovics, 1998). By establishing meaning in everyday life, resilient people build bridges from present-day trials and hardships to the vision of a better future. This sense of meaning helps the troubles of the present feel more manageable and provides hope for the future.

The authors are a group of educators, health care managers, researchers, and service providers who work in the rehabilitation field. We have backgrounds in psychology, social work, occupational therapy, and speech-language pathology. Because we represent a variety of academic disciplines, we bring diverse perspectives to the writing of the chapters in this book. Our own biases, assumptions, and preferred ways of thinking about the world have undoubtedly affected the interpretations we have made and the conclusions that are drawn in this book. We have, however, done our utmost to keep the interpretations grounded in the stories told by the study participants.

Why did we write this book? It is based on a research study that provided fascinating insights into the topic of resilience, which we felt would be of interest to a wide range of people (beyond the typical research article in an academic journal). We initiated this research study on resilience because of our previous research experiences. We knew that many people with disabilities do well in life—they reach their goals and dreams and are viewed by themselves and others as successful (King, Cathers, Miller Polgar, MacKinnon, & Havens, 2000). Yet research studies indicate that having a disability puts people at greater risk for poor outcomes in life, such as unemployment, underemployment, poverty, or social isolation (Clark & Hirst, 1989; Fawcett, 1996; Hechtman, 1991). We wanted to find out what makes people resilient (i.e., able to bounce back from adverse events) and what supports from others, personal characteristics, and sequence of events assists in this process of resilience. The idea of turning points—critical life events and experiences—seemed like a good way to see what helps and hinders people over their life course.

When we heard what people said about their turning points, we were caught up in their experiences, struggles, and triumphs. We learned a great deal as we considered how people made sense of and got through their turning points. We were particularly struck by the commonalities in people's experiences, despite their unique personalities and life circumstances. Common themes emerged even though people's stories of their turning points were different and unique. When the study participants met together to discuss the findings, some of them also were struck by the similarity of their experiences.

In *Stones from the River,* a novel by Ursula Hegi (1997), the protagonist is a young girl with a disability. This young girl uses a metaphor of stones in a river to communicate the same concept of surface differences but underlying commonalities. From the surface of the river, the girl sees the river as a whole but, when she looks under the surface, she sees the different stones that make up the riverbed. Our special differences make us unique but we should not ignore the fundamental commonalities in how people view and deal with life experiences. These are the three themes of belonging, doing, and understanding that we heard when we listened and reflected on people's stories of their turning points in life.

We begin the book by describing the study in which these stories were shared. In chapter 1, "How We Got Here," Jacqueline Specht, Janice Miller Polgar, and Gillian King describe the research study on which this book is based. They discuss previous research on resilience and explain why and how we did the study. They outline the process that was used to gather the stories and discover the common themes. You, the reader, are introduced to the people whose stories you will come to know. Information about the nature and effects of cerebral palsy, spina bifida, and attention deficit disorder is provided. We use the word *disability* to refer to these chronic health conditions because this was the term generally used by study participants. Chronic health conditions have a biochemical or physiological basis and are of a long-term nature (World Health Organization, 2001). Attention deficit disorder sometimes is assumed to have less significant effects on people's lives than conditions such as cerebral palsy, but this is not always the case, as the stories shared by study participants will show.

Chapter 2, by Gillian King, Tamzin Cathers, Elizabeth Brown, and Elizabeth MacKinnon, is "Turning Points: Emotionally Compelling Life Experiences." This chapter explores the nature of people's turning points along with the settings and times of life in which they occurred. The chapter considers the role of emotions in these experiences, and how turning points start and end. The major focus is on how study participants gave meaning to life events and came to terms with their critical life experiences. Some of these experiences involved their disabilities and some did not. The chapter highlights commonalities in people's descriptions of life-changing moments and indicates how the meaning of turning points of people with disabilities is similar to those of people without disabilities. The chapter focuses on the importance of belonging, the necessity of doing things that are important to us, and the value of understanding ourselves and others.

Chapter 3, "The Resilient Self—What Helps and What Hinders?" by Colleen Willoughby, Elizabeth Brown, Gillian King, Jacqueline Specht, and Linda Smith, looks at the factors that help or hinder us in life. In the study, participants shared what was helpful and what constricted them during their life journey. They mentioned the importance of being believed in, valued, validated, listened to, loved, encouraged, and understood by another person. The chapter also discusses the important roles of personality traits, how people view themselves, and spiritual beliefs.

In chapter 4, " 'Choral Music' for Community Change," Elizabeth MacKinnon, Elizabeth Brown, Janice Miller Polgar, and Lisa Havens consider how members of society can respond to the concerns that were shared by people in the study. They had many suggestions for change. This chapter builds on their recommendations and challenges all of us to consider what we can do to encourage attitudes and actions that broaden understanding and inspire a community that welcomes and celebrates the diversity of its members.

Chapter 5 ties things together. In "Tying It All Together: Frames of Reference and Meaning in Life," Gillian King describes how the three common ways in which we create and make meaning in our lives—belonging, doing, and understanding—are intricately connected. She explores how different professional disciplines, including psychology, social work, and occupational therapy, emphasize the primacy of one or more of these paths to meaning in their explanations of various life experiences. The chapter discusses the various frames of reference or points of view that professional disciplines and individuals adopt to make sense of their worlds. The chapter concludes by focusing on the importance of our participation in multiple roles and endeavors, because this is how we develop our resilience and make meaning in our lives. Through our involvement in an array of work, leisure, and social activities, we feel that we belong, contribute to our communities, and come to understand ourselves and other people.

The book will take you, the reader, on an interesting journey toward understanding turning points, resilience, and meaning in life. Along the way, you'll see that people have fundamental commonalities but are uniquely different; how turning points and change are more the status quo than are continuities in life; how turning points often reflect the dynamic interplay between loss and gain; and how personal qualities, social support, and spiritual beliefs can lead to resiliency. You'll see how frames of reference both provide structure to our world and limit our perspectives, how adversity can lead to meaning in life, and how meaning in life is created and maintained.

Hearing people's stories will provide insights into the experience of having a disability. We all have various assumptions about what having a disability means. We may believe, for example, that the major difficulties facing people with disabilities are their physical challenges, and we therefore may underestimate the role of other people's attitudes, expectations, and reactions. It is important to note that this book is about resilience and meaning in people's lives—people who happen to have disabilities. Sometimes their turning points reflect experiences related to their disabilities, and sometimes they do not. People with disabilities face some turning points that are no different from those of people without disabilities, including divorce and marriage. Their stories do, however, illuminate the added challenges they face.

Hearing people's stories about turning points can be powerful. People's stories can make us pause and look at our own lives. Hearing about others' experiences can spur us to think about what has helped and hindered us in our own turning points. We can be challenged by what we hear from others. Their stories may confirm our own thoughts and experiences, or may encourage us to refocus our energies in our daily lives.

This is an invitation to you to listen to stories of people with disabilities and to consider what these stories tell us about universal human experiences. Students in the applied health and social sciences fields, educators, people with special needs and their families, and other members of the community can benefit from the insights shared in this book. By challenging our beliefs about people and life, we can create new awareness about the diversity and commonality of human experience. This book promotes a greater understanding of the profound similarity in how we experience the world—the fundamental aspects of life that are important to us all.

REFERENCES

Clark, A., & Hirst, M. (1989). Disability in adulthood: Ten year follow-up of young people with disabilities. *Disability, Handicap & Society, 4*, 271–283.

Fawcett, G. (1996). *Living with disability in Canada: An economic portrait.* Hull, QC: Human Resources Development Canada.

Hechtman, L. (1991). Resilience and vulnerability in long term outcome of attention deficit hyperactive disorder. *Canadian Journal of Psychiatry, 36*, 415–421.

Hegi, U. (1997). *Stones from the river.* New York: Simon & Schuster.

King, G., Cathers, T., Brown, E., Specht, J.A., Wllloughby, C., Miller Polgar, J., MacKinnon, E., Smith, L. K. & Havens, L. (2003). Turning points and protective processes in the lives of people with chronic disabilities. *Qualitative Health Research, 13*(2), 184-206.

King, G., Cathers, T., Miller Polgar, J., MacKinnon, E., & Havens, L. (2000). Success in life for older adolescents with cerebral palsy. *Qualitative Health Research, 10*(6), 734–749.

O'Leary, V.E., Alday, C.S., & Ickovics, J.R. (1998). Models of life change and posttraumatic growth. In R.G. Tedeschi, C.L. Park, & L.G. Calhoun (Eds.), *Posttraumatic growth: Positive changes in the aftermath of crisis* (pp. 127–152). Mahwah, NJ: Lawrence Erlbaum.

Specht, J., King, G., Brown, E., & Foris, C. (2002). The importance of leisure in the lives of persons with congenital physical disabilities. *American Journal of Occupational Therapy, 56*(4), 436–445.

Specht, J.A., Miller Polgar, J., Willoughby, C., King, G., & Brown, E. (2000). A retrospective look at the educational experiences of individuals with disabilities. *Exceptionality Education Canada, 10*(3), 25–39.

World Health Organization. (2001). *International classification of functioning, disability and health.* Geneva, Switzerland: World Health Organization.

Chapter 1

HOW WE GOT HERE

*Jacqueline Specht, Janice Miller Polgar,
and Gillian A. King*

What do we know about people who do well in life despite the fact that they have faced some type of adversity? The purpose of this chapter is to show the authors' journey from this initial general question to how we arrived at doing a qualitative research study involving extensive interviews with people with disabilities.

We use the word *disability* to refer to chronic health conditions or disorders that have a biochemical or physiological basis, are of a long-term nature, and may affect a person's engagement in activities and roles in life. More appropriately, we should use the term *chronic health condition,* following the World Health Organization's (2001) International Classification of Functioning.

THE BEGINNING

Perhaps it is best to start at the beginning. This research study was the logical next step in a series of studies that we had been involved with in the past. We had investigated various issues of importance to children and youth with disabilities. These included topics such as how people with disabilities view themselves (i.e., their self-concept, self-esteem, and self-efficacy) (King, Shultz, Steel, Gilpin, & Cathers, 1993; Specht, King, & Francis, 1998) and what *success in life* means to them (King, Cathers, Miller Polgar, MacKinnon, & Havens, 2000). The findings showed that some of the children and adolescents fared well, but others did not. We

decided it was time to investigate the factors and supports that give individuals with disabilities the strength to cope with adversity. The term
resilience describes this notion of doing well in life despite adversity
(Garmezy & Masten, 1991; Rutter, 1985).

Situations that may involve adversity include being raised in poverty,
being hospitalized for surgery or a chronic illness, and having a disability.
These situations put a child at risk for not doing well in life. As a result of
these situations, children may experience psychological or physical health
problems that affect, in turn, their ability to successfully attain either their
own goals or goals that society sees as important (e.g., learning to read and
write, finishing school, getting a job, finding a life partner). For example,
we know that children of single mothers often live in poverty (Fellegi,
1997) and that living in poverty is associated with poorer health and a
lower likelihood of being successful at school (Duncan & Brooks-Gunn,
2000). Of course, many children raised by single mothers do well in life.
These children have been considered resilient or stress resistant.

There are a number of concepts related to the idea of *resilience,* including hardiness, sense of coherence, and learned optimism. All these terms
refer to individual differences in the ability to adapt to stress. Martin Seligman, a leading psychologist, has developed a theory of *learned helplessness* based on the key idea of control—whether people feel they can
influence the good and bad things that happen to them (Seligman, 1975).
People with optimistic attitudes believe they have a lot of control. They do
better in school, persevere more in the face of obstacles, and enjoy new
challenges. Aaron Antonovsky, another psychologist, has developed a
similar concept called *sense of coherence* (Antonovsky, 1987). People
with a strong sense of coherence feel that life is sufficiently ordered to be
understandable, manageable, and meaningful. Likewise, people who are
hardy believe they can control events, are committed to the activities of
their lives, and perceive change as a positive challenge to their further
development (Kobasa, 1979).

In addition to being thought of as a characteristic of an individual,
resilience can refer to a process of successful adaptation (Garmezy &
Masten, 1991). The research literature contains two main ideas about the
experiences and events that lead to resilience. These are the ideas of *protective factors* and *protective processes. Protective factors* are the circumstances—personal qualities or supports—that protect an individual from
risk. These protective factors come from different sources: individuals
themselves (i.e., their characteristics, beliefs, and traits), their families,
and/or their communities (Garmezy, 1983; Rutter, 1990).

Protective processes deal with how these factors operate in people's lives to protect them from risk (Rutter, 1987; Zimmerman & Arunkumar, 1994). According to Michael Rutter, a leading researcher in the area of risk and resilience, there are four main ways in which turning points can change the trajectory of our lives, so that we end up in a different place than we would have otherwise (Rutter, 1987). The first way is that the risk factor itself—whether it is being raised in poverty, being hospitalized, or having a disability—is altered through how we come to understand the turning point experience. Another process that can change expected outcomes is an experience that reduces or stops a negative chain of events. Michael Rutter's third process deals with the kinds of experiences that can result in feelings of self-worth, self-confidence, or self-efficacy—the conviction that we can successfully cope with life's challenges. Finally, turning points can change life's direction by opening up opportunities for people.

When we looked carefully at the literature on risk and resilience, we found that many research studies have investigated resilience in children who are at risk due to situational or environmental factors such as poverty or hospitalization (e.g., Garmezy, 1993; Rutter, 1985). Few studies have examined the resilience of children with chronic disabilities or disorders. There also has been a good deal of research on adults' adjustment to chronic illnesses such as cancer (e.g., Peters-Golden, 1982; Wortman & Dunkel-Schetter, 1979). This work on adjustment to chronic illnesses deals with acute events, whereas our interest was in how individuals adjust to chronic disabilities that begin—but perhaps are not diagnosed—early in life. The literature on the well-being of adults with chronic illnesses tends to focus on the importance of their interpersonal relationships (e.g., Dakof & Taylor, 1990), whereas our interest was broader and encompassed characteristics of the self, such as traits and competencies, in addition to interpersonal relationships and social supports.

In our review of the literature, we found little research on the resilience of children or adults with chronic disabilities. Few studies have focused on the factors that protect individuals with disabilities from adverse life experiences (none have looked at protective processes). Although researchers often discussed how important protective processes were (e.g., Rutter, 1987; Zimmerman & Arunkumar, 1994), the specific nature of these processes were seldom examined. For example, we know that *being believed in* is an important protective factor (Brooks, 1992; King et al., 2000; Weiss & Hechtman, 1993). What we do not know is when and how it comes to be important for people.

Michael Rutter calls significant life events, experiences, and realizations *turning points* (Rutter, 1979). We saw turning points as the key to unlocking the mystery of resilience. Like Michael Rutter, we were interested in how protective processes surround turning points and lead to new directions in life. Our particular interest was in the processes operating for individuals with disabilities. Thus, we were interested in resilience as a process of successful adaptation to stressful conditions or events associated with having a disability.

Nadine Lambert, a psychologist, sees turning points as times when the processes that place children and adolescents at risk can be altered (Lambert, 1988). She suggests that, at a turning point, we have to make some big decisions. Turning points force us to make sense of our world in new ways. We can't often see turning points coming until we hit that fork in the road. Sometimes we don't realize we have gone through a major turning point until we look back on an event and see it, in hindsight, as pivotal to where our lives have gone. However, if we are aware of potential turning points that lie ahead, we can be better prepared for these often highly emotion-filled experiences.

A book by Harilyn Rousso presents the stories of ten women with disabilities, in which they talk about their life experiences (Rousso, 1988). In this book, Rousso talks about a key turning point in her own life: a realization that occurred as a result of meeting a woman with a disability who had a dynamic career, was married, and had children. For the first time, Rousso realized she might be able to have these things. Before that time, she had assumed that because she had a disability, she could not date, marry, or have children. She felt she could not create a relationship with a partner or have children in her life. This experience changed the possibilities she saw ahead of her and gave her new goals in life.

Is a turning point different from a traumatic experience? Traumas are emotional experiences or shocks that may have lasting psychological effects, such as being in a car accident or in a war, or being abused. Many traumas are sudden and have an aspect of crisis to them (Tedeschi, Park, & Calhoun, 1998). In our view, traumas are one type of turning point. Turning points may not have the intense emotional impact of a trauma and turning points can be positive in nature (such as getting married). The defining features of turning points are that they are highly significant to the person experiencing them and they are felt to mark an important change in the person's life course.

Studies of trauma are relevant, however, in that they indicate two things that may be true of the broader notion of turning points. First, traumas shatter people's core assumptions about themselves or the world in which they live (Janoff-Bulman, 1992). Being robbed can shatter the assumption that the world is a safe place. Experiencing a divorce can shatter the assumption that one can put faith and trust in another human being. Turning points may have similar effects on people's core beliefs.

Second, it appears that many people are able to rebuild their shattered assumptions by finding some positive meaning in the traumatic experience. In fact, more than 50 percent of people who have experienced a traumatic event or life crisis, such as a divorce or an accident, report that some benefit arose from it (Cleveland, 1980; Schaefer & Moos, 1992; Wallerstein, 1986). These positive outcomes include the development of new skills, new life goals, improved relationships, and changed perspectives (Schaefer & Moos, 1992; Tedeschi & Calhoun, 1995). In the aftermath of crisis, people speak of the lessons they learned, such as gaining a different sense of themselves, a different understanding of the world as a benevolent or hostile place, or a newfound appreciation of life or oneself (Janoff-Bulman, 1992). This appreciation appears to be associated with the realization that things of value in life are fragile, and so one must treasure them all the more.

Thus, studies of trauma provided a good backdrop with respect to our interest in turning points. These studies illuminate the wisdom-producing experiences of individuals in difficult circumstances and show the potential for human development (Tedeschi et al., 1998). Few research studies, however, have explicitly investigated the processes by which important life changes occur (O'Leary, Alday, & Ickovics, 1998).

WHAT DID WE WANT TO LEARN?

We conducted the study to find out four basic things. First, we wanted to be able to describe and understand the nature of key turning points in the lives of people with disabilities. Second, we wanted to be able to identify the key protective factors that helped their adaptation at these turning points and the factors that hindered their adaptation. Third, we wanted to understand people's experience of the protective factors and the ways in which these factors unfolded in their lives (the idea of protective processes). Fourth, we wanted to hear people's recommendations for changes in the educational, health, and social service systems that would foster positive life experiences.

We believed that this study would add to the knowledge of resilience in a number of ways. As we've already noted, little research has focused on protective factors and processes that help individuals with chronic disabilities adapt to their disabilities and their lives. Second, few studies have looked at all of the factors (individual, family, and community) from childhood to adulthood. Dennis Harper, a psychologist from the University of Iowa working in the area of childhood disability, has suggested that individuals with disabilities may require different supports at different times in their lives (Harper, 1991). Furthermore, different protective factors and processes may be important at different developmental stages (Brandtstädter, 1999; Masten et al., 1988). Understanding what is important throughout the lives of adults with disabilities will provide ideas about how to keep life on a positive road. These ideas will be relevant to people with and without disabilities, parents, and service providers.

WHO DID WE WANT TO INVOLVE IN THE STUDY?

We gave careful thought to which people to invite to participate in this study. You will see in the later chapters of this book that participants' disabilities often were not important in their turning point experiences. However, because our focus was on how individuals with disabilities can do well in life despite the difficulties their disabilities may bring, we had to start by deciding which types of disabilities to include and we also had to consider the age of participants.

We decided to interview people with disabilities that started relatively early on in life (i.e., before seven years of age) because there is evidence that disabilities acquired later on, such as spinal cord injuries, have a different impact on people's lives (e.g., Duggan & Dijkers, 1999). We decided to focus on the experiences of individuals with three different types of diagnoses, to see whether their experiences were similar or different from one another. The three diagnoses were attention deficit disorder (with or without the component of hyperactivity), cerebral palsy, and spina bifida. These conditions all appear early on in life but are not always formally diagnosed at that time. Cerebral palsy and spina bifida generally are diagnosed when the child is young, but this is not always the case for attention deficit disorder (ADD). The ability to diagnose ADD has improved over the years, but some participants in our study did not receive a diagnosis until later on in life.

We decided to include participants between the ages of 30 and 50 years. According to developmental psychologists, middle age begins at 30. Erik Erikson has characterized this stage of life as one in which we take stock of our lives to see if we are contributing to the next generation (Erikson,

1963). We thought that this reflective mind-set at midlife should provide the introspection necessary to identify turning points and consider things that helped or hindered at these times.

A number of other characteristics of participants were considered. Since we needed to audiotape the interviews so they could be transcribed, it was important for those who took part to have intelligible speech. Finally, the participants required an ability to conceptualize and verbalize their life story. We did not include people who were currently receiving therapy for psychological issues or who were on medication for such issues because we felt that these situations might interfere with how people viewed their lives in hindsight.

Part of the reason for including people with physical disabilities or difficulties with attention was that we were interested in seeing the extent to which there were differences and commonalities in the turning points and life experiences of people with a visible or an invisible disability. According to Conway Saylor, people who have an invisible disability can engage in *passing,* which means they can hide the existence of their disability (Saylor, 1990). Until they are required to perform a function that is affected by their impairment, they can appear to behave in a typical manner. For example, a woman with a learning disability who has difficulty reading may say she forgot her reading glasses in order to avoid reading and thus revealing her disability. Of course, this is substituting one impairment (poor vision) for another impairment (a learning disability) that is less common and perhaps less socially acceptable.

Invisible disabilities may cause stress if people deny their special needs in order to appear to function in a typical manner. Similarly, people with a visible disability may attempt to cover the full extent of their disability by not using some sort of assistive device that may make functioning easier because this device would call attention to their impairment. A person may persist in using a walker rather than a wheelchair because a walker suggests a lesser degree of disability than does a wheelchair. Similarly, people may not use hearing aids or glasses because these devices call attention to a physical impairment.

Before we introduce you to the study participants and tell you something about them, we feel it is important to provide some background material about the causes, nature, and typical effects of cerebral palsy, spina bifida, and attention deficit disorder on people's lives. Study participants endorsed this idea of providing educational material in order to dispel myths about the nature of various disabilities. At the same time, we are very aware that focusing on the disabilities of participants makes this "difference" very salient. One of the study participants said, "Remember the individual is a person first and disabled second." Please keep this in mind as you read the following descriptions. Our intent is to inform, not to put people into "boxes" where they are defined solely in terms of their disabilities. Our position is that all people have uniquenesses and differences.

WHAT IS A DISABILITY?

The World Health Organization provides a very useful scheme for considering the consequences of health conditions. This scheme is called the International Classification of Functioning, Disability and Health (World Health Organization, 2001). This scheme uses three terms to classify the negative effects of health conditions on the person: impairment, activity limitations (or disability), and restricted participation in life situations.

Impairment refers to any loss or abnormality of function, including physical, psychological, or anatomical structures. An activity limitation occurs when there is a restriction on the way in which a person performs an activity, such as walking, which results from an impairment. Participation restrictions are problems an individual may have in the manner or extent of his or her involvement in life situations, including the activities of personal maintenance, mobility, social relationships, education, leisure, spirituality, and community life.

Throughout this book we use the term *disability* extensively, largely because this is the word that study participants most often used to describe both their impairments and their activity limitations. Our use of the term *disability* should not be taken to mean that we are not aware of people's strengths and abilities. In fact, our interest in resilience is driven by an awareness of and interest in people's strengths.

WHAT IS CEREBRAL PALSY?

Cerebral palsy refers to an impairment of a person's central nervous system caused by structural abnormalities in the brain or lack of oxygen during or around the time of birth, or during the first few years of life (Carter & Low, 1989). For every 2,000 children who are born, approximately three have cerebral palsy (Onley & Wright, 1995).

People with cerebral palsy have an impairment that is not progressive. It does not become better or worse over time, but a person's symptoms, such as muscle contractures, can vary significantly over time. Cerebral palsy is broken into subgroups according to the type of motor disability and how a person's body is affected (Onley & Wright, 1995). When a person has an increase of muscle tone in certain muscle groups, the person has spastic cerebral palsy. This may involve all four limbs (quadriplegia), predominantly the legs (diplegia), or the arm and leg on one side of the body (hemiplegia). People with athetoid cerebral palsy have uncontrolled movements. They may move their arm in a wavelike manner when attempting to reach for an object. Individuals with ataxic cerebral palsy have difficulty with balance and the ability to coordinate their movements.

Activity limitations associated with cerebral palsy can range from minimal to severe. Individuals with minimal limitations may have difficulty manipulating objects or performing the skilled motor activities needed for many team sports. They may have minor difficulties speaking, but generally need little or no assistance to engage in daily activities. Individuals with more severe limitations may not be able to walk, stand, sit, or roll over on their own. They may have great difficulty speaking or may not speak at all. In terms of daily activities, they require assistance to eat, dress, perform hygiene activities, play, or work. They may use various devices to assist them in performing activities such as moving around their environment or communicating with others. The devices they use can be as simple as a brace for the feet, a cane, or a wheelchair, or as complex as a computer system controlled by voice input or eye gaze that enables the person to communicate. People with cerebral palsy do not always have cognitive impairments. Their cognitive abilities can be impaired, but many have average or above average intelligence (Carter & Low, 1989).

WHAT IS SPINA BIFIDA?

Spina bifida is a condition caused by the failure of the vertebral column (the spine) to close during the development of the fetus (Chutorian, 1989). It is typical to surgically close the child's spinal lesion within a few days of birth because infection may occur if this is not done. It appears that a combination of genetic and environmental factors cause the vertebral column to fail to close. This failure to close can occur at any point on the spine but is most common lower down. This often affects a person's bowel and bladder function and their ability to walk.

There are two main types of spina bifida. In spina bifida occulta, the bones of the spine fail to close but the underlying spinal cord remains intact. The second classification, spina bifida with meningocele or meningomyelocele, involves damage to the spinal cord in which either the covering of the spinal cord or portions of the spinal cord protrude. In this case, a person's control of function is affected below the level of the area of the spine that has failed to close during gestation (Hinderer, Hinderer, & Shurtleff, 1995).

Spina bifida is associated with a number of impairments. A common accompanying impairment is hydrocephalus, which literally refers to "water on the brain." When an individual has hydrocephalus, the volume of fluid in their brain is increased. If the excess fluid is not released, damage to the brain tissue can result. This is typically done through the use of a shunt that drains the excess fluid into a person's abdomen. As the child grows, the shunt may have to be lengthened. Further medical attention must be paid to prevent bladder infections as well as other effects on the child's bones and spine (Chutorian, 1989). Spina bifida also is associated with club feet and dislocated hips.

As with cerebral palsy, the activity limitations associated with the condition of spina bifida can range from mild to severe. Individuals with mild limitations may walk without any form of assistance and have few or no problems with bowel and bladder function. Other individuals are able to walk using crutches or braces, which provide some stability. Others use a wheelchair for mobility. Some individuals do not gain control over their bowels and bladders. Providing that there is no associated damage to the brain (such as may occur with hydrocephalus), people's cognitive ability is often not affected (Chutorian, 1989).

WHAT IS ATTENTION DEFICIT DISORDER (ADD)?

Attention deficit disorder (ADD) is a condition that encompasses a host of characteristics, which are not displayed in all children with ADD. The causes of ADD are not well known but it does appear that there is a familial link and that the brain chemistry of people with ADD is different from those without ADD (Selikowitz, 1995). Approximately 1–7 percent of the population has ADD (Hinshaw, 1994). About three times as many boys are diagnosed with ADD than girls (Hinshaw, 1994).

Children with ADD often have problems concentrating on the task at hand. Children with attention deficit hyperactivity disorder (ADHD) can have the following types of difficulties: impulsivity, overactivity, disorganization, learning problems, poor social skills, or defiant behavior (Selikowitz, 1995). According to the American Psychiatric Association (1994), a child is only diagnosed as having difficulties in attention when the behaviors are present for at least six months, are developmentally inappropriate, and cause problems in two main settings in the child's life—that is, at school, at home, or with the child's peer group.

It used to be believed that the child with ADD would "grow out of it."
We now know that this is not the case. Although many people with ADD
experience decreasing symptoms in adolescence, the characteristics are
still present (Selikowitz, 1995). However, many individuals with ADD are
not bothered by its effects in adulthood. It is estimated that about 20 percent have no behavior difficulties when they are adults. About 60 percent
of individuals with ADD have minor problems as adults, but they choose
career paths that accommodate their difficulties. The remaining 20 percent
continue to have the same difficulties that they did as children (Selikowitz,
1995).

ADD interferes with the daily activities of people's lives. In school,
children with ADD tend to stand out because they fidget in the classroom
and may appear to act out. It appears that children with ADD have difficulty telling themselves to focus on the task at hand or to stop and think
before they act. On many occasions their so-called noncompliant behavior is not purposeful. Rather, it seems to result from the different speed at
which the child with ADD processes information compared to the child
without ADD (Selikowitz, 1995). Consider the situation of a teacher
going around the classroom asking children questions. A child with ADD
may respond to a question with the answer to a previous question because
he or she needed the extra time to process the first question—and did not
even hear the second question being asked. This makes the child appear
to be defiant, when in reality the child has a problem with processing
information. Impulsivity can lead to danger for children with ADD
because they cannot stop to think of the consequences of their actions
(Wodrich, 1994).

Children with ADD often do not do as well in school as their peers
(Hechtman, 1991). In adolescence, they can experience difficulties
with substance abuse or problems with the law. Difficulties with alcohol and other types of addictions can continue into adulthood (Hinshaw, 1994).

WHAT CHALLENGES ARE FACED BY PEOPLE
WITH DISABILITIES?

Whether people have cerebral palsy, spina bifida, attention deficit disorder, or some other type of disability, they often face the same types of challenges (Pless & Pinkerton, 1975). This is surprising to some people
because it is often thought that the challenges people face are tied more
directly to the nature of their disability.

Although many gains have been made over the past few decades in the development of devices that can compensate for some of the physical impairments associated with disabilities, physical barriers to inclusion and participation continue to exist. Some restaurants indicate that they are accessible to people with disabilities when, in fact, the only level entrance is the service entrance. This may require a person in a wheelchair to pass by the garbage, which is not a very appealing prospect prior to eating. Even where adapted bathroom stalls exist, the entrance to a washroom may require passing through a double set of doors, with a possible turn, which is not easy to navigate for a person in a wheelchair or for a person who has difficulties walking.

Dependable transportation is a recurring complaint of people with a physical disability (Murphy, 1987). Where accessible transportation exists, it is often unreliable, expensive, and inconvenient. People often have to book their transportation days in advance, which eliminates spontaneous activities from their lives. Everything needs to be planned in advance.

The biggest barrier to the participation of individuals with disabilities in community life, however, is the attitudes of community members. Many people who write about living with a disability indicate that social barriers—not physical barriers—have the biggest impact on them (e.g., Morris, 1991; Sherr Klein, 1997). Several authors of the present book conducted a qualitative research study examining adolescents' perceptions of what "success in life" meant to them (King et al., 2000). These adolescents with disabilities indicated that the limiting and negative attitudes of others were a major barrier to attaining success in life.

Many myths exist about the abilities and life experiences of people with disabilities. For example, the presence of a physical disability is often considered to be synonymous with a cognitive impairment in people's minds (Morris, 1991). Many young people with learning disabilities or attention difficulties are told they are stupid because others do not understand the reason for their academic difficulties. Individuals with disabilities may be viewed as incapable of making judgements, of looking after themselves, or of having intimate relationships.

Gaining employment is difficult because some employers do not believe that people with disabilities are capable of meeting the demands of the job. Consequently, many people with physical disabilities are unemployed, underemployed, or not paid for their work (Satcher & Hendren, 1993). Although employers are required by law in many jurisdictions to make necessary accommodations for people with disabilities, these accommodations may not be sufficient to enable people with disabilities to meet job requirements (Crichton & Jongbloed, 1998).

People with ADD may be successful in obtaining a job because their disability is invisible. However, to be successful in their jobs, they may need accommodations such as the elimination of distractions and different means of accessing and producing information. Without these accommodations, their productivity may be reduced. Rather than seeing the physical environment as inadequate or the issue being the fit between the person's needs and the environment, employers or colleagues can localize the fault within the person with a disability, so that he or she is viewed as lacking in ability or skill.

Intimate relations are another area in which societal attitudes limit full involvement. Sexual aspects of daily life are often overlooked for people with disabilities (Matthews, 1983; Morris, 1991). Although the provision of rehabilitation services is the most obvious situation in which to provide information about sexuality, the issue is seldom raised and information is seldom provided (Matthews, 1983). People with disabilities often are not seen as a potential life or sexual partners because they do not always match society's views about what an attractive or desirable partner is or looks like.

Expectations that other people hold for individuals with a disability can either enhance or hinder their success in life. When significant people such as parents, teachers, and siblings believe in the person's abilities, then that person expresses more confidence in pursuing goals in life such as employment, education, or intimate relationships (King et al, 2000; Weiss & Hechtman, 1993). People may have lowered expectations of people with disabilities (Morris, 1991). Lowered expectations are shown, for example, when someone rushes to assist a person with a disability even though no assistance has been requested. Another example is when someone speaks slowly and uses simple language because they believe the person will have difficulty understanding them.

Jan Morris has written about the prejudice encountered by people with disabilities in their daily lives (Morris, 1991). According to her, it is most damaging when people are denied opportunities because others in positions of power do not recognize their full abilities. One example is streaming young people with disabilities into a lower academic level or an educational program that limits their ability to pursue higher education. Another example is engaging individuals in a volunteer capacity and not being willing to pay for their contribution.

Another damaging attitude is devaluing the person with a disability (Morris, 1991; Schlaff, 1993). People without disabilities assume that individuals with physical disabilities are less happy and less satisfied with life (Anderson & Clark, 1982). People with disabilities have indicated that they feel they are more disadvantaged by attitudes of society than by their disability (Hall, 1995). The fact that physical access to public buildings and the right to live independently often must be legislated are indications that the lives of these people are not as valued as they should be.

When parents take the life of their child with a physical disability or a court grants the right to passive euthanasia (through starvation or removal of a respirator), concern arises about the value that is placed on the lives of people with a disability. In many of these situations, sentiments are expressed that decry the great tragedy of life with a physical disability. It is beyond the imagination of many people that a person with a disability could live a satisfying and productive life. Yet it is often not the physical disability but the social situation in which individuals must live that brings them to the point of despair. Social and financial supports often are insufficient to enable a person with significant physical needs to live reasonably independently. As well, parents often do not receive the financial and social support they need to care for a child with a physical disability (Sloper, 1999; Sloper & Turner, 1992).

Labeling is another way in which individuals with a disability are discredited (Link, Mirotznik, & Cullen, 1991). People with ADD may be labeled *not smart* in school because their particular learning needs are not recognized. In response to this label, some individuals may misjudge their own intellectual capacity and become unmotivated to do well at school. This is the idea of a *self-fulfilling prophecy,* whereby what has been expected by teachers actually becomes true (Rosenthal, 1974).

People with a disability are often labeled by their disability (e.g., a cerebral palsied or a learning disabled child). Such labeling defines people by their disability rather than by their other attributes. It makes the disability the most important aspect of the person (Murphy, 1987).

In conclusion, social attitudes can be more disabling than barriers in the physical environment. To some individuals, these social barriers feel insurmountable and so they may withdraw from or limit their interactions with other people. To others, these attitudes create responses of anger or determination—"I will prove them wrong." As you will see in the following chapters, our work on resilience examines why and how people react in these different ways to having a disability and to adverse life events of all kinds.

WHO WERE THE ACTUAL STUDY PARTICIPANTS?

Fifteen individuals (six women and nine men) with an average age of 37 years took part in our study. Six people had attention deficit disorder, five had cerebral palsy, and four had spina bifida. As you will see when we describe the study, we asked these 15 individuals to tell us a little bit about themselves. In particular, we were interested in their life experiences (employment, attending school, living situation, etc.) and their satisfaction with their life experiences.

Let's consider their life experiences first. Participants had a wide mix of employment and schooling experiences. Most (five people) were taking part in both paid and unpaid employment, and some of these individuals also were attending school or working at home. Five others were taking part in unpaid employment, and some of these also were attending school or working at home. Three individuals were in paid, full-time employment, and one was attending school full-time (one chose not to supply this information). The group was well educated, with 93 percent having completed at least a high school education. Approximately one-third had obtained a university degree.

How did people's condition or disability impact on their life? Almost half of the participants felt that their condition limited their life somewhat, whereas 27 percent felt that their life was limited to a fair or great extent. The remaining 20 percent felt that their life was limited to either a small degree or not at all. The participants indicated that their condition had a wide range of impacts with respect to the different areas of their life. The area that was most affected was their work. Family life was the area least affected.

We asked people about their satisfaction with their lives in four areas known to be important to people in general: their competence, their ability to manage their own lives, their engagement in meaningful activities, and their overall life satisfaction (Campbell, 1997; Spekman, Goldberg, & Herman, 1993). The majority were very satisfied with their lives (93%), felt able to manage their lives (93%), and felt engaged in meaningful activity (87%). Two-thirds felt competent.

The picture this information paints is of a group of people who are very satisfied with their lives, who feel in control, and who are engaged in worthwhile pursuits (including school and various combinations of unpaid and paid employment). Only 3 of the 15 participants were, however, in full-time employment.

We would like to introduce you to these people now. We have used pseudonyms to protect people's identities.

Neil is 36 years of age. He is married and has children. He has a university degree and is engaged in full-time unpaid work. He has cerebral palsy.

Cory is 37. He lives alone and is a part-time student. He has attention deficit hyperactivity disorder and has had difficulties with drug and alcohol dependence.

Alisha is 34 and lives with her parents. She has a university degree and has cerebral palsy. She has a full-time paid job.

Grace has spina bifida. She is 51 years of age, divorced, and now living alone. She has two university degrees. She works part-time on a voluntary basis.

Evan has cerebral palsy that affects all four of his limbs. He is 37. He lives in a group setting and takes part in a combination of paid and unpaid work.

Helen is 39. She lives with her children and is a student at university. She has attention deficit disorder.

Loreena has completed college. She is 36, has spina bifida, and lives alone. She has a full-time paid job.

Perry, at 28, is the youngest of the group we interviewed. He has completed high school and lives with his mother. He has spina bifida.

Bernie is 53. He has completed some high school and some college. He has spina bifida and experiences chronic pain. He is married and works both at home and in unpaid part-time work.

Rick is 34 years of age. He is a student at an adult education center. He has attention deficit disorder and lives alone.

Scott is married and is 32 years of age. He completed college and has a full-time paid job. He has attention deficit disorder.

Dan has cerebral palsy. He is 34, lives alone, and has completed high school. He is involved in part-time work of a voluntary nature.

Trudy is married and has children. She has completed some college and takes part in a variety of work roles, including paid and unpaid work and working at home. She has attention deficit disorder. She is 39.

Frank has a learning disability and attention deficit hyperactivity disorder. He is married and is 33 years of age. He has a full-time paid job and has completed a master's degree at university.

Karen is 37. She lives alone, takes part in both paid and unpaid work, and has completed high school and some college. She has cerebral palsy.

WHAT DID TAKING PART IN THE STUDY ENTAIL?

All of the research literature that we read pointed to the usefulness of a qualitative approach. Qualitative research is especially well suited to an in-depth exploration of an issue that is not well understood (Charmaz, 1990). We wanted to discover the turning points in the lives of individuals with disabilities. We could have asked participants simply to tell us the three key turning points of their lives. However, this straightforward approach would only have informed us about the nature of people's turning points. It would not have provided us with any information about the helpful factors or the factors that hindered people at these times. Furthermore, we would have gained little insight into how the factors played out in people's experiences—what led to what and how turning point experiences started and were resolved.

We could have presented people with a list of key turning points that we developed based on past studies and our own hunches, and asked participants whether they had experienced such turning points. However, this would have meant that we started with predetermined beliefs about turning points. Instead, we wanted people to tell us, with minimal prompting, what their turning points were and how they uniquely experienced them. This is the value of a qualitative approach—it allows people to convey their own experiences in a relatively unstructured manner.

We therefore decided it would be best to interview people about their turning points, the processes surrounding these turning points (the things that came before and the things that came after), and the factors that helped and hindered them at these points in their lives. We felt that interviews with people would be the best way to understand people's experiences. We decided to conduct two interviews. In the first interview, people identified the main turning points in their lives. In the second interview, held about three weeks later, people talked about the meaning and effects of the turning points, and the factors that helped or hindered at these times.

The method we used is known as *recursive interviewing*. In recursive interviewing, participants are given a transcript of their first interview and asked to reread it before the second interview. We saw a number of benefits to this approach. First, people can correct any misperceptions or errors in their interviews because they have the opportunity to read and reflect on what they have said. Second, when information is shared in this way, the process is more participatory and more meaningful to those taking part. Third, we hoped that reflecting on turning points by reading the first transcript would allow participants to feel very ready for the second interview about helpful and hindering factors.

We sought participants through advertisements distributed with the kind cooperation of a number of health and social service agencies in London, Ontario. The advertisement mentioned that we were interested in listening to the life stories of people with nonprogressive disabilities such as cerebral palsy, spina bifida, and attention deficit disorder. The advertisement outlined our specific interest in turning points in people's lives. A contact number was provided for people who were interested in participating.

In the initial phone call, the study's research assistant determined whether the person was suitable for the study (based on the criteria mentioned earlier, which included their diagnosis, age, and ability to take part in an interview). If the person was suitable and interested, a letter was mailed explaining the study in more detail. This letter told participants that we wanted them to think about how turning points came about, what made those events or experiences important in their lives, and what helped or hindered them at these times.

The interviews took place either in participants' own homes or at a children's rehabilitation center (Thames Valley Children's Centre in London, Ontario, Canada). We wanted people to feel as comfortable and safe as possible, so we asked them to choose the location they preferred. Each interview lasted about two hours. All interviews were audiotaped and transcribed. The first transcribed interview was sent to each participant for review, and the second interview was scheduled to occur approximately three weeks later. This time lapse was designed to give participants enough time to read and think about the first interview.

Because of the potentially personal nature of the interviews, all identifiers were removed from the transcripts (i.e., names of friends, cities where people grew up, and so on). A list of the researchers' names was shown to the participants and anyone they recognized by name was not allowed access to their transcripts. All of these measures were taken to ensure confidentiality and anonymity for the participants. It was very important to ensure anonymity so that participants felt as comfortable as possible in sharing their life stories.

The interviews started in May 1997 and were completed approximately 10 months later in March 1998. The interview process continued until 15 people had completed their interviews with us. Because each person took part in 2 interviews, there was a total of 30 interviews, each approximately 50 pages in length. This gave us a wealth of information—about 1,500 pages of key experiences in people's lives. Yvonna Lincoln and Egon Guba, two respected researchers in the field of qualitative research, recommend that qualitative studies involve between 12 and 20 participants in order to get enough breadth and depth of information (Lincoln & Guba, 1985).

To obtain some general information about participants, participants were asked to complete a questionnaire at the end of the second interview. As mentioned previously, this questionnaire asked about their life experiences (employment, education, living situation, etc.) and about their satisfaction with their life experiences.

After collecting all of the information, the daunting task of analyzing the data began. All members of the research team carefully read over the transcripts to gain an overall sense of people's life stories. Next, we generated a list of all the main ideas discussed in the interviews. At this point, two of the researchers (Elizabeth Brown and Gillian King) took on the task of developing the detailed coding scheme. They read and reread the interviews of the participants to get a feel for the themes surrounding turning points, life lessons, helpful factors, and hindering factors. These larger themes were divided into many smaller ones. The coding scheme they developed was shared with the other researchers to ensure its appropriateness. In qualitative data analysis, researchers need to immerse themselves in the information to determine the key themes. Many weeks were spent on this process and the coding scheme was refined over and over as new transcripts were read and thought about in terms of their major chunks of meaning.

Once we were happy with the coding scheme, Elizabeth Brown assigned code words to each major idea in the transcripts. In the end, we had over 1,400 codes to help us give order to the stories. Clearly, coding life is a lot of work. To make sure the codes were being applied consistently, Gillian King and Elizabeth Brown separately coded the same randomly selected portions of a number of the transcripts and then compared the codes they had used. They agreed 79 percent of the time, which is quite amazing given the number of codes they were working with. This number is above the accepted levels of 65 percent to 75 percent agreement, which are considered to indicate good reliability in qualitative research studies (Boyatzis, 1998).

At the end of this process, which took about six months of intensive work, participants were invited to take part in one of two groups to check the accuracy of the themes (or key ideas) that came from the analysis of the interviews. The idea behind these *member checking* sessions is for the researchers to share the interpretations of the main themes with the study participants and to check the accuracy or trustworthiness of the ideas with them (Fiese & Bickman, 1998). We are happy to report that the member checking sessions affirmed that the coding scheme and resulting interpretations—the study themes—truly reflected participants' experiences. In other words, what we share in the rest of this book about turning points and the factors underlying resilience did concur with how study participants saw their experiences.

We turn now in chapter 2 to what turning points are all about. You will learn about their emotional nature, where they take place, how they begin and end, and—above all—what they mean.

REFERENCES

American Psychiatric Association. (1994). *Diagnostic and statistical manual of mental disorders* (4th ed.). Washington, D.C.: Author.

Anderson, E.M., & Clark, L. (1982). *Disability in adolescence.* London: Methuen.

Antonovsky, A. (1987). *Unraveling the mystery of health: How people manage stress and stay well.* San Francisco: Jossey-Bass.

Boyatzis, R.E. (1998). *Thematic analysis and code development: Transforming qualitative information.* Thousand Oaks, CA: Sage.

Brandtstädter, J. (1999). Sources of resilience in the aging self: Toward integrating perspectives. In T.M. Hess & F. Blanchard-Fields (Eds.), *Social cognition and aging* (pp. 123–141). San Diego: Academic Press.

Brooks, R.B. (1992). Self-esteem during the school years. *Pediatric Clinics of North America, 39*(3), 537–550.

Campbell, S.K. (1997). Therapy programs for children that last a lifetime. *Physical & Occupational Therapy in Pediatrics, 17*(1), 1–15.

Carter, S., & Low, N. (1989). Cerebral palsy and mental retardation. In L.P. Rowland (Ed.), *Merritt's textbook of neurology* (8th ed.) (pp. 458–466). Philadelphia: Lea & Febiger.

Charmaz, K. (1990). "Discovering" chronic illness: Using grounded theory. *Sociology of Health and Illness, 30,* 1161–1172.

Chutorian, A. (1989). Spina bifida and cranium bifidum. In L.P. Rowland (Ed.), *Merritt's textbook of neurology* (8th ed.) (pp. 475–480). Philadelphia: Lea & Febiger.

Cleveland, M. (1980). Family adaptation to traumatic spinal cord injury: A response to crisis. *Family Relations, 29,* 558–565.

Crichton, A., & Jongbloed, L. (1998). *Disability and social policy in Canada.* Toronto: Captus Press.

Dakof, G.A., & Taylor, S.E. (1990). Victims' perceptions of social support: What is helpful from whom? *Journal of Personality and Social Psychology, 58*(1), 80–89.

Duggan, C.H., & Dijkers, M. (1999). Quality of life—peaks and valleys: A qualitative analysis of the narratives of persons with spinal cord injuries. *Canadian Journal of Rehabilitation, 12*(3), 179–189.

Duncan, G.J., & Brooks-Gunn, J. (2000). Family poverty, welfare reform, and child development. *Child Development, 71,* 188–196.

Erikson, E.H. (1963). *Childhood and society.* New York: W.W. Norton.

Fellegi, I.P. (1997, September). *On poverty and low income.* Statistics Canada Cataglogue No. 13F0027XIE. Accessed May 20, 2001, from http://www.statcan.ca/english/concepts/poverty/pauv.htm.

Fiese, B.H., & Bickman, N.L. (1998). Qualitative inquiry: An overview for pediatric psychology. *Journal of Pediatric Psychology, 23*(2), 79–86.

Garmezy, N. (1983). Stressors of childhood. In N. Garmezy & M. Rutter (Eds.), *Stress, coping, and development in children* (pp. 43–84). New York: McGraw-Hill.

Garmezy, N. (1993). Children in poverty: Resilience despite risk. *Psychiatry, 56,* 127–136.

Garmezy, N., & Masten, A. S. (1991). The protective role of competence indicators in children at risk. In E. M. Cummings, A. L. Green, & K. H. Karraker (Eds.), *Life-span developmental psychology: Perspectives on stress and coping* (pp. 151–174). Hillsdale, NJ: Lawrence Erlbaum.

Hall, D. (1995). Commentary. *Archives of Disease in Childhood, 73,* 91–99.

Harper, D. C. (1991). Psychosocial aspects of physical differences in children and youth. *Pediatric Rehabilitation, 2,* 765–779.

Hechtman, L. (1991). Resilience and vulnerability in long term outcome of attention deficit hyperactive disorder. *Canadian Journal of Psychiatry, 36,* 415–421.

Hinshaw, S. P. (1994). *Attention deficits and hyperactivity in children.* Thousand Oaks, CA: Sage Publications.

Hinderer, K., Hinderer, S., & Shurtleff, D. (1995). Myelodysplasia. In S. K. Campbell (Ed.), *Physical therapy for children* (pp. 571–620). Philadelphia: W. B. Saunders.

Janoff-Bulman, R. (1992). *Shattered assumptions: Towards a new psychology of trauma.* New York: The Free Press.

King, G., Cathers, T., Miller Polgar, J., MacKinnon, E., & Havens, L. (2000). Success in life for older adolescents with cerebral palsy. *Qualitative Health Research, 10*(6), 734–749.

King, G. A., Shultz, I. Z., Steel, K., Gilpin, M., & Cathers, T. (1993). Self-evaluation and self-concept of adolescents with physical disabilities. *American Journal of Occupational Therapy, 47,* 132–140.

Kobasa, S. C. (1979). Stressful life events, personality, and health: An inquiry into hardiness. *Journal of Personality and Social Psychology, 37,* 1–11.

Lambert, N. M. (1988). Adolescent outcomes for hyperactive children. Perspective on general and specific patterns of childhood risk for adolescent educational, social, and mental health problems. *American Psychologist, 43,* 786–799.

Lincoln, Y., & Guba, E. (1985). *Naturalistic inquiry.* Newbury Park, CA: Sage.

Link, B., Mirotznik, J., & Cullen, F. (1991). The effectiveness of stigma coping orientations: Can negative consequences of mental illness labelling be avoided? *Journal of Health and Social Behavior, 32,* 302–320.

Masten, A. S., Garmezy, N., Tellegen, A., Pellegrini, D. S., Larkin, K., & Larsen, A. (1988). Competence and stress in school children: The moderating effects of individual and family qualities. *Journal of Child Psychology and Psychiatry, 29,* 745–764.

Matthews, G. (1983). *Voices from the shadows: Women with disabilities speak out.* Toronto: The Women's Press.

Morris, J. (1991). *Pride against prejudice: Transforming attitudes to disability.* Philadelphia: New Society Publishers.

Murphy, R. (1987). *The body silent.* New York: Henry Holt and Company.

O'Leary, V.E., Alday, C.S., & Ickovics, J.R. (1998). Models of life change and posttraumatic growth. In R.G. Tedeschi, C.L. Park, & L.G. Calhoun (Eds.), *Posttraumatic growth: Positive changes in the aftermath of crisis* (pp. 127–152). Mahwah, NJ: Lawrence Erlbaum.

Onley, S., & Wright, M. (1995). Cerebral palsy. In S.K. Campbell (Ed.), *Physical therapy for children* (pp. 489–524). Philadelphia: W.B. Saunders.

Peters-Golden, H. (1982). Breast cancer: Varied perceptions of social support in the illness experience. *Social Science and Medicine, 16,* 483–491.

Pless, I.B., & Pinkerton, P. (1975). *Chronic childhood disorder: Promoting patterns of adjustment.* London: Kimpton.

Rosenthal, R. (1974). On the social psychology of the self-fulfilling prophecy: Further evidence for Pygmalion effects and their mediating mechanisms. New York: MSS Modular Publications.

Rousso, H. (1988). *Disabled, female, and proud! Stories of ten women with disabilities.* Boston: Exceptional Parent Press.

Rutter, M. (1979). Protective factors in children's responses to stress and disadvantage. In M.W. Kent & J.E. Rolf (Eds.), *Primary prevention of psychopathology (Vol. 3), Social competence in children* (pp. 49–74). Hanover, NH: University Press of New England.

Rutter, M. (1985). Resilience in the face of adversity: Protective factors and resistance to psychiatric disorder. *British Journal of Psychiatry, 147,* 598–611.

Rutter, M. (1987). Psychosocial resilience and protective mechanisms. *American Journal of Orthopsychiatry, 57,* 316–331.

Rutter, M. (1990). Psychosocial resilience and protective mechanisms. In J. Rolf, A.S. Masten, D. Cicchetti, K.H. Neuchterlein, & S. Weintraub (Eds.), *Risk and protective factors in the development of psychopathology* (pp. 181–214). Cambridge, UK: Cambridge University Press.

Satcher, J., & Hendren, G. (1993). Employer agreement with the Americans with Disabilities Act of 1990: Implications for rehabilitation counseling. In M. Nagler (Ed.), *Perspectives on disability* (2nd ed.) (pp. 463–469). Palo Alto, CA: Health Markets Research.

Saylor, C. (1990). Stigma. In I.M. Lubkin (Ed.), *Chronic illness* (pp. 65–85). Boston: Jones and Bartlett.

Schaefer, J., & Moos, R. (1992). Life crises and personal growth. In B. Carpenter (Ed.), *Personal coping: Theory, research, and application* (pp. 149–170). Westport, CT: Praeger.

Schlaff, C. (1993). From dependency to self-advocacy: Redefining disability. *The American Journal of Occupational Therapy, 47,* 943–948.

Seligman, M.E.P. (1975). *Helplessness.* San Francisco: W.H. Freeman.

Selikowitz, M. (1995). *All about A.D.D.* South Melbourne, Australia: Oxford University Press.

Sherr Klein, B. (1997). *Slow dance: A story of stroke, love and disability.* Toronto: Knopf Canada.

Sloper, P. (1999). Models of service support for parents of disabled children. What do we know? What do we need to know? *Child: Care, Health and Development, 25*(2), 85–99.

Sloper, P., & Turner, S. (1992). Service needs of families of children with severe physical disability. *Child: Care, Health and Development, 18,* 259–282.

Specht, J., King, G., & Francis, P. (1998). A preliminary study of strategies for maintaining self-esteem in adolescents with physical disabilities. *Canadian Journal of Rehabilitation, 11,* 103–110.

Spekman, N. J., Goldberg, R. J., & Herman, K. L. (1993). An exploration of risk and resilience in the lives of individuals with learning disabilities. *Learning Disabilities: Research & Practice, 8,* 11–18.

Tedeschi, R. G., & Calhoun, L. G. (1995). *Trauma and transformation: Growing in the aftermath of suffering.* Thousand Oaks, CA: Sage.

Tedeschi, R. G., Park, C. L., & Calhoun, L. G. (1998). Posttraumatic growth: Conceptual issues. In R. G. Tedeschi, C. L. Park, & L. G. Calhoun (Eds.), *Posttraumatic growth: Positive changes in the aftermath of crisis* (pp. 1–22). Mahwah, NJ: Lawrence Erlbaum.

Wallerstein, J. S. (1986). Women after divorce: Preliminary report from a ten-year follow-up. *American Journal of Orthopsychiatry, 56,* 65–77.

Weiss, G., & Hechtman, L. T. (1993). *Hyperactive children grown up: ADHD in children, adolescents, and adults* (2nd ed.). New York: Guilford Press.

Wodrich, D. L. (1994). *What every parent wants to know about attention deficit hyperactivity disorder.* Baltimore: Brooks Publishing Co.

World Health Organization. (2001). *International classification of functioning, disability and health.* Geneva, Switzerland: World Health Organization.

Wortman, C. B., & Dunkel-Schetter, C. (1979). Interpersonal relationships and cancer: A theoretical analysis. *Journal of Social Issues, 35*(1), 120–155.

Zimmerman, M. A., & Arunkumar, R. (1994). Resiliency research: Implications for schools and policy. *Social Policy Report: Society for Research in Child Development, 8*(4), 1–20.

Chapter 2

TURNING POINTS: EMOTIONALLY COMPELLING LIFE EXPERIENCES

Gillian A. King, Tamzin Cathers, Elizabeth G. Brown, and Elizabeth MacKinnon

> There are definitive moments, moments we use as references, because they break our sense of continuity, they change the direction of time. We can look at these events and we can say that after them things were never the same again. They provide beginnings for us, and endings too.
> — Margaret Atwood, *The Robber Bride*

Life is a complicated mystery involving learning, change, and growth. It is a journey rather than a destination. Turning points are critical junctures in life that provide a window to see change and growth at work. In this chapter we will consider how turning points come about, what they mean, and how they can lead to the creation of meaning in life.

How do we learn? There are things we do because people (usually our mothers) tell us to. We eat our vegetables, wear clean underwear, try not to be late, and always do our best. Other things we learn through the wisdom of the ages, expressed by sayings such as "He who hesitates is lost," and its opposite, "Act in haste, repent in leisure."

We also learn through the various media, including books, magazines, newspapers, and talk shows. Newspapers are full of people's life stories and the meaning of these. Their stories are told as tragedies, triumphs, and a combination of the two. This book (and this chapter in particular) is different. It is about the learning we can harvest from looking at turning points in the lives of people with disabilities. We can learn so much from the life experiences of others. The wisdom others share can guide our life choices at specific developmental turning points (such as leaving home, starting a family) and, hopefully, help us deal with the more unexpected types of turning points, such as the sudden death of someone we love or the experience of being fired from a job. In this chapter, we will consider how we grow through life-changing experiences and realizations—through life's turning points.

Turning points and their meanings can be profoundly touching and moving because they speak to our own life experiences. In conducting the study on which this book is based, we did not set out to explore the ways in which people acquire or create meaning in life but ended up there anyway. Sometimes the most direct route to something is to sneak up on it from behind.

What did we, the authors, learn from people's shared experiences? We learned some very basic and important things. The things we learned shed light both on study questions we intended to address and on questions we did not set out to examine. As with most journeys, we had a basic road map and itinerary, but our major joys came from the unexpected findings along the way. We took the time to stop and explore the smaller, unexpected delights of people's life stories. Our planned itinerary was to determine whether there were common types of turning points in people's lives and the nature of these turning points. We wanted to gain a rich sense of turning points in terms of their settings, the key people involved, and the way in which the turning points unfolded over time—the things that trigger turning points and the ways in which they are resolved. The aim of our journey was to understand the nature of resilience—the things that help and hinder people in their life journeys and adaptation to the bigger changes in life. Turning points were the vehicle by which we went on our journey of discovery about the ways people get through life.

Some of the more unexpected learnings involved larger things than turning points or resilience. We learned about the many roads to one place and the commonalities of human experience. The "many roads" are the three paths to meaning in life (the "one place"): the paths of doing, belonging, and understanding. We ended up developing a model of the meaning of life experiences that integrates what participants told us with what is known across diverse literatures (this model is described in detail in chapter 5). We learned about the links between a host of life experiences, including happiness, enjoyment, meaningfulness, and resilience. We also experienced smaller treasures and delights along the way, such as understanding the role played by emotion in turning points, learning what it means to feel supported by others, and appreciating a number of paradoxes about life.

Aside from books on spirituality, books written about meaning in life often view meaning as coming from things in life. They reduce the mystery and richness of life to a consideration of things that we have or wish to have, like money, a nice house, or a car. Complex, meaningful events are described by a few short, dry phrases that give little insight into the real meaning of events—phrases such as *getting married* or *contributing to society*. In what ways are these events important and significant? How do these experiences play out in the larger context of people's lives? Does it make a difference if we marry for love or because we want to leave home and be independent from our parents? Surely there is much more to life events than is typically portrayed in books. This chapter aims to provide broad and deep insights about life experience by weaving the stories and experiences of people with disabilities into what is known about topics as varied as resilience, optimal experience, self-help, risk taking, spirituality, work, friendship, and ceremony.

TURNING POINTS, TRANSITIONS, AND CHANGE

> Life is only a moving picture. Nothing in life is a permanent fixture....Life is only what you make of it. You make the verses rhyme and all the pieces fit.
>   —The Kinks, "Moving Picture"

There are many books about historical turning points. These are more appropriately called *historical markers*. Historical markers are not the same as the life-changing experiences we explore in this book. There are common historical markers in our North American culture to which everyone of a certain age can relate. Our experience with the marker event makes it familiar and recognizable. The assassinations of John F. Kennedy, Martin Luther King, and John Lennon provide this common touchstone for baby boomers. Members of the previous generation may have an "aha" feeling of instant recognition, which also incorporates emotional understanding, when they think of the Hindenberg disaster or the kidnapping of the Lindberghs' baby. The death of Diana, Princess of Wales, speaks to the experiences of the current generation, as does the date September 11.

The sinking of the *Titanic* is one of those tragedies with an impact that cuts across generations, due in large part to the motion picture and the power of film. In addition to tragedies, miraculous events stick in the common collective consciousness, such as the first footsteps made on the moon ("One small step for man, one giant leap for mankind"). What is it about these events that has the power to move us and etch their details in our memories?

We can begin to answer that question by looking at people's life-changing experiences. These experiences reveal much about human nature and the things that are important to us. The word the authors of this book use for these significant experiences, events, or realizations is *turning points* (Rutter, 1987). These times of life also have been called *critical junctures* or *epiphanies,* which are sudden illuminations (Denzin, 1989; Mandelbaum, 1973). Turning points are profound and transforming experiences or realizations in people's lives. At these times of transformation, we enter into new roles, start fresh relationships, or acquire a new sense of ourselves (Bruner, 1994; Clausen, 1993). Turning points therefore introduce change into our lives—into our behavior, our relations with others, and the way we view ourselves and our lives.

Margaret Atwood, a well-known Canadian author, defines a *turning point* as a definitive moment, after which "things were never the same again" (1994, p. 4). Obviously, we cannot objectively demonstrate this. Saying that something was a turning point is a subjective judgment, made in hindsight. According to Ian Gotlib and Blair Wheaton, two psychologists who have written about turning points and life trajectories, turning points are only knowable after the fact (Gotlib & Wheaton, 1997). Turning points involve a fundamental shift in the meaning, purpose, or direction of a person's life, and the person is aware of the significance of the change. What makes an event or experience a turning point, therefore, is the awareness and sense that there has been significant change in the pattern of one's life.

The theme of turning points is everywhere—in books, movies, and newspapers. *Old Flames,* a novel by Kim Moritsugu (1999), deals with a turning point triggered by turning forty—the consideration of what life might have been like if an opportunity in love had been taken. The book considers the sense of loss that can arise if we allow our dreams to fade and how this sense of loss (the road not taken) can make life feel aimless. *The Shawshank Redemption,* voted the top movie ever made (according to the Internet Movie Database), deals with how a person triumphs over the adversity and hopelessness of being in prison through the power of perseverance and friendship. Again, the theme is one of turning points in life. In the wake of schoolyard violence, U.S. politician Al Gore called amendments to gun possession laws a "turning point for our country." Vancouver mystery writer L. R. Wright talks about her interest in writing mystery stories: "I think my primary preoccupation, for example, is with characters who for a variety of reasons lose control over the trajectory of their lives. I'm fascinated by this. By the events that placed them in this situation, and by the choices they make to try to re-establish authority over their own destinies" (Wright, 2000, p. D17).

Why are turning points so important in books, movies, and newspapers? This may reflect the fact that we live in a time of tremendous social change. World economies fluctuate widely, our health care and educational systems are undergoing massive restructuring, and the institution of the family is in transition. The major challenge in living these days is to learn to adjust, cope, or survive. We experience changes and challenges in all aspects of our lives, including in our work, our parenting roles, and our intimate relationships. More frequently than in the past, we are forced to reconsider the values and beliefs by which we live. Self-help books are tremendously popular because they guide us in how to determine direction in our lives. They help us clarify the things that are most important in this time of change and uncertainty.

The stories of people's turning points are helpful in a similar way. Although the participants in our study had disabilities, their turning points were not always related to their disability. (Our interest was in understanding what people felt were important junctures in their lives, regardless of the link to disability.) Their stories can help us learn to recognize significant junctures in our own lives. In this way, we can become aware of what we are going through when we are going through it. And it helps to see that there is light at the end of the tunnel. It can help to know that we aren't the only ones who have ever had a life-changing experience. In fact, a survey by John Clausen (1990), a researcher interested in psychological turning points, indicated that 85 percent of people feel they have had turning points in their lives. It is rare to feel that our lives have unfolded in an orderly manner.

LIVES AS CHANGE: STRESS, COPING, AND ADAPTATION

Nothing is constant except change.
—Anonymous

To be alive is to be under stress.
—Lawrence Hinkle, a researcher in the field of stress

As far back as 1957, Adolf Meyer (1957), an eminent social scientist, talked about the importance of the ways in which people meet key life changes and transitions. If we look at life as a series of continuities and discontinuities, turning points are the times of significant change and transition. These times of change can lead to tension and thus to feelings of stress, which can be experienced by a person along a continuum of positive to negative affect.

It is now commonly accepted, due to the pioneering work of stress researchers Richard Lazarus and Susan Folkman (1984), that not all stress is bad. Stress can be experienced positively when a state of tension exists that feels challenging to a person rather than overwhelming or immobilizing. Richard Lazarus and his colleagues focused on feelings of stress arising from daily hassles and major life events. They defined these events in objective terms rather than in terms of how they are subjectively experienced by the person feeling the stress. They did not explicitly consider turning points.

Stress is not an automatic result of turning points. Turning points can give rise to positive emotions—physiological states we label as happiness or joy—rather than more negative emotions such as anger, fear, or disappointment. There are many examples of how the same life event, such as getting married, losing a job, or getting divorced, can be a turning point for completely different reasons. Getting married can be a positive turning point when it is considered to be a wonderful experience. For others, the wedding day can be a time of disappointment, where everything goes wrong and the event (and perhaps even the whole marriage) does not live up to the high expectations that were set. Losing your job after twenty years of devotion and belief in what you were doing can be one of the most earth-shattering experiences. Then again, some people who lose their jobs see this, in retrospect, as a wonderful opportunity to try new things in life. For some people, a divorce is a great abandonment, causing anger and depression. Others see divorce as the best thing that ever happened to them because it allowed them to escape from an intolerable situation that was harmful to them or their children. Sometimes what appears to be quite an innocuous event, such as a child walking down the street to visit a friend unaccompanied by an adult for the very first time, can create turmoil in a parent. Other parents may rejoice in the newly found independence of their child. Surprisingly, doctors who do genetic screening are finding out that telling people they don't have faulty genes can be just as difficult to cope with as hearing bad news (Abraham, 2000). In other words, good news can be bad news when a person is expecting a reduced life expectancy and is living life according to that expectation. It is all in how the event is seen, experienced, and felt. What affects how we react to events? What determines the meaning that we give to them? This is something we will consider.

RESILIENCE AND SUCCESSFUL ADAPTATION TO CHANGE

> Coping [is] a process which unfolds over time.
> —Dennis Drotar, "Psychological Perspectives in Chronic Childhood Illness"

> The basic purpose of all human action is the protection, the maintenance, and the enhancement not only of the self but also of the self-concept.
> —Jean Watson, *Nursing: The Philosophy and Science of Caring*

Our research on how people with disabilities view turning points in their lives was motivated by a desire to find out if there were factors that helped or hindered them at these times. The most important goal was to find out what makes some people more resilient than others in the face of potentially threatening life events. Why are some people able to bounce back from stressful experiences more readily than others or at particular times in their lives and not others? The word *resilience* captures this idea of bouncing back.

As discussed in chapter 1, resilience deals with the general notion that some people are better able than others to fend off the negative consequences of experiences that expose them to increased risk for poor outcomes in life. These experiences include prenatal or birth complications, poverty, severe family discord, and chronic illness or disability. Children and adolescents who have psychological strengths and receive support from others despite a history of prolonged stress have been called invulnerable, stress resistant, or resilient (Anthony, 1974; Garmezy, 1991). Resilience therefore is seen as a process of successful adaptation to stressful events or conditions (Wyman, Sandler, Wolchik, & Nelson, 2000). The things that help us deal with stress—such as our personal qualities and the support of others—are called *protective factors* (Garmezy, 1983; Rutter, 1990). They protect us from the negative consequences often experienced by those exposed to the risk.

There is general agreement that stress is the normal and natural result of change that arises through living (Aldwin, 1994). The social and physical environment constantly affects our sense of self, our pursuit of goals, and our view of the world, sometimes in ways that are seen as threatening. Changes are viewed as stressful in a negative sense when they involve some sort of threat of harm to the individual. Thus, change leads to a sense of threat only because of the meaning it has, not because of some intrinsic property of change itself.

We must constantly adapt to a stressor-laden environment. Adaptation, therefore, is best understood in terms of the interaction between the person and his or her environment. Daniel Levinson, famous for his 1978 book on life stages called *The Seasons of a Man's Life,* talks about the pattern of relationships between the self and the world and introduces the idea that the self and the world are each part of the other. This notion of interdependence has been discussed by many others, including psychologist Ellyn Kaschak (1992), who uses the word *interconnected* to describe the relationship between the self and the world. The link between the self and the world will be explored further in chapter 3.

Adaptation or coping involves the capacity to deal with opportunities, challenges, frustrations, and threats in the environment (Murphy & Moriarty, 1976). Resilience, like adaptation, always reflects the fit between a person and his or her given social, cultural, and historical context (Masten, Best, & Garmezy, 1990). Thus, resilience, coping, and adaptation all refer to the effective functioning of people within their environments.

The field of study that encompasses the concepts of risk, protection, resilience, stress, and coping or adaptation across the life span is called developmental psychopathology (Pellegrini, 1990). A basic assumption of this field is that changes in the environment induce tension or disturbances in a person's equilibrium. These environmental changes lead to coping strategies and behaviors. Another basic assumption is that stress and adaptation occur throughout life. It's always something! Just when one crisis occurs or is averted, along comes the next, throwing our plans and lives into disarray.

People used to think that continuity or harmony was the status quo in life. Now it is increasingly accepted that discontinuity or disequilibrium is the norm, interspersed by periods of harmony. Thus, periods of tension or disquiet or upset are more common than we have thought. We need to shift our thinking to see that change is the norm and calm is the exception.

Turning points are a time of major discontinuity in life. They are often described as leading to adaptations that contribute to the successful fit of the individual in his or her world. George Singer and Laurie Powers, from the Darmouth Medical School, have said that difficult life events (one type of turning point, as we shall see) can challenge preestablished ways of viewing the world so that new meanings or ways of understanding need to be acquired (Singer & Powers, 1993). People therefore respond to stress by creating new meanings. They need to work through an event, sometimes by attaching meaning to the event that is then incorporated into their belief system or self-concept. For example, the death of a loved one can be made sense of by the belief that "It was meant to be."

A newspaper article reported that the Italian opera singer Andrea Bocelli had been troubled by criticisms about the shortcomings of his voice (Posner, 1999). In reaction, he became determined to work harder and make more sacrifices for his art. He said, "Do you know something in this life that can be good without sacrifice?" This is a positive way of viewing a shortcoming—the belief that it can be overcome with effort. Such beliefs, a type of coping strategy, can be learned from families and friends or picked up from books, movies, and other media. In this way, the social groups to which we belong, as well as our broader society, exert an influence on the meanings we give to difficult life events.

We all know that growing children develop in many ways—emotionally, intellectually, physically, and socially. Contrary to popular belief, it is not just children who develop. Adults can develop different attitudes, beliefs, and values as they age (Levinson, 1986). This makes sense when we think about it. We all know people who have changed, such as friends who became strangers, lovers who became enemies, and enemies who became allies.

Daniel Levinson is a major proponent of the idea that adults develop. He states that growth in understanding and in making meaning occurs throughout life, primarily in response to stressful events and experiences (Levinson, 1986). Without these triggers to shake up our existing ways of viewing ourselves or the world, there would be little reason for us to change our beliefs, assumptions, attitudes, or values. Some researchers have in fact argued that development is accelerated during periods of instability or lack of equilibrium (e.g., Breunlin, 1988). This is the time when people are most able to develop new skills and come to new realizations about themselves and the world.

Adult development consists of exits and entrances, disengagements and reengagements, losses and gains (Brandtstädter, 1999; Klinger, 1977). Throughout adulthood, we cross from one life stage to another, marked by events such as developing an intimate relationship, having children, or starting retirement. Since the life course refers to the engagement of the self with the world, it is not surprising that adults change in response to key turning points, new learnings, and new understandings.

We've been considering what has been written about adaptation, across the life span, to events seen in a negative light. Does this apply to all turning points? By definition, turning points are times of tension, times when equilibrium in life is upset, times requiring adaptation. What are the ways in which adaptation to these significant experiences comes about? To what extent do turning points deal with events and experiences perceived as negative rather than positive? We will consider these things after a small detour to consider the nature of *meaning*.

THE MEANING OF MEANING: MAKING SENSE OF OUR WORLDS

> The life we want is not merely the one we have chosen and made. It is the one we must be choosing and making.
>   —Wendell Berry, poet

What is the meaning of *meaning*? Perhaps the easiest way to explain meaning is that it refers to "making sense." Literally, something has meaning when it makes sense—when it fills more than one of our five senses in a coherent pattern—we can see it, touch it, smell it, taste it, and/or hear it. Things therefore have meaning when we experience them on these many levels—when they fill multiple senses simultaneously. As Diane Ackerman (the best-selling author of *Natural History of the Senses*) puts it, our senses "tear reality apart into vibrant morsels and reassemble them into a meaningful pattern" (Ackerman, 1990, p. xvii).

Things also make sense when they fit our existing beliefs or ways of viewing the world. According to both Thomas Schwandt (1994), a social scientist interested in how we construct meaning, and Mihaly Csikszentmihalyi (1990), a researcher interested in optimal experience in life, we create meaning to establish order among unrelated or conflicting information. That is, we change or modify our beliefs in the light of new experiences to keep our world seamless and whole. Because we evaluate the fit between new ideas and existing concepts, we are active makers of meaning. We construct meaning by inventing new concepts to make sense of experience.

This process of making meaning is influenced by the meaning given to events and experiences by others around us, including the groups to which we belong and society at large. There have been historical shifts in what is valued by society that undoubtedly affect our construction of meaning. Gail Sheehy, best-selling author of *Passages* (1977) and *Pathfinders* (1982), discusses the valuing of the home in the 1950s and the self in the

1960s (the so-called me generation). These different societal values influence how individuals make meaning. According to Mihaly Csikszentmihalyi (1990), every human culture contains meaning systems that guide and shape the meaning and purposes of individuals. Social conventions and the language commonly used in our society to describe events and experiences also play a role in how individuals create meaning for their life experiences.

GIVING MEANING TO LIFE EXPERIENCES

> The very meaninglessness of life forces man to create his own meanings.... However vast the darkness, we must supply our own light.
> —Stanley Kubrick, film director

What makes some experiences attain the status of a turning point in life? What makes a person describe an event as a *life-changing moment*?

As we have discussed, people are meaning makers. When something happens, we ask, "What does it mean?" Managers sitting around a boardroom table often discuss events that could have negative or positive effects on their business. What they are trying to do is make sense of the event—and figure out what the implications may be—so they can act to capitalize on an opportunity or to prevent a negative outcome, such as a mark on the business' reputation or a reduced market share. On the level of the individual, the huge market for self-help books reflects our intense desire to find meaning in our lives and to grow and cope with adversity. These books range from those dealing with positive thinking, yoga, and meditation to those dealing with spirituality and ways of understanding the world.

The act of making meaning can be seen as a creation, and we can have an intense desire to understand what *meaning* is. If life is a tapestry and the interwoven threads are our experiences, it is as if we are trying to gain a vantage point from which to see the tapestry's pattern—life's meaning. We are continually looking for the pattern and perhaps wondering whether there is any pattern at all. But because the self and the world are interwoven with one another, it is impossible to back away from the tapestry far enough to see the pattern. Listening to people's stories is an oblique, and thereby effective, way of seeing the pattern.

"Stories give shape to the events and emotions that make up our lives. And they provide a sense of permanence, a way of remembering what has happened to us. Without stories, we lose our sense of the past and its connection to our present and future" (Vera Rosenbluth, storyteller, 1997,

p. 7). When people tell stories, other people should listen carefully. Stories are the vehicle by which people communicate their own personal meanings to others. Through stories, people communicate a coherent explanation for things. Stories also can be a safe way of talking about emotions. They can legitimize our feelings by giving a particular perspective and providing a reason for the feelings we experience. Emotions play a big role in turning points, as we shall see.

To understand the meaning of turning points, we need to know what occurs before a turning point and what comes after. Meaning therefore comes from the context—the timing of the turning point in a person's life. Daniel Levinson (1978) refers to this idea when he says that the meaning of a stage in life is defined by its part in a sequence. This is why life stories are so intriguing and useful as a way of looking at the meaning of experience. The convention in telling a story is to describe a cast of characters and a series of events leading up to a climax, and to end with a satisfying resolution to the problem. If only life were so simple.

Researchers who study the unfolding course of human lives (e.g., Baltes, 1987) show us that it is important to take a life-span perspective when looking at meaning. Things that are important at one stage in life can become relatively unimportant at another stage. Conversely, new areas of meaning can become apparent as we mature. It is now commonly accepted that, in Western culture, both adolescence and midlife are not always times of stress and struggle. When adolescents have the responsibility and independence they desire, that time in life can reflect the opposite of the *teenager from hell* (Eccles et al., 1993). Midlife also has had short shrift in our popular conception. The midlife crisis is not inevitable. In fact, a 10-year study, conducted by the MacArthur Foundation Research Network on Successful Mid-life Development, which involved nearly 8,000 Americans between 40 and 60 years of age, showed that only 23 percent reported having a midlife crisis and only a third of this group described this crisis as having to do with the realization that they were aging (Goode, 1999). Rather, midlife seems best described as a time of psychological well-being, productive activity, and community involvement. Thus, adolescence and midlife are not necessarily times of crisis or major turning points, despite the myths that have grown around these periods of life.

TYPES OF TURNING POINTS

> In the light of subsequent events…it might even be said that
> this small decision of mine constituted something of a key turn-

ing point; that that decision set things on an inevitable course towards what eventually happened.

— Kazuo Ishiguro, *The Remains of the Day*

Turning points can be cumulative episodes or sudden events (Denzin, 1989). They can be events we have control over (active decisions we make) or fortuitous happenings (Cohler, 1987). They can be gradual understandings or sudden illuminations (Denzin, 1989). In her book *Pathfinders,* Gail Sheehy (1982) distinguishes between two types of adult life crises—those that are predictable because they are a typically encountered stage, or "passage," in life and those that are unpredictable, such as accidents. Researchers have in fact found evidence for these two types of turning points at midlife: normative or commonly experienced transitions and unscheduled or unanticipated events (Wethington, Cooper, & Holmes, 1997). Regardless of their nature, turning points always have a personal, subjective meaning. It is sometimes difficult for others to see that some event has been meaningful, whereas other situational life events, such as the death of a close family member, are quite commonly seen as turning points.

The turning points described by the people in our study were a mix of events or experiences and sudden or gradual realizations. The events sometimes reflected common developmental issues such as leaving home, getting a job, getting married, buying a home, and having children. Other events described as turning points were nondevelopmental but things most of us would see as highly meaningful, such as emigrating to a new country, losing a foster child, receiving a diagnosis, or experiencing a divorce. Other turning points were realizations about differences between self and others.

We now embark on our journey to explore turning points, as told to us by the participants in our study. What are the key characteristics of turning points? Where do they tend to take place, who do they tend to involve, what emotions are associated with them, how do they start and end, and, above all, what do they mean?

THE SETTINGS OF TURNING POINTS

One might think that life-changing experiences could happen anywhere and that there would be no pattern to where they occur. People's turning points, however, tended to occur in particular settings (times and places). The most common setting was the educational environment—

elementary school, high school, and university. Turning points concerning struggles in the educational system seem to be particularly important for people with attention deficit disorder. Children who display hyperactive behavior (and struggle to pay attention in class) tend to have poorer educational outcomes than other children of the same age (Hechtman, 1991). Individuals with chronic physical conditions also had turning points in the educational system. Their turning points involved a variety of issues—getting along with peers, the limiting attitudes of some teachers, and difficulties in participating due to inaccessible playgrounds and classrooms.

It is possible that the age of the participants (most were in their 30s) had an influence on their reports about turning points in the educational system. School had been the major occupation in many of their lives. It would be interesting to see what senior citizens would say about turning points and whether school is a distant and relatively unimportant setting in their life stories, as seen from a vantage point further on in life. Bruce Headey and Alexander Wearing, political scientists at the University of Melbourne, have reported that young people experience both more favorable and more unfavorable life events than do older people (Headey & Wearing, 1989). If this is the case, perhaps the school environment may be a setting for major life experiences from any vantage point in life.

Another common type of setting was an institution, organization, or program providing services, support, or advocacy for those with disabilities, health problems, and/or mental health difficulties. The third most common type of setting was a group, organization, or association that did not provide services, such as a fraternity or a senior citizens' center. Job sites also were mentioned fairly frequently as a setting for turning points.

We do not know whether another group of people would describe their key turning points as taking place in similar types of settings, but we would hazard a guess that the educational environment is a key contender for life-changing experiences for everyone. In our early years, we spend so much time at school. In elementary school, we are young, impressionable, and often uncertain of our academic ability. In high school, we are often uncertain whether we fit in and may try to be one of the so-called in group. Many people who go to university are intensely focused on good marks to ensure a good job. Others avidly pursue a social life. Regardless of our aims and uncertainties, the educational environment is a key place in which life-changing experiences and their resolution unfold. The school system has a profound impact on children, youth, and young adults.

KEY INDIVIDUALS IN PEOPLE'S LIVES

According to Michael Rutter (1985), a researcher interested in how resilience develops, it is a truism that relationships with people form the basis of much that is helpful in our lives. Gerben Sinnema, a clinical psychologist from the Netherlands, states that social relationships are the cornerstones of our sense of self-worth (Sinnema, 1991). Other people make us feel valued, assist us in acquiring new meanings for distressing experiences, and help us in practical matters. As we have seen, the key settings for people's turning points in our study were social settings, which reflects the idea that other people play key roles in our lives. As described in chapter 1, study participants took part in interviews that were transcribed so we could closely examine the information they shared. To qualitatively analyze this information, we created a coding system that contained over 1,400 codes. Of all these codes, the most frequent code (occurring more than 680 times) was "people."

Who are the most significant people in our lives? For participants, they were (in no particular order) friends, mothers and fathers, parents, doctors, teachers, and wives and husbands. Why are these people part of significant times in life? These people are important to us because they can help us and hurt us. We often care what they think of us and we realize the influence they have over us. They are the ones who believe in us, advocate for us, comfort us, guide us, and support us. They are the ones who make us angry or fearful. They can hold expectations for us that are narrow and limiting, and make assumptions about us that we don't like. They can hold out an ideal vision of the person they would like us to be, so that we either become our best selves due to their expectations or rebel against this vision.

People therefore are key players in the stories of turning points. They may be lead actors who do something with tremendous impact on us, such as abandoning us or believing in us. They may be supporting actors who help pick up the pieces and patch the wounds. They may be Good Samaritans on our journey in life, people who lie in wait in the bushes, or just fellow travelers we encounter on the way.

TURNING POINTS AND EMOTIONS

> Emotions play a central role in individual experience and interpersonal relations.
> — Phillip Shaver, Judith Schwartz, Donald Kirson,
> and Cary O'Connor, "Emotion Knowledge:
> Further Exploration of a Prototype Approach"

There is no doubt that we *react* on an emotional level to events in our lives. What may not be so clear is that emotions also spur us into *action*. Carroll Izard, a researcher noted for her work on emotion, states that, whether consequences or antecedents, emotions give meaning and significance to human existence (Izard, 1971). Some people are driven to risky activities, such as mountain climbing and parachute jumping, because these activities give an emotional thrill, an exhilarating feeling of being truly alive.

If turning points are emotionally compelling events, experiences, and realizations, then what are the emotions most often associated with them? The emotions most often described by people when talking about their turning points were anger, joy, fear, hurt, pain, and devastation. There are hundreds of terms that refer to emotions, but the most basic ones seem to be love, joy, surprise, anger, sadness, and fear, which are very similar to those mentioned by participants.

Anger was due to others' assumptions, not being understood, being abandoned, or feeling betrayed. Research indicates that anger occurs when something interferes with reaching a goal or harms a person in some way, and this is seen as unfair or wrong (Shaver et al., 1987). As expressed by our study participants, joy encompassed feelings of happiness, enjoyment, and excitement, and was sometimes due to achievements. Joy is typically associated with getting something we desire, whether it be producing something, achieving recognition, receiving affection, or just being involved in an activity we love. Fear was due to the threat of failure or anxiety about being alone. According to Phillip Shaver and his colleagues (1987), fear commonly begins with an anticipation of physical harm, loss, rejection, or failure. Sadness occurs after a person has experienced an undesirable outcome, such as the death of a loved one or the loss of a relationship. Sadness involves discovering that one is helpless to change the circumstances. Devastation is similar to sadness: it is a feeling of being overwhelmed and shattered by events.

The participants in our study gave vivid portrayals of these various emotions. Neil is 36 years old. He is married and has children. At eighteen, he was cut off from services he had been receiving (for cerebral palsy) since childhood.

Being eighteen and being cut off from a support system, something you have known for thirteen years—it sets you back. It really gets you angry.... You don't have that support system so you start back at square one and you flail for a while until you find your feet again.... Now, on a positive note—it is sort of positive in a way because it sort of makes you mad—I have always found anger is a very good motivator for actual change, provided, of course, that you don't get so angry that you run your head up against a brick wall.... I've always found the best change in my life comes out of that deep-seated anger, knowing there was something wrong and knowing that the only way to do anything about it was to launch into a positive mode and try and do things.

Anger was a key emotion associated with turning points. We often think of anger as a bad thing, something we want to control in ourselves and our children. Anger is associated with being out of control and with aggression and violence. Anger, however, can be a positive motivating force that drives people to prove others wrong and proceed to achieve a life goal, such as graduating from school.

Karen is a 37-year-old woman who, like Neil, has cerebral palsy. She lives with her dog and receives attendant care to meet her daily living needs. She talks about a turning point involving her graduation from grade eight, when she felt joy and pride from having proved others wrong.

It was very exciting. I felt very proud.... Many of the doctors and other people that were in my life in the past had always said that I would never graduate, I would never become anything.... They said it to my parents and they said it to me. I think a lot of times doctors talk about the child when they are right there. They don't think that the child understands or comprehends, but I don't believe that. A lot of those messages go into the brain and stick there.

Another emotion often expressed when describing turning points is devastation. Loreena, who has spina bifida, talks about a devastating experience with a friend.

This girl that I met, she changed my life and my way of thinking about different things.... She was somebody I opened up to and I told her my deepest, darkest secrets that I had never told anybody in my entire life. Also, I told her about my physical difficulties. Most people only see the fact that I walk differently. Having spina bifida, obviously there are other complications that nobody really can see. She knew all that about me and that was the first time I'd ever let anybody know anything about myself physically.

When I moved away from the city, our friendship sort of grew apart, but in December I dropped off her Christmas gift. I didn't hear anything from her for about 10 days and I thought this was really strange because usually we called each other every weekend.... About 10 days later, I got a package in the mail. She sent back all my Christmas gifts and all the gifts I'd ever given her, and a 10 page "I hate you" letter. It was the most devastating day of my life and I thought, "What did I do?" She told me things that she'd never said to me before.... That I was trying to buy her friendship.... It was just a devastating day.... I called my sister and she said, "Don't worry about it. Leave her alone. If she decides that she wants to come back, she'll come back." And I haven't heard from her since.

It took me a few weeks to get over it and then I just said there's nothing I can do about this, so let's move on and concentrate on what we're doing and friends that are here, rather than worry about if she might come back and if she might not. So I just let it go.... We were really good friends, but I hung on too tight.... I heaped things on her—at that point I was in a depressed state. Friends will take you through the good times and the bad, but when you go through two years of bad, it's got to be really hard on the friendship too.... Now I'm very cautious and I don't put everything on my girlfriend all the time. I try to work it out myself now.... It was very important to me to realize that there are some days that I can deal with myself and I do now. It gives you that extra step of confidence that you can depend on yourself. You don't have to have someone else to help you. You can get through it on your own.

This devastating experience—the loss of a friend—was a turning point for Loreena. It led her to the decision not to rely so much on others and to the realization that she had the ability to deal with life's problems on her own.

Grace and Helen talked about the devastation of divorce. Grace is 51 years old, has two university degrees, and has spina bifida.

I got divorced 17 years ago and that was a major, major turning point, a bad one.... It shattered all my former beliefs and values and I had to redefine myself. It just shattered my confidence.... Within a year's period, I lost my marriage, I had a major illness, I lost my home, I lost my job.... A lot of it I blamed on my disability. It took a lot of work and a lot of soul searching, and a good support network, to make me come back to normal.... I thought the marriage wouldn't have broken up if it hadn't been for the disability.... And looking back on it, it probably was the natural thing to do because it took me a long time to look inside myself and see where I may have contributed to those factors.

Having survived the initial year, a renewal took place. I regained my confidence. I discovered my sense of self but most amazing to me was when I set about building a new future. Here I would say my experience with a disability came into play. I think the way I had to deal with that gave me the tools to deal with this.... I felt a strength and determination which drove me to redefine my life entirely.... I feel this strength developed out of a need to deal with the early years of disability, except now it was being utilized to reorganize an entire way of life.

After the initial devastating period, I embarked on a new career, the pursuit of a degree, and added a whole new circle of friends and interests.... I did a complete house clean, metaphorically and physically.... I can remember the motivating feelings—there was the shock and the anger and the betrayal and all the stuff that goes with it and the utter hopelessness of it.... But there came a point when I felt this sense of relief and this sense that there is so much that I could be doing.... There was this inner desire to purge myself of what was, retain the things and people that were important to me, but then redefine everything else. I do remember at one point thinking this is a golden opportunity to do something with the rest of my life that would not have been possible for me had I remained married.... That turning point in my mid-thirties set me on a totally different course, simply because I had expected to be married for the rest of my life.

Grace's sense of devastation came from a combination of losses—the loss of her marriage, health, home, and job. Her beliefs and confidence were shattered. After a period of time, she began to rebuild her life and establish new hope for the future. She set out to recreate her life and redefine her sense of self. Crises often force us to consider how we want to live (Brown & Harris, 1978). By helping us clarify our goals and values in life, turning points can come to be seen as positive experiences that provide new opportunities for growth. It is interesting that the Chinese symbol for "crisis" stands, in part, for the notion of "opportunity." Through crises, new opportunities are seen or develop.

Helen, who has attention deficit disorder, describes a similar experience with a divorce.

About a month after my son was born, my husband decided that he couldn't cope with married life and being a father, and he left. Now I can't say that there have been too many more traumatic experiences in my life than that one, but at the time I was so busy being a single parent that I can't say that that necessarily triggered anything.... It wasn't until eventually a couple of years later that my husband said he wanted to come back.... He was seeking forgiveness but I wasn't interested in forgiveness. I was very angry, bitter, and upset with him and decided that a reconciliation was out of the question. I was still very, very angry and had decided on some level that I couldn't trust him. I couldn't trust him with my love, my emotions, the well-being of my children. I was making it. I was doing it. He had broken the big dream of the white picket fence and I wasn't interested.

> I really wanted to try in my heart of hearts to forgive him and understand why he did the things that he did and not take it personally....I knew that the anger that I was carrying was not a good thing for me as a person or as an influence on my children....I wanted to let that go and say, okay, these are the good things that have come out of it. I don't have to argue with someone else about any decisions around this house. I don't have to argue about how to raise the children....I really want to use lemons to make lemonade. I really want to live that way because it is better for me and it is better for my children.

Helen had a dream of "the white picket fence" and all that entailed, which was broken by her husband's leaving. She describes experiencing a delayed response of anger and distrust to this abandonment. Her emotional roller coaster ended when she decided to let go of the anger and began to see the good that arose from the bad. At this point, she made a conscious decision to live her life focusing on the positive—the lemonade rather than the lemons. Similar to Grace's decision to rebuild her life in a new way, Helen's turning point ultimately led her to make a choice about how to live. Her decision to focus on the good coming from the bad exemplifies the type of thinking that can carry us through a turning point and make us stronger and more resilient. In *A Woman's Book of Life,* Joan Borysenko (1996) states that many women who have gone through divorce experience a personal growth in their sense of control. People who successfully remake their lives after a divorce often develop a strong belief in their capacity to cope with difficult life experiences. It has been said that "That which doesn't kill us makes us stronger." This is the idea of strength or "steeling qualities" arising from adversity (Rutter, 1987, 1990).

Loss and anger, followed by a spiritual resolution, is shown in a turning point described by Bernie, who has chronic pain and spina bifida and has had problems with alcohol. Bernie had been fostering a child who was placed in another home.

> When he left I had a lot of guilt. I felt I let him down....He left in November and I was ready to start drinking in January. I was saying to God, "What's this all about, what's the point in all this? I prayed and prayed that you would give me somebody that I could pass the things I've learned on to, and you give him to me and then you just jerk him out of here." And through that frustration and dealing with all those feelings and the pain I went through, that's when I embraced Jesus Christ as Lord the Savior. That was my conversion time and I consider myself a born-again Christian today....So for me the devastation, the pain, and the hurt of losing that kid was also the door that opened me up to finally humble myself to accept the next grace level....The

rage is still there, the anger is still there, but it is muffled. I have a sense of gentleness and humbleness and compassion for others.

To feel devastated means to feel overwhelmed and helpless. Our view of the world is in disorder and we need to put the fragments back into a coherent whole. Bernie achieved this through his embracing of Christianity.

There are other kinds of losses besides the loss of people. Losses can be symbolic (Watson, 1985). We can experience a sense of loss around events we have no control over and around experiences in which we make choices. When a sense of loss occurs due to a choice we have made, such as allowing dreams to fade or choosing one potential partner over another, it can be difficult to deal with this sense of loss. A state of cognitive dissonance (thoughts not fitting together) occurs any time we make a decision where the unchosen alternative has more positive features than the chosen alternative (Festinger, 1957).

We also can experience loss of a part of ourselves through things we have no control over, such as illnesses, accidents, or physical impairments. In these cases, a sense of loss occurs when we must relinquish something in the way we see ourselves or a hope or desire about our physical function. Alisha and Karen talk about a loss concerning their physical capabilities. Alisha has cerebral palsy and is 34 years old. She got a motorized scooter for the first time when she was attending university.

> My big turning point was getting the scooter. Getting used to relying on the scooter for my mobility, which allows me to use my energy elsewhere. ...Once the scooter came I realized how much more energy I had at the end of the day because I wasn't physically defeating myself with getting to class....I had to accept it and my friends and family had to accept it as well....Now I was getting a chair and they were looking at it as "You're getting lazy."...They couldn't understand why I needed this chair....They said: "She hasn't needed one all this time, why would she need one now?" Well, you go and look at the campus and then you tell me that....I had to learn to accept it, plus it felt like at times I had to teach my friends and family to learn to accept it too. But it got to a point where I just said: "I have got the scooter. You learn to accept it, I have."...It just taught me how to accept that I have a disability and that I have limitations....Getting my scooter was bad at the time, but eventually it was good.

Getting a scooter was originally seen as a bad thing by Alisha. However, she came to accept the scooter and to realize its benefit—the fact that she had more energy at the end of the day. She also learned something about herself from the turning point. This was an acceptance of her disability as part of herself.

Karen also has cerebral palsy. She talks about a similar experience concerning the meaning of having a wheelchair.

> By the time I was 12 my hip started to dislocate so, after many medical examinations, I had to decide whether to have surgery to lock my hips in place or to stop walking and go to a wheelchair.... And that was a big turning point in my life.... Having a wheelchair gained me a lot more freedom. I could come and go when I wanted. I didn't have to wait for my braces to be locked.

Karen sees the event of choosing a wheelchair as a positive decision that gave her much more physical mobility. Before a person comes to terms with a loss of physical capacity, it can be difficult to cope with the sense of diminishing capacity. It may not be something that we often realize, but we can lose what we have never had—an idea of what we might become or might possess (Brown & Harris, 1978; Parkes, 1971).

Through people's descriptions of turning points, we see that turning points truly are emotionally compelling events, experiences, and realizations. Emotions of anger, joy, fear, hurt, pain, and devastation surface again and again in people's stories. Proving others wrong is an experience associated with joy. The experiences of loss and abandonment are associated with strong, negative emotions but, over time, people come to see the positive, growth-enhancing aspects of turning points.

THE MEANINGS OF TURNING POINTS

Seek and ye shall find.
—Matthew 7:7

Is there one single meaning of life? Is it love? Is it understanding ourselves? Is it immersing ourselves in something we love to do? Is it believing in God? We next consider the three paths to meaning in life that resoundingly emerged from people's descriptions of their turning points—belonging, doing, and understanding the self and the world.

BELONGING

[Some hold the] belief in "belongingness" as the ultimate need of the individual.
—William Whyte, Jr., *The Organization Man*

As a theme by which participants created meaning in their lives, *belonging* was by far the strongest. Baumeister and Leary (1995) have in fact proposed that the need to belong is a fundamental human motive. Based on an extensive review of research findings, they concluded that people are motivated by a strong desire to form long-term, caring relationships. Their work supports the view that a sense of belonging, formed through human connections, is a fundamental way in which people create a sense of meaning in their everyday lives.

People belong, or are connected with others, in different ways. The most basic type of belonging is belonging to our family of origin. Throughout our lives, we belong to different social groups—our class at school, groups of friends, activity-based groups of various kinds, and work groups. As we mature, we also form romantic attachments and develop intimate relationships.

While some people think that the point of growing up is to become independent, it is more accurate to realize that, throughout our lives, we are interdependent with others. Al Condeluci, program director of United Cerebral Palsy of Pittsburgh, has introduced this notion of interdependence in the lives of all people (Condeluci, 1995). Whatever our age or abilities, we are always reliant to some extent on others. We rely on others for emotional support, for practical support, and for opportunities. We rely on our intimate partners, our children, our friends, and our doctors. They, in turn, rely on us for our support, our assistance, and our patronage.

Joseph Viszmeg was an award-winning Edmonton filmmaker who directed a documentary about his experience with adrenal cancer, *In My Own Time: Diary of a Cancer Patient*. He described the tumultuous journey of coming to terms with his illness as a "monster truck rally" in which he learned the importance of love and relationships (Downey, 1999).

Relationships were very important to participants in our study. Evan, who has cerebral palsy, discusses what it meant to him to return to his hometown and family after living in supportive housing in another city for 20 years.

> I was really, really feeling the blues....I was lucky enough to realize that I had to get out of that situation and go home....I realized that the city wasn't what I need in my life. What I need is here. This is the center for me and it always will be....I didn't feel a part of the city. I didn't feel like I belonged....I said to myself: "Enough is enough, let's go home."...I wasn't happy at all. I thought, I'm missing everything like my nephew and niece growing up and I want to be there....I thought, man, I am stuck here in another city and missing everything else in my life.
>
> I realized that my mom and dad are not going to be around forever....I took all that into consideration and decided on an action and the action was to come back here....A couple of months ago, my sister had her second

baby.... I was glad that I was a part of that. I finally got up to her place and held the little one in my arms. If I was in another city, that never would have happened.... Now I am closer to my family. It was one of the best things I ever did.... Family has always been number one with me. Coming back only reaffirmed that.

Evan is very clear about his family's importance to him. Living in another city, he felt he was missing the experience of watching his niece and nephew grow up, and he realized that his parents would not be around forever. His turning point—moving back home—helped him to be closer to his family, which he sees as the most important thing in life.

Bernie also discusses the meaning of belonging to a group: "I think the real turning point is my joining Alcoholics Anonymous. It's that sense of belonging, that I fit in. I don't feel so unique anymore. AA gave me the tools to step away from those things."

Bernie's experience illustrates that having a common bond with others makes us feel part of something—not alone. Members of self-help or mutual aid groups share a similar condition or difficulty, which can allow them to understand each other as no one else can. Because they are in the same boat, they often have a strong sense of a common predicament or concern.

Many self-help groups, such as Alcoholics Anonymous, have a particular philosophy and set of teachings that show members how to cope with life events and how to interpret their life situation (Humphreys & Rappaport, 1994). Changes in world view frequently occur as a result of membership in these groups. According to Keith Humphreys, a leading researcher on self-help, these changes in perspective can occur in several areas, including the person's view of the problem, their spirituality or sense of universal order, their self-understanding, and their relationships with others (Humphreys & Rappaport, 1994). Thus, self-help groups do more than create a sense of belonging. By effecting changes in how people view themselves and their world, self-help groups can lead to fundamental shifts in what is meaningful to people, and thereby contribute to their adaptation and resilience.

What is it about relationships with others that is meaningful? Sharing a common bond, feeling understood, feeling valued, and having our perspectives validated all are consequences of close relationships. Some participants used the words *being believed in* to describe the support that close relationships gave to them.

Frank is 33 years old, married, and has attention deficit hyperactivity disorder and a learning disability. He describes how it feels to have a partner in life. Note that this turning point has nothing to do with Frank's disability.

> I think it was on the ride home that I knew that this was the girl that I was going to marry....I thought: "You know, here is a wonderful, wonderful lady."...It was only two weeks after I had met her....That realization at that point was wonderful....We just got along really well and I just felt so comfortable with her....Here was a young lady who was bright, who was intelligent, who was beautiful, who laughed at my stupid jokes....She was happy with who I was. She was confident with who I was and I was confident with who she was and there was a mutual admiration on both parts.
>
> Our wedding day was absolutely wonderful. It was the best day of my life! Guys don't usually say these things, but it is that ego thing where everybody is there for you. You have a wonderful time and it goes so fast. It was a beautiful day and I couldn't ask for things going as well as they did....Everybody that meant something to you was there, so it was just an absolutely wonderful time.
>
> She gives me so much confidence and so much belief in myself....She has given me a more positive life and tells me when I am beating up on myself too much, when I am expecting too much....I just can't think of ever being without her.

Frank's story shows the importance of being believed in by someone else. Robert Brooks, an expert in children's resilience, considers being believed in by someone we care about to be an important aspect of social support for all people, including those with disabilities (Brooks, 1994). Social support refers to the perception that we are cared for, esteemed, and valued by other people. It makes a huge difference to know that someone understands you, knows both your strengths and your weaknesses, and still values you.

Part of the way we come to value ourselves is through the love and acceptance of others, which shows us that others see our worth. The other way we gain a sense of self-esteem is through our competencies, such as knowing we are good at sports or school work, or good at making friends. According to Susan Harter's (1982) theory of self-concept development, we make judgments of our ability in several key life areas, including our academic, social, and athletic performance, and our physical appearance.

Being believed in therefore has the direct effect of bolstering our self-esteem. Also, if someone believes in us, this can give us the confidence to take risks and try new things, so that an opening up of new opportunities can occur. Through these opportunities, we can gain new skills and new perceptions of our abilities, with a corresponding impact on our self-esteem.

> The difference between a productive life filled with excitement, joy, satisfaction, and accomplishment and a life punctured with despair, envy, underachievement, and self-defeating coping strategies may be based on the presence of at least one "charismatic adult," an adult who shows acceptance and respect and who provides experiences that constantly convey the message, "You are unique and worthwhile, you have much to offer and contribute, and you have the abilities to assume responsibility for what occurs in your life." Children and adolescents who incorporate this message develop high self-esteem and experience life as a challenge to confront and master rather than as a stress to avoid. (Brooks, 1992, pp. 548–549)

Gabrielle Weiss and Lily Trokenberg Hechtman asked young adults with attention deficit hyperactivity disorder what, if anything, had been most helpful to them while growing up (Weiss & Hechtman, 1993). Not surprisingly, the most frequent response was someone who believed in them. People with attention deficit hyperactivity disorder often experience an inconsistency between being able to grasp ideas easily but struggling with the more rote aspects of learning (Lambert, 1988). When a person doubts his or her own intelligence and does not fully understand the reasons for difficulties at school, this can lead to a poor self-concept with respect to academic performance. If you are that person, having someone who believes in you can make the world of difference. His or her positive regard provides you with emotional support in your efforts to succeed. His or her belief that you can master the challenge makes you feel worthwhile and optimistic about your future. By listening to you and providing feedback, the person who believes in you helps to shape your thoughts and helps you see the legitimacy of your feelings. According to Mihaly Csikszentmihalyi (1990), cherished companions also provide the gift of helping to bring order into our consciousness. All of this helps to reduce the feelings of anxiety that we experience when something isn't right in our world.

DOING

> [W]ork . . . is often the most enjoyable part of life.
> —Mihaly Csikszentmihalyi, psychologist

Passion refers to a strong emotion that has an overwhelming or compelling effect on us. We are passionate about the things we love to do—the things that we would do for free!

At 18, Tal Bachman, son of Randy Bachman (lead guitarist of the Guess Who and Bachman-Turner Overdrive), had a turning point (Niester, 1999). At university, reading Plato's *Republic,* he was struck by Plato's declaration that music is sovereign and that it shapes the customs of society. This led him to question why he was not pursuing music as his passion in life. He quit university and devoted himself to pursuing what he now sees to be his calling. At 18, Eddy Gofsky, who has attention deficit disorder and was skipping classes, had an epiphany (Martin, 2000). Eddy read the book *Think and Grow Rich* and decided to change his life. He decided that he wanted to have $100,000 by the time he was 24. He took a second job, threw himself into online investing in the stock market, and met his goal. Barry Blanchard, an accomplished Canadian mountain climber, was on the way to being a juvenile delinquent when a teacher gave him a book to read about mountain climbing that changed his life. Each of these examples shows the power of books in leading people to new activities that they passionately embrace.

Engagement in absorbing activities that satisfy our creative urge is often seen as the answer to the question of what is most meaningful in life. The businessperson who has trouble slowing down and finding meaning in hobbies after retirement epitomizes the notion that we primarily find meaning in the work that we do. We are not necessarily talking about paid work here, which is something valued by Western culture. The point is that, regardless of our cultural background, we derive meaning from engagement in activities, whether paid work, volunteer work, caring for others, hobbies, sports, or other activities.

People need to engage in activities they find fulfilling and engrossing. Involvement in activities is also the way we achieve the goals we set for ourselves. For people with disabilities, in particular, achieving a sense of independence can be an important goal. Getting a job is an achievement that can bring a sense of independence, as is buying a house.

Alisha, who has cerebral palsy, describes getting a full-time job as a turning point.

> It filled my expectations of what I was going to do with my life. . . . I had set a time frame out for myself. I was going to go to school, get my degree, get a job, get married, have my life all planned out. I never envisioned not working. . . . So getting a job reinforced my ability to be a productive member of society and it increased my independence. . . . It helped me keep that independent life. . . . It reinforced that you have to do things. I am an adult and my disability is not playing a role that is deterring me from doing anything.

Before my job, I was on disability pension and the whole system was awful. Every single penny you earned you have to report to them. It was like someone always looking over your shoulder. From day one it was like: "I am not living my life like this. I am going to be independent and it is me that is going to watch my finances, not somebody else."...I remember the day I got full time here and I wrote a nice letter to Family Benefits saying: "Thank you very much. You know I really appreciated the help going to school and such but I will no longer be needing your assistance." It was like a day of freedom. It was honestly unbelievable freedom I felt.

To Alisha, getting a full-time job meant many things. It meant that she achieved a goal she had set for herself, that she was independent, and that her disability was not deterring her from achieving things in life. Having a job symbolized freedom and autonomy. Thus, we see how employment can have tremendous implications for how we view ourselves and our lives, especially in North American culture.

Karen lives alone (except for her dog) and has cerebral palsy. She tells a story about hiring people to provide attendant care for her.

I now hire my own staff, train my own staff, and do up the payroll on the computer....I love it because I have more freedom than I have ever had in my life. I have staff that can come when I want them to. I make up the schedule and I book them for whenever I need them. I can sleep in or I can get up early. If I have to go to the mall and get shopping done, they can drive me there....They cook, clean, all that.

I know the people coming in. There is no more not knowing who is going to come because all the people that come are trained and I know them....And that makes a whole lot of difference. I am more relaxed. I don't have to worry about some stranger coming into my house to do my shower or whatever. So it is probably one of the best things that has happened.

All my life I have been doing things at other people's convenience. I am grateful that they were able to help but now I have my life....I can do more things for others because of it. I can take my niece out for supper or shopping....I can do simple things like that, which makes my life more exciting and fruitful and fun.

I feel a burden has been lifted off of me and off of my family. I have a totally different relationship now with my parents. It is more of a daughter-parent relationship where before it was daughter-parent/caregiver. At thirty plus years, you need to have that bit of space and privacy. Able-bodied thirty year-olds don't have their parents dressing them or cooking all the time.... We are getting to the point now where it is more fun to be together because my mom doesn't feel she has to help out.

Karen's turning point shows that attendant care is a lot more than having someone provide assistance. Through the act of managing the hiring of these staff, Karen experiences a sense of independence. Her self-confidence has been increased through doing and achieving things on her own.

Loreena, who is 36 and completed college (and has spina bifida), describes buying her own home as a major turning point in her life.

A major, major change in my life was buying my own home. I was so stressed out. Being single and the only income earner and paying a mortgage, I was just petrified. But I knew that it was something I had to do because I was spending so much in rent and it made no sense anymore. As somebody said, you might as well be writing a check and throwing it off the edge of the balcony.... At least now I've got something that's building a little bit of equity. The first year, I looked up my mortgage payments and went, "Gee, I own the front door now!"

I really, really like having my own place.... When I come home, I feel like I'm home.... It's the nicest feeling to come home, plop myself on the couch and go: "Aah. This is my home. This is mine."... It has taken me a long time to get to this point in my life, and it has taken a lot of hard work too.... It's my biggest accomplishment and one of my proudest accomplishments because it was a goal I set for myself years ago.... I had now achieved the same level of success as my brothers and sisters.... They are all married and have their own places and I hadn't reached that level of success in my own eyes.

It was the best decision I ever made.... It has made me feel that much more confident. You just keep building your confidence level by taking more steps and more risks.... I think my parents saw I'd made a smart decision and they respected that.... It's really nice to know that your parents are proud of what you've accomplished in life.... Our relationship has changed.... The whole thing has just changed my outlook on life.

Here we see multiple meanings intertwined in the story of buying a home. To Loreena, buying a home meant gaining self-confidence, achieving a life goal, and putting her relationship with her parents on a new footing. Daniel Levinson (1978), well known for his work on life stages, talks about the developmental task of leaving our parents. The goal at this life stage is not to end the relationship but to move it to a different level, involving new qualities of mutual respect. Loreena and Karen describe exactly this sort of change in their relationships with their parents following their achievements of independence—as told in their stories of buying a home and managing attendant care.

People become competent by engaging in activities that help them develop skills, including interpersonal skills, analytical skills, skill in caring for others, and artistic skills. Only through doing and achieving do we develop a sense that we are capable individuals with something of value to offer. Ann Masten, Karin Best, and Norman Garmezy (1990), researchers in the area of resilience, echo this when they say that a key protective factor in life is to be competent in some area that is valued by the person themselves or by society. Of course, what is valued can differ from person to person, family to family, and society to society.

Meaningful engagement in activities is also thought to be necessary for a person to become an adult with the capacity to enjoy life. Gordon Mathews (1996) says that people are happiest if they can spend the majority of their time engaged in activities to which they are deeply committed. When we engage in activities we love and do well, there are benefits to our sense of self. We develop feelings of competency and self-efficacy (Bandura, 1986). In addition, depending on the nature of the activity, involvement in an activity we love can make us feel that we are making a valued contribution to some enterprise or goal beyond ourselves, such as to our family, our workplace, or our society. A general sense of mastery can arise from doing well at specific tasks, so that we feel in control of the forces that affect our lives.

Among the many books written on the importance of doing things that have meaning to us, two are particularly worthy of note. The first, *Working,* by the journalist Studs Terkel (1972), is a classic in the world of business. Based on three years of interviews with over 100 people in various jobs, including a strip miner, a bar pianist, an assembly line worker, and a firefighter, this book allows us to see the common factors underlying seemingly different jobs. One of the most powerful messages is the importance of having meaning in work above and beyond the reward of a paycheck. Terkel was astonished by what he calls the "extraordinary dreams of ordinary people" and their common view that work should acknowledge a person's being and sense of self.

The second book, *Flow: The Psychology of Optimal Experience,* by Mihaly Csikszentmihalyi (1990), deals with the importance of flow experiences in people's lives. When people are totally involved in some activity which has clear goals that fit their abilities and is seen as challenging but not overwhelming, a state of deep concentration can occur, called "flow," that is enjoyable. Flow is a state of mind that occurs when our thoughts are focused on the activity at hand (harmoniously ordered) and we want to pursue whatever we are doing for its own sake. When in a state of flow, people feel strong, active, creative, focused, and motivated. They are not aware of themselves as separate from what they are doing; they are totally absorbed in the activity. People report flow experiences at work, when creating art or sculpture, and when gardening, hiking, jogging, or engaging in any kind of sport or hobby that stimulates them by requiring high skill but does not overchallenge. This book therefore sheds light on how doing things—engaging in certain activities—can be so meaningful to us. Flow experiences occur for people of all ages and people in all cultures. Teenagers in Tokyo and grandmothers in Korea report these same experiences.

Charles Fipke, a geologist, epitomizes a person whose experiences lead to flow. As described by Vernon Frolick (*Fire into Ice: Charles Fipke and the Great Diamond Hunt,* 1999), Fipke, tired of being broke, appears to have experienced a turning point where he made the decision to become the master of his own fate. This decision led him to discover one of the largest diamond mines in the world. Before striking it rich, he was asked what he would do if he could do anything he wished. The question puzzled him. "I'm doing it," he answered (Knoll, 1999). Fipke's single-minded drive had a price, as we shall see in chapter 5.

Chris Loscerbo, who broke his neck in a diving accident, spent many years struggling to come to terms with not being able to use his arms or legs ("Singing Praises," 2000). He felt profoundly irrelevant and had no sense of accomplishment because he had no activity to fully engage him. Then he discovered sailing. By using sip-and-puff technology that allows people to steer and work the sails by breathing through a straw, Chris was able to sail single-handedly. Being able to sail brought about a transformation in his life. He experienced a sense of liberation, a restoration of joy in his life, and a sense of fun and passion. He says "There's a fire in my eye again.... When you've got something like sailing, it really puts the joy back in living" ("Singing Praises," 2000).

UNDERSTANDING OURSELVES OR LIFE IN A NEW WAY

> The ultimate goal of life remains the spiritual growth of the individual.
>
> —M. Scott Peck, *The Road Less Traveled*

We change in our definitions of ourselves and the world, in our modes of response and adaptation, and in our orientations and

values. Sometimes particular transitions require radical adaptation in behavior and in our role identities. Other change is gradual.
But we do change—not only our role contexts, but our selves.
                        —John R. Kelly, *Leisure Identities and Interactions*

We have seen the importance of belonging and the importance of engaging in activities we care about. An alternate viewpoint, especially within
Western culture, is that the most important aspect of living is achieving
self-understanding or a new set of beliefs or values that guide how we live.
According to Janoff-Bulman (1992), all of us develop personal theories of
reality that guide our behavior and automatically structure our experiences. These theories of reality include assumptions about the self and
assumptions about the world. Many self-help books start with the premise
that self-understanding is the ultimate goal of living in this world. Erik
Erikson, a psychologist, saw conflicts and crises as being valuable and
necessary in the sense that they lead to the healthy development of the personality (Erikson, 1963).

What evidence is there for the role of self-understanding in people's stories of their turning points? A key self-understanding reached by many
participants is revealed in the following stories told by Alisha, Rick, and
Trudy.

Alisha, who earlier described getting a full-time job and what it meant
to get a scooter, talks about the experiences that "opened her eyes" to how
others viewed her as a person with a disability (she has cerebral palsy).

> I was being considered for integration into the school system. . . . I always
> expected to go to school with my brothers and sisters because, at that point,
> I could see no difference in me as opposed to my sister except that I went to
> a different school. . . . My mother was a firm believer in integration: "She
> will go to the school where she wants to go and she wants to go to the school
> where her sisters and brothers go."
>
> I was probably one of the first people who was integrated into the school
> system and that was a learning experience. It opened up my eyes because
> it showed me that I was different only because the school system treated
> me differently. Not badly, just differently. They had never had anybody
> with a disability in there before so they weren't sure what to do. . . . I wasn't
> allowed to go outside at recesses to play. I had to stay inside and it was just
> driving me nuts and I said: "Mom, look, I have to go outside." So I had her
> write a note. She was forever writing notes that said: "Let her do this."
>
> Shortly after I arrived, another person came with a disability, so what
> they did was let us go outside, but we had to sit on chairs right against the

wall, side by side. Well, all of a sudden we were getting these crowds of people around us and, to me, it was: "What are those people staring at us for?" That opened my eyes to see that there was a difference between me and my sister because, in my family, there was no difference—I was always able to do whatever I wanted to do. So that was a big turning point—realizing the differences.

Alisha describes realizing that others saw her differently as a key turning point in her life. In a similar vein, both Rick and Trudy talk about the experience of being diagnosed with attention deficit hyperactivity disorder, which occurred later on in their lives. Rick, who is 34 and lives alone, considered receiving a diagnosis to be a turning point in his life.

> I've basically been able to fake being able to think straight up to now.... I used to go home and I would just go in my room and grip my head, it was going so fast. At that point I didn't know what was wrong with me.... I didn't get tested for ADHD until about a year and a half ago.... It felt good to finally know what was wrong with me. I'm not alone in the world, I'm not the only one that has this.
>
> I went to a meeting for people with learning disabilities.... It was different because I had never met anybody else that had it.... They were talking about their lives and I was saying: "Hey, that sounds like me."

We often think of labels in negative terms because they can perpetuate stereotypes; however, labels can have benefits as well. On the one hand, a diagnosis can identify a distinction that we find useful because it explains the situation to ourselves and others. On the other hand, we sometimes don't appreciate having a diagnostic label because we want to belong and fit in. Our reaction to having a label therefore depends on how we see it—as a vehicle for self-understanding or as an impediment to belonging.

Trudy, who is 39 and married, reports a positive experience concerning the importance of receiving a diagnostic label. One of Trudy's children was diagnosed as having attention deficit hyperactivity disorder. She then discovered that she herself had attention deficit hyperactivity disorder.

> They told us he [her son] had ADHD and that he was a very highly challenged child. And then there was working through that. After hearing that, it was like you have reason to feel tired, to feel frustrated, to feel like pulling out your hair. But you are not a failure. That was wonderful.... The turning point was the assurance that we had done everything possible that we know of.

> You have a turning point in your life and then that makes sense of some
> of the experiences you've gone through.... When I was growing up, there
> was the low self-esteem and the frustration and the feeling that something
> was different with me. I had trains instead of brains. But after all of this with
> my child and then being diagnosed myself—it put everything in perspec-
> tive. I understood why things were happening.... I now understand why my
> mother was so frustrated, why kids laughed at me—the whole thing.... I felt
> for the first time that I could walk with my head high and proud.

The experience of receiving a diagnosis can be profound for individuals
with attention deficit disorder or attention deficit hyperactivity disorder.
Many individuals with learning disabilities experience academic difficulties and a sense of failure, and have feelings of being different, difficulty
making friends, and low self-esteem (Brooks, 1994; Hechtman, 1991). Not
understanding what is happening to them is the underlying issue that causes
many of these feelings. One often-expressed viewpoint is that people with
disabilities need both to understand their disability and to incorporate it into
their conception of themselves. This process, called "acceptance of disability" (Starr & Heiserman, 1977), provides a sense of self-worth and also
frees people to seek satisfaction in activities they value, rather than in activities society endorses as appropriate.

As we have seen, some participants came to realize things about themselves, through turning points, that concerned their disability. Other types
of self-understandings also occurred as a result of turning points. For
example, Loreena described coming to an understanding that she had
expected too much of a friend. Bernie described coming to an understanding of Jesus Christ.

Spiritual understandings like Bernie's can be important turning points in
life. They are inner realizations or life-changing beliefs of a very personal
kind. Spirituality has been defined in various ways. For some, spirituality
refers to a connection to God or a Creator. Others define spirituality in terms
of how we view the purpose of our lives (Egan & Delaat, 1994). For others,
spirituality refers to the ultimate values and meanings in terms of which we
live (Griffin, 1988). Spirituality can be simply the experience of meaning in
everyday life activities (Urbanowski & Vargo, 1994) or the experience of
"just being"—being fully aware in the here and now, as in Buddhist teachings. Regardless of the particular definition of spirituality, it appears that, to
live a spiritual life, we need to be connected in some personally meaningful
way with ourselves, others, or the rest of creation (Egan & Delaat, 1994).
Through these connections, we find our own personal meaning in life.

Linda Treloar, who has a nursing background, conducted a research study examining the spiritual beliefs of adults with disabilities and their family members (Treloar, 1999). She describes some participants as deciding to live their lives in a certain way in response to the challenges of living with a disability. They chose to live with joy and thankfulness rather than with bitterness. So here we see a decision arising from the stresses associated with having a disability that affected the future course of people's lives.

Spiritual questions can arise as a result of turning points. Joan Borysenko (1996) discusses how, as we mature, disappointments, deaths, failures, and traumas can bring the questions of meaning into sharp focus. Without a turning point to spur us to consider and resolve such questions, we can be too busy, preoccupied, or complacent to consider them. Mihaly Csikszentmihalyi (1990) states that turning points can lead to new clarity of purpose by helping us see the inessential choices in life. They can clarify for us what is truly important and what is not. Turning points therefore can be the trigger for self-understandings of a spiritual nature, especially for adults. Chapter 3 will return to the theme of spiritual beliefs by considering how such beliefs are a major helping factor in life (rather than a new understanding arising as a resolution to a turning point). Chapter 3 also will provide a rich discussion of two key self-understandings (self-concept and self-esteem) that we have just considered briefly so far.

MULTIPLE MEANINGS

The Japanese word *ikigai* refers to "that which most makes one's life seem worth living." Gordon Mathews, a social anthropologist, uses this notion to compare the views of people in Japan and the United States. His book, *What Makes Life Worth Living?: How Japanese and Americans Make Sense of their Worlds,* largely deals with contrasting the Western ideal of self-realization to the Eastern ideal of commitment to the group (Mathews, 1996). His study revealed that most people in both Japan and the United States made sense of their lives through balancing the pursuit of self-realization with commitment to others. Thus, whereas some people seem to have a single, major life theme, others find meaning through a combination of the themes.

Some of the turning points we've heard have involved more than one type of meaning. For example, Frank's marriage meant finding a sense of belonging and self-confidence. Helen's divorce initially meant abandonment and the loss of the dream of "the house with a white picket fence."

This loss eventually evolved into her decision to live her life in a way that focuses on the positive and not that "which might have been."

Some of the life stories people told us showed even more clearly the intertwining of multiple meanings. Frank describes two turning points with these multiple meanings.

> The special education teacher—her influence with me at a particular point in time was a major turning point in my life because I think, if she hadn't been there, I would have continued to go backwards.... But she was there in the right place at the right time to help me and to give me enough confidence to get on to do the rest of my life.... She had the training, the education, the will-power to help me with my difficulties.... My self-esteem was at an extremely low level as with most people with learning disabilities. She provided me with the education and the exercises to help me feel good about myself, but also challenged me in a way that I could learn.... I think that it definitely affected my self-confidence.... That period of time showed me that I could do things, that I could accomplish things if I put my mind to it, if I worked hard at it. I knew that I had to work harder, but I knew that I could accomplish things.
>
> So instead of being in my own world, I felt part of the regular world.... It was always my goal to be part of the "in" crowd or to be part of what I considered the "regular people" in school. It took me a long time to figure out nobody is regular and nobody is average. Everybody has their problems. But at that particular time it was me and other people separated from the regular class, and that was disconcerting for me. I always wanted to be just a plain individual, not noticed, not singled out.... So that period with [the special education teacher] provided me with the tools and the ability and the self-confidence to get to a stage where I could do my own learning. She gave me the tools and I used them.... When I graduated from university, I tried to get in contact with her to say, "Thank you. You know I wouldn't be here without you."...I think that shows how much she meant to me at that particular time.

Here we see a teacher providing an all-important influence in someone's life. This experience led Frank to gain a sense of self-confidence that allowed him to accomplish things. It led him to realize ultimately that all people are different, and it led to him to be able to belong to the "regular world" in the way he desired. We know that effective support systems involve people who listen to, guide, and encourage others. These supportive people provide clear, consistent, and realistic expectations that encourage and enable others to do their best. They have been called *reliable allies* (Turnbull & Turnbull, 2001). These are people who provide instrumental, practical, and affective support in times of emotional distress. Reliable allies are described as understanding and kind, and as providing a sense of support by believing in the other person. Mentors are supportive people within a work context. Mentors tutor and coach others in some endeavor or profession and function as trusted counselors or guides.

When he was at university, Frank had another experience that shows how belonging can increase a sense of self-confidence.

> I met some people and they invited me to join their fraternity.... I really started to enjoy that because there was a group of people that I had a connection with.... The fraternity sort of started things rolling. I was asked to live with two guys who are life-long friends.... Before that I had lived here and there and really hadn't lived with anybody who was a good friend of mine or that I really got along well with.... It was nice to share the university experience with a group of guys and I hadn't done that before as much.
>
> Everything sort of came together that year it seemed.... I finally felt like I had things together. I had a good group of friends. I was doing okay in school.... I took a couple of courses in an area and my interest was finally twigged. I finally found something that I was really interested in and I thought this was good and it was going to go somewhere.... My self-confidence was high. I was enjoying myself.... I felt that I had a purpose.... Things had come together. So, for my self-esteem, for my ego, for everything, it seemed to be a real turning point. Here are people that I know that I have a connection with, that I am good friends with. That's really important to me.

Belonging to a group and finding courses that he was interested in boosted Frank's sense of self-confidence, with all three factors culminating in a sense of purpose—a sense that his experience at university was meaningful.

We mentioned previously that Karen, who has cerebral palsy, lives with her dog Sam.

> Another turning point is Sam. He's a special skills dog.... He is a wonderful dog. He is very protective.... He was in training for two years before I got him, and when they brought him, they stayed with me for a week to train him.... I can live on my own because of him. He's meant a lot of freedom.... If I drop something, he can pick it up for me. I don't have to wait for somebody to come in to pick it up. I don't have to bother other people to do this or that.... He closes doors, opens doors, just makes my life a little bit easier.... With the attendants, there is only enough funds to give you six hours a day. Sam is here twenty-four hours a day, seven days a week. He can't do everything, but he can do a lot.
>
> He does a lot for my own personal self-confidence.... He just gives me that little bit of feeling that I will be okay on my own.... Also, people in public generally have more acceptance of me now as a person since I got the

dog, because people have a common thread—they love dogs. . . . I hear more dog stories than you can imagine! People will stop and talk to me now because of the dog. It's a very unique situation.

Sam has taught me a lot about life in general. When I work too long he always comes over and nudges me. It's like, "Come on, it is time to play. This can wait. I need some attention" and it has been good for me to get away from work. . . . You learn that guide dogs are supposed to be perfect and they're not. That was a big thing I learned because when I first got him, my Sam was perfect. He could do nothing wrong. Just the same when bringing up a child. But I was wrong and it was a very valuable lesson, because I think sometimes we put too much emphasis on people being perfect, and we are all different. . . . You don't have to have a perfect life or body to be somebody. You make or break your own destiny.

Also, one other thing that he gives me—that I don't think people realize—is that I have someone to look after. I can't have children but I have a dog that needs me to look after him. He needs me to feed him. He needs me to take him to the vet. He needs things done for him. I think people never think that people with disabilities need to be needed. But it is all part of being a person and it is an important part. I never really thought about that until I got him and realized that I was now needed and that that was an important part of being who I was.

Getting Sam was a turning point for Karen because he increased her self-confidence and led her to learn various life lessons about the need to balance work and play, and not to overemphasize perfection. Sam also fulfilled her need to be needed.

Belonging, doing and achieving, and understanding self and the world are the meanings that emerged again and again in people's stories of significant turning points in their lives. Why is this? Are these universal needs that transcend cultural contexts? Do they underlie our life experiences regardless of our age, gender, society, or historical context? Are they fundamental needs whose expression is simply dampened or enhanced by the societies and historical times in which we live? These issues will be considered in chapter 5.

TRIGGERS AND RESOLUTIONS OF TURNING POINTS (BEGINNINGS AND ENDINGS)

> What is true of beginnings is true of endings.
> — John Dewey, *Experience and Nature*

With the stories of people she'd known since her childhood it was like that: one incident in their lives might come to an end-

ing, but others would lead into new veins, and what was fascinating was to look at the whole of it and discern a pattern, a
way of being, that had shaped those passages.
                              —Ursula Hegi, *Stones from the River*

Margaret Atwood writes that turning points "provide beginnings for us,
and endings too" (1994, p. 4). Do we see this in people's stories? How do
turning points start and how do they end?

We've seen that turning points begin with a sense of tension caused by
an event or experience that can be traumatic or even quite innocuous.
The life stressors that lead to turning points can be good or bad in people's eyes. Stressors are perceived negatively when they pose a direct
threat to long-held plans or intentions or to people's view of themselves.
The stressors experienced negatively (at least initially) by study participants included divorces, difficulties at school, the loss of a friend, feeling out of place in a big city, and recognizing one's physical limitations.
Stressors are perceived positively when they represent attainable challenges or achievements, such as buying a house, getting a full-time job,
getting married, joining a fraternity, or hiring one's own attendant care
providers. Thus, on a fundamental level, turning points involve perceptions of loss and perceptions of gain.

We've seen that emotions such as anger, joy, and devastation play a big
role in turning points. We've also seen that resolution to the events perceived as negative comes when meaning is restored. Understandings and
realizations therefore seem to be common endings to the turning points
characterized by negative stress. Many of the turning points characterized
by positive stress, such as buying a house and getting a special skills dog,
also led to new understandings. Nicholas Hobbs, James Perrin, and Henry
Ireys (1985) have written extensively on how people cope with chronic illnesses. They state that the final stage in people's response to a diagnosis of
chronic illness is one of adaptation, which involves a lessening of intensity
of feelings and a reorganization of perspective that emphasizes the positive aspects of the situation. Both processes they describe—the lessening
of emotion and the development of new understandings—characterized
the resolution stage of the turning point experiences of participants in our
study.

As suggested by Margaret Atwood, newly acquired understandings are
not just endings. They can be beginnings too. After her divorce, Grace
redefined herself, went back to school, and started a new career. Other positive outcomes that can be thought of as new beginnings include accepting
disability, forging a new relationship with our parents, establishing inde-

pendence, making new friends, transcending or rising above our limitations, and making new discoveries about ourselves.

Part of the process of coming to a new understanding seems to be actively making a decision. You may have noticed that the resolution of turning points often involved people coming to decisions that they stated to themselves. The literature indicates that making decisions or personal resolutions is one way in which people begin to grow after a crisis (Tennen & Affleck, 1998). These decisions often come about after a period of deliberate and effortful thinking (Calhoun & Tedeschi, 1998; Epstein, 1990). Jerome Bruner (1994), a psychologist known for his work on children's development, has suggested that turning points are ultimately attributed to a change *inside* a person, such as a decision to adopt a new belief or a new outlook on the world. The process of coming to a new conviction is illustrated in the story of Richard Hillary, a hero of the British RAF in 1940, who suffered severe burns when his aircraft was shot down. He later felt compelled to write about his experiences, having felt that he had undergone some kind of personal transformation. As Sebastian Faulks writes in his book *The Fatal Englishman* (1997), "...although his grief at his own disfigurement and the deaths of his friends may have provided the emotional triggers, the change was ultimately an intellectual one. It was a change of conviction: he came to believe that the War was not only worth fighting but was an historic emergency with universal moral implications" (p. 171).

Many people described a particular moment when they made a statement to themselves that crystallized a decision and allowed them to move on. These statements are of the following sort: "I just got to the point where I said to myself...that I can't live like this anymore, that I need to move back home, that I can't do anything about this because it is her problem." Some people turn bad into good by encapsulating the lesson learned from the experience ("I decided I couldn't live my life that way") so that the experience provides a guide for future behavior. Jerome Bruner (1994) has suggested that it is a characteristic of turning points to carry a strong moral message. Other people come to a specific decision about an action to take ("I decided that it was up to her"). In fact, according to Jerome Bruner, turning points often lead to a new and intense line of activity (e.g., a new circle of friends or a new career), what we have been calling a new beginning. Thus, active decision making around a new understanding seems to be a watershed time at which the turning point is left behind and the person moves on.

The key thing about the resolution or ending of a turning point is that the person comes to some understanding or meaning of the experience that has implications for action or the way they intend to live their life. Thus, turning points end when a person's new life direction has been set. John Dewey (1958), a philosopher and author of the book *Experience and Nature,* says that when a challenging event is given meaning, thinking stops. Because the event has been made sense of, there is no need to go on thinking about it, and so the person moves on. The quest is over—for the time being, at least.

By considering how turning points start and end, we gain insight into their desirable qualities. However hard they may be at the time, turning points can lead to growth. Gail Sheehy (1977) talks about the stages of life passages, which can be thought of as turning points involving the life choices we make. Feelings of depression and anxiety can occur during the decision and transition phases in these life passages, as we decide, for example, whether to go back to school or to leave a relationship. Once the passage is over, however, people often experience a sense of exhilaration from having successfully negotiated it. As philosopher Friedrich Nietzsche said over a century ago, our greatest joys are often associated with our greatest pains.

What are the ways in which turning points can change a person's life trajectory? This will be considered next.

GOING DOWN A NEW PATH: HOW TURNING POINTS CAN CHANGE LIFE'S DIRECTION

Most studies of resilience have focused on children rather than adults. Emmy Werner and Michael Rutter are the gurus of the study of risk and resilience in children faced with poverty or deprived backgrounds of some kind. Emmy Werner and Ruth Smith conducted a groundbreaking study of children growing up in Hawaii/Kaui and the factors that led them to experience productive and satisfying lives (Werner & Smith, 1977, 1989). Building on their work, Michael Rutter has been interested in the ways in which turning points affect people's lives. As mentioned in chapter 1, Michael Rutter (1987) believes there are four main ways in which turning points can change the trajectory of our lives, so that we end up in a different place than we would have otherwise.

The first way is that the risk factor itself—whether it is being raised in poverty, being hospitalized, or having a disability—is altered through how we come to understand the turning point experience. Children who are hospitalized at a young age can be traumatized by this experience or they can come to learn about unconditional love by being supported and cared for by their parents. Children raised by unloving parents can attribute this to problems that their parents have rather than being an unlovable child. In both of these examples, the inherent riskiness of the event is reinterpreted or altered in a way that reduces the riskiness. The experience of successfully coping with a hazard gives rise to "steeling qualities" in the individual. This is similar to the notion of how inoculation provides immunity to a disease.

Grace, one of the participants in our study, showed awareness of the steeling qualities of having a disability when she spoke of how the coping skills she had developed to deal with her disability assisted her later on when she was going through a devastating divorce. Neil showed how determination to prove others wrong can influence the life course. Determination or perseverance is often thought of as a crucial personality trait because it reflects a strength of will or motivation to succeed in life. Neil's experience shows that people's assumption that all individuals with disabilities have limited ability can sometimes lead to a strong determination to prove them wrong. We have seen then, that a steeling quality (determination) can arise from the past experience of coping with a disability. Rather than end up with a negative outcome, people who develop a strong sense of determination to achieve their goals can overcome the risk. This process alters the expected direction of their life.

Another process that can change expected outcomes is an experience that reduces or stops a negative chain of events. Frank's turning point at school illustrates this process. In grade 3, he was receiving remedial classes but still slipping backwards in his academic achievement, particularly in his reading. He felt that he would have continued to slide backward if not for the teacher who came along at the right place and the right time. She gave him the self-confidence and tools he needed to take charge of his life.

Michael Rutter's third process deals with the kinds of experiences that can result in feelings of self-worth, self-confidence, or self-efficacy—the conviction that we can successfully cope with life's challenges (Rutter, 1987). Two types of experiences are crucial here: a secure and harmonious relationship, and success in accomplishing tasks that are central to our interests. These are precisely the types of experiences that psychologist Susan Harter (1983) believes contribute to the development of high self-esteem, as we shall see in chapter 3. Participants' stories showed that self-esteem can arise from relationships with others and from success in accomplishing tasks. For instance, Frank gained a belief in himself as a result of being believed in by his wife. Loreena experienced a growth in self-confidence through buying a home, a goal accomplished after many years of planning and hard work. Sometimes the link between achieving a goal and developing self-confidence is mediated by the perception that we have attained some degree of independence. Attaining independence and a sense of freedom was a key theme in Alisha's turning point concerning getting a job and Karen's turning point about hiring people to provide attendant care.

Turning points also can work their magic by opening up opportunities for people. This is the final process described by Michael Rutter (1987). Grace turned her negative divorce experience into a positive one by reshaping her life drastically—getting a degree, pursuing a new career, and redefining her sense of self. Whether an event initially seen as bad is ultimately seen as an opportunity or a lifelong, lingering slap in the face is all in how we cope with it and ultimately come to see it.

People's stories of turning points revealed three other ways in which turning points can ultimately influence life outcomes, which have not been explicitly considered by Michael Rutter. These are reevaluating loss so it becomes a gain (*transcending*), recognizing new things about ourselves (*self-understanding*), and making decisions about relinquishing something in life (*accommodating*). All three processes deal with the development of new understandings that affect our actions in the future. Each process reveals a different path by which a different type of new understanding comes about. All deal with a *contextual reframing,* whereas Rutter's first process (*reevaluating the risk experience*) involves a *content reframing*. Content reframing involves changing the meaning of the situation itself whereas contextual reframing involves placing an event into a larger perspective (Sandidge & Ward, 1999).

The first process (transcending) involves reevaluating loss so it becomes a gain. As we have seen, turning points that deal with the experience of loss can lead to a new sense of self or way of viewing the world. The turning points of four participants in our study (Grace, Helen, Loreena, and Bernie) all are about loss—loss of husbands, a foster child, and a friend. All find something in the end (a new sense of self, a belief in Jesus, a new ability to be more self-reliant). This process of initial loss transformed into ultimate gain is described repeatedly in the literatures on grief and depression (Klinger, 1977) and on aging (Baltes, 1987; Brandtstädter, 1999). It is analogous to "finding the silver lining" in a bad experience or seeing that good comes out of bad. These new understandings can be major realiza-

tions that alter or shift a person's life course. We all know people, raised
by parents with poor parenting skills, who turned out to be wonderful
fathers or mothers, perhaps precisely because of what they learned from
their childhood experience. Brian Clark, one of the survivors of the col-
lapse of the World Trade Center's South Tower, sees positive changes in
his view of life as result of the experience. "I enjoy life more now, I concentrate on the present. That has been a tremendous joy" (Cheney, 2002).
Michael J. Fox, the Canadian actor, has commented on the positive aspects
of being diagnosed with Parkinson's disease: "There's discomfort. It's
progressive. I can't do all the things that I used to do. But at the same time,
too, it's…changed me so fundamentally. It's been a gift in the sense that
it's really opened me up to not taking things for granted, for having a more
empathetic view of other people's situations" (Mickleburgh, 2002).

Turning point experiences also can lead to new understandings about
ourselves that are not precipitated by loss, but which change the directions
of our lives. For example, recognizing our need to be creative or to care for
others, can lead to seeking out a new career, hobby, or activity. Self-
realizations can be profound illuminations that can lead to actions that
change our lives in some fundamental way (Bruner, 1994). A number of
participants described a life-changing moment in which they realized they
were different. For Rick and Trudy, having a label for this difference
helped them to make sense out of past events in their lives, which led to a
new sense of self-confidence.

Another pathway that has not been considered previously by Michael
Rutter or other researchers involves decisions that allow us to relinquish
something and thereby set us on new paths. This is the process of *accommodating*. Alisha and Karen described how they adjusted to increasing
restrictions in mobility by getting a wheelchair or a scooter. They both
came to the point of seeing the advantage of these assistive devices, which
was to provide them with more freedom and independence. To get to this
point, they had to accept their physical limitations and let go of the idea
that they should keep trying to walk by themselves, despite the cost
(reduced energy or the need to have surgery). Alisha also had to work hard
to convince her family to accept this reality because they felt that getting a
scooter meant that she was being lazy and not trying hard enough. Of
course, relinquishing a hope or dream about ourselves can be seen as a loss
of sorts. It is a loss of part of the person we would have liked to be. Coming to accept our limitations can be seen as something positive—a sign of
strength or a gain—because this new type of understanding allows a person to reinvest energy in another direction rather than trying to fight a los-

ing battle. A balance between persevering to achieve goals (pushing the limits) and changing one's goals (accepting or redefining the limits) is what is needed to be resilient in life (Brandtstädter, 1999). Wishing for things we can't have is not adaptive because it can lead to negative, repetitive thoughts and unhappiness (Martin, Tesser, & McIntosh, 1993). In fact, the ability to be flexible and pursue alternate goals is thought to be one of the most important life skills a person can have (Carver & Scheier, 1998). Mature wisdom is involved in knowing when to persist in pursuing a goal and when to disengage.

In summary, the three new processes deal with different ways of acquiring or creating meaning from life events. They are different from the first process described by Rutter in which the risk factor itself is altered through a person's understanding of the experience. The processes of reevaluating loss so it becomes a gain, recognizing new things about ourselves, or deciding to relinquish a hope or dream describe protective processes that are different from an alteration of the meaning of the risk experience itself or the development of steeling qualities (personality traits such as determination). The risk-causing experience is still there, but something new has emerged—a larger perspective or a new understanding about the self or a way of seeing the world rather than a simple reevaluation of the risk event itself. The mechanisms involve new beliefs that allow people to go forward in new directions, rather than new ways of looking at past events that allow us to put them to rest. Rutter's focus has been on dangerous or risky events or situations, such as hospitalization or living in poverty, and he acknowledged that more work is needed to understand psychological hazards. By asking participants to focus explicitly on turning points, we explicitly targeted meaning making and so it should be no surprise that we found evidence of contextual reframing in addition to content reframing.

TURNING POINTS, RESILIENCE, AND MEANING: A TANGLED WEB

Examining people's turning points in life was the vehicle we used to explore the factors associated with resilience in the face of life's adversities. By examining the various types of turning points and how they play out, we came to see three key ways in which we make and maintain meaning in life. These are through belonging, doing, and understanding ourselves and the world. Turning points are the microcosm or hothouse in which the seeds of resilience sprout and the lessons about meaning in life are harvested. Turning points make us reflect. Only in situations of uncertainty or alternatives do we search, question, and reflect. The coping strategies and meaning we take from turning points affect how we deal with other turning points down the road.

There are strong connections between resilience, personal well-being, and the ability to create and derive meaning from experiences. As shown in the following chapter, these characteristics develop from our upbringing, others' belief in us, and broader societal attitudes and supports. According to Joan Borysenko (1996), resilient people find or create positive meaning in their suffering. Resilient children have been found to have a sense of meaning in their lives, along with a belief that life makes sense, and that they have some control over their fate. According to Gail Sheehy (1982), a sense of personal well-being is associated with believing that life has meaning and direction. She describes people high in well-being as radiating humor, energy, and optimism. There is a clear parallel here with the three ways in which people create meaning in life, as revealed by our study of life's turning points: humor reflects meaning derived through feeling and belonging, energy reflects meaning derived through purpose and doing, and optimism deals with meaning derived through hope and understanding.

TYING TOGETHER THE STRANDS OF MEANING

> Believe that life is worth living, and your belief will help create the fact.
>
> —William James, philosopher

By definition, turning points involve change. This change entails, in all cases, a shift in perspective. On a day-to-day basis, we make little adjustments and shifts in our views of ourselves and of others. At critical junctures, we undertake the major kind of working through that characterizes the resolution stage of a turning point. This is where we gain new insights into our worlds and where we acquire meaning about who we are and what is important to us. Turning points therefore are times when life challenges spur us to make meaning and give purpose to our lives. Turning points have been defined as periods or points in time when a person undergoes a major transformation in commitments to important relationships, involvement in significant life roles such as job and marriage, and/or views about the self (Bruner, 1994). It is remarkable that this definition parallels the three paths to meaning in life shown in our study—belonging, doing, and understanding.

People have multiple needs. We need to feel a shared bond and commitment to others (belonging), do what we want to do and make the contribution we want to make (doing and achieving), and know ourselves and live our dreams (understanding and hope). How do these three strands of meaning relate to one another in our life experiences? Think of braiding someone's hair, with each braid being one of the three strands of meaning. The act of creating the braid is the act of living. At one point in time, the strand you place on top could be *belonging*. At another time, the top strand could be *doing*. All the strands are there, but sometimes one is hidden behind the others and we pay most attention to the topmost strand.

At times, we make conscious decisions about what is most important in our lives. Having a baby can be an all-encompassing experience that leads parents to put the child's needs first, and their own pursuits in the background. After the preschool years, this ordering of priorities can shift and parents may rediscover their relationships with their partners and their connections to friends, and they may start to pursue their own interests with more intensity.

Although the three strands of meaning have been discussed as if they were separate, they are, in reality, intricately connected. We have seen that a single turning point can have multiple meanings: this is much more the rule than the exception. We have described the strands separately, but now want to reassemble these strands into a whole that reflects how we experience life.

The strands can be thought of as a braid or rope. Let's give this braid a twist. If we do that and then join the two ends, we create a Möbius strip—a 2-dimensional shape with only one surface (Figure 2.1). We can use the Möbius strip as an analogy for life. Created by the German mathematician August Ferdinand Möbius, who lived in the early 1800s, the Möbius strip has no beginning and no end. If you start at any point on the strip and draw a line down the middle, you will reach the point from which you started. Your single line has crossed both sides of the original piece of paper. This property of the Möbius strip symbolizes the idea that meaning in life has no beginning or end—it is determined by the complex interplay of the strands of meaning in life.

Although we view phenomena in terms of one strand causing another, the Möbius strip shows us that this is illusory in the bigger scheme of things because of the interconnections between the strands.

A *phenomenon* is a fact, circumstance, or experience that is apparent to the senses and that can be described. Let's take turning points as an example of one of the many phenomena in life. We've considered how the loss

Figure 2.1: Möbius Strip Illustrating the Model of Life Experience

of an important relationship can be experienced as a loss of meaning concerning belonging. This can have an influence on both of the other strands
of meaning: It can influence our sense of ourselves (are we worthy of
being loved?) and the goals we set for ourselves (do we want to find
another intimate relationship?). But, if we back up in time (i.e., move
backwards on the Möbius strip), it is also true that our life goals and how
we view ourselves both contribute to the impact that the loss of a relationship has on us to begin with. For example, if we grow up wanting more
than anything to be a spouse and a parent, then going through a divorce
will be harder for us because we have defined our identity so strongly in
terms of those roles.

   As another example of the links or threads between the strands, we have
seen how doing can lead to a sense of achievement, to self-efficacy, and to
self-knowledge (these are three of the many threads that exist between the
strands of doing and self-understanding). The following quote illustrates
one thread between doing and self-understanding, where doing is seen as
the cause and understanding is seen as the effect: "Success is the point of
self-deception. Failure is the point of self-knowledge" (Graham Greene,
novelist, quoted by biographer Norman Sherry, 1994, p. 456).

   Continuing with the Möbius strip analogy, we can describe many life
experiences in terms of the strands of meaning that they entail, and the

relationships between the strands—that is, which strand is seen as the cause and which is seen as the end result. For example, ceremonies and rituals can be seen as joining the strands of doing and belonging in a cause-and-effect way. In a newspaper article "The Power of Ritual: Reinventing Ceremony in a Secular Time," Robert Fulford (1999) argues that rituals and ceremonies (including audience participation at sports events and music concerts, and religious services and festivals) intensify our feelings through joint symbolic action. There is something about being part of a group of people experiencing the same emotion and performing the same agreed-upon actions that can heighten our own emotions. The key to this seems to be the repetition of action in social settings that underlies rituals. Repetition of an action, such as dance, movement, or song, can lead to states of tranquility or exhilaration in which time seems to be suspended and reality heightened. Thus, action (doing) leads to a heightened sense and feeling of belonging.

Friendship is another phenomenon that incorporates the three strands. Friends make us feel that we belong, we do things with friends, and friends help us grow as individuals. The meaning of friendship is repeatedly discussed, in self-help books and research articles, in ways that correspond to the three strands. Friends are said to validate or reinforce our sense of self by being a touchstone for our perceptions of events and ourselves. They also can expand our sense of ourselves by introducing us to new ideas and activities, and can provide the impetus for our emotional and spiritual growth (Antonovsky, 1987; Sinnema, 1991). Friends help us understand and make sense of the things that happen to us. They help us "keep perspective" on things and also to change perspective, depending on the circumstances. They help us do and achieve things in life by believing in us, giving us practical assistance, and showing us how to be competent (Hupcey, 1998; Shumaker & Brownell, 1984). By joining in activities with us, they reinforce the importance of these activities and our enjoyment of them. Friends give us unconditional love and support, which allows us to be our true selves. By listening and caring, they endorse our unique worth as individuals. Thus, friendships give us many things. We learn from friends, feel connected to our world through friends, and grow through our friendships. Clearly, friendships are a fundamental way to derive meaning in the world. Friendships can encompass all of the ways in which we make sense of our worlds.

By linking the three strands of meaning into a single entity that loops back on itself—the Möbius strip—we see the interconnectedness of meaning on a larger level. We see that the three ways of creating meaning in life are interlaced. One does not supersede the others and each can influence the others. When we look at phenomena such as collective rituals or friendship, in some sense we are artificially cutting the stream of life experience in order to fully understand the phenomenon. This can give the illusion that one strand or stream of meaning causes the others, when it may make most sense to consider their effects in multicausal, reciprocal ways. "There are only imaginary boundaries. Each aspect of experience contains all the others" (Ellyn Kaschak, psychologist, 1992, p. 29).

As in life experiences, where the boundaries between aspects of meaning are essentially illusory (but useful to consider), differences between people fade into the background when we consider our fundamental similarities.

DIFFERENCES AND SIMILARITIES: THE ILLUSION OF PARADOX

> Every person is, in certain respects, like all others (universal norms), like some other persons (group norms), and like no other persons (idiosyncratic norms).
> —Jean Watson, *Nursing: The Philosophy and Science of Caring*

One of the major findings of this research study deals with a paradox. It is intriguing (but not surprising) that a study exploring disabilities—or differences—can end up yielding such a strong appreciation of commonality. Some participants taking part in the groups we held to check the accuracy of the interpretations of their stories experienced an "aha" moment when they recognized the remarkable similarity of their experiences to those of others.

According to the dictionary, a *paradox* is something that has contradictory qualities. It is something that doesn't make sense or is inconsistent with common experience. Paradox occurs due to our human need to differentiate and categorize aspects of the world around us, in order to make sense of the world, and to function adaptively within it. Paradoxes occur when we categorize events or experiences, which really lie on a continuum, into units or boxes. Paradoxes occur when we quantify qualities. According to the philosopher John Dewey, contradictions or paradoxes are simply evidence that we are engaged in an arbitrary sorting of things into different boxes when, in reality, these experiences are not distinct and in nature are always present "in conjunction and interpenetration" (Dewey,

1958, p. 61). As soon as we give up certain assumptions, certain things cease to be perplexities.

When you look at a rainbow, you can see the clear divisions between the colors, but, if you look more closely, you begin to see that the colors actually blend into one another. The sense of distinct differences in color is illusory. There is actually a continuum of color in a rainbow that reflects an underlying continuum of similarity. In the same way, there are underlying similarities in people, despite—or in addition to—surface differences. We need to move beyond seeing things in black and white or valuing one pole of a continuum more than another. We need to appreciate the full spectrum in between.

This journey through life's turning points has revealed that people have a fundamental similarity in the need to establish or create meaning in life. Furthermore, we all use the same three paths to create meaning. Some of us will use one path more than another, but the three paths—belonging, doing, and understanding ourselves and the world—are followed by all of us to some degree or another. This is the idea of *universality* of experience. It does not mean that we are the same: it means that there are fundamental similarities in human nature as revealed by the processes by which we make meaning in life. As individuals, we are unique and different. Our special differences make us unique but we should not ignore the fundamental commonalities in how people view and deal with life experiences.

In *An Anthropologist on Mars,* the writer and neurologist Oliver Sacks (1995) talks about a paradox concerning illnesses and disabilities: the fact that disease and "disability" can bring out strength and "ability." Rather than "succumb" to a physical condition or illness, people often rise above these situations by establishing meaning in life in ways that fit their situations. This is much more common than is generally thought. It is a myth to think that only remarkably strong or special people are resilient. As revealed in the stories of people's turning points in this chapter, we all share a common drive to create meaning in life and we follow common paths in this quest; furthermore, most of us experience some degree of success in this mission. Thus, it really does not make sense to put people into the box of disability, which implies lack of ability and strength, or into the box of being a remarkable person with a disability, which implies that only certain people (like Terry Fox, Rick Hansen, or Stephen Hawking) can find meaning in life. According to Jerome Bickenbach and his colleagues, disability is actually a fluid and continuous condition that is experienced by all of us at some stage of our lives (Bickenbach, Chatterji, Badley, & Ustun, 1999).

The challenge is to go from seeing differences to seeing the essential reality of our common human needs. Seeing commonalities in experience to those we think of as different from ourselves can lead us to new understandings—perhaps not life-changing understandings, but at least life-enhancing ones. This focus on similarity rather than difference—on the big picture rather than the smaller differences—dovetails with a humanistic-altruistic value system, which is a view of humanity entailing love and appreciation of diversity and individuality. Combining the two ideas of commonality and diversity results in a vision of a community that values and recognizes both similarity and plurality (rather than homogeneity and difference). Such a community recognizes basic human needs but also embraces diversity. This is a vision that we should strive for. It is a vision that will give meaning to the existence of us all.

REFERENCES

Abraham, C. (2000, April 15). He lived fast, certain he'd die young. *The Globe and Mail,* p. A15.

Ackerman, D. (1990). *A natural history of the senses.* New York: Random House.

Aldwin, C. M. (1994). *Stress, coping, and development: An integrative perspective.* New York: Guilford Press.

Anthony, E. J. (1974). The syndrome of the psychologically invulnerable child. In E. J. Anthony & C. Koupernik (Eds.), *The child in his family: Children at psychiatric risk.* New York: Wiley.

Antonovsky, A. (1987). *Unraveling the mystery of health: How people manage stress and stay well.* San Francisco: Jossey-Bass.

Atwood, M. (1994). *The robber bride.* New York: Doubleday.

Baltes, P. B. (1987). Theoretical propositions of life-span developmental psychology: On the dynamics between growth and decline. *Developmental Psychology, 23*(5), 611–626.

Bandura, A. (1986). *Social foundations of thought and action: A social cognitive theory.* Englewood Cliffs, NJ: Prentice Hall.

Baumeister, R. F., & Leary, M. R. (1995). The need to belong: Desire for interpersonal attachments as a fundamental human motivation. *Psychological Bulletin, 117*(3), 497–529.

Bickenbach, J. E., Chatterji, S., Badley, E. M., & Ustun, T. B. (1999). Models of disablement, universalism and the international classification of impairments, disabilities, and handicaps. *Social Science and Medicine, 48,* 1173–1187.

Borysenko, J. (1996). *A woman's book of life: The biology, psychology, and spirituality of the feminine life cycle.* New York: Riverhead Books.

Brandtstädter, J. (1999). Sources of resilience in the aging self: Toward integrating perspectives. In T. M. Hess & F. Blanchard-Fields (Eds.), *Social cognition and aging* (pp. 123–141). San Diego: Academic Press.

Breathnach, S. B. (1998). *Something more: Excavating your authentic self.* New York: Warner Brooks.

Breunlin, D. C. (1988). Oscillation theory and family development. In C. J. Falicov (Ed.), *Family transitions* (pp. 113–155). New York: Guilford.

Brooks, R. B. (1992). Self-esteem during the school years: Its normal development and hazardous decline. *Pediatric Clinics of North America, 39*(3), 537–550.

Brooks, R. B. (1994). Children at risk: Fostering resilience and hope. *American Journal of Orthopsychiatry, 64,* 545–553.

Brown, G. W., & Harris T. O. (1978). *Social origins of depression: A study of psychiatric disorders in women.* London: Tavistock.

Bruner, J. (1994). The "remembered" self. In U. Neisser & R. Fivush (Eds.), *The remembering self: Construction and accuracy in the self narrative* (pp. 41–54). Cambridge, UK: Cambridge University Press.

Calhoun, L. G., & Tedeschi, R. G. (1998). Posttraumatic growth: Future directions. In R. G. Tedeschi, C. L. Park, & L. G. Calhoun (Eds.), *Posttraumatic growth: Positive changes in the aftermath of crisis* (pp. 215–238). Mahwah, NJ: Lawrence Erlbaum.

Carver, C. S., & Scheier, M. F. (1998). *On the self-regulation of behavior.* New York: Cambridge University Press.

Cheney, P. (2002, March 13). "Teflon man" moves on and finds new joys in life. *The Globe and Mail,* pp. A4–A5.

Clausen, J. A. (1990, August 11–15). *Turning points as a life course concept.* Paper presented at the American Sociological Association meeting, Washington, D.C.

Clausen, J. A. (1993). *American lives: Looking back at the children of the great depression.* New York: Free Press.

Cohler, B. J. (1987). Adversity, resilience and the study of lives. In E. J. Anthony & B. J. Cohler (Eds.), *The invulnerable child* (pp. 363–424). New York: Guilford.

Condeluci, A. (1995). *Interdependence: The route to community* (2nd ed.). Winter Park, FL: GR Press.

Csikszentmihalyi, M. (1990). *Flow: The psychology of optimal experience.* New York: Harper & Row.

Denzin, N. K. (1989). *Interpretive interactionism.* Newbury Park, CA: Sage.

Dewey, J. (1958). *Experience and nature.* New York: Dover Publications.

Downey, D. (1999, June 23). Joseph Vismeg: Edmontonian's film on cancer won Genie. *The Globe and Mail,* p. A19.

Drotar, D. (1981). Psychological perspectives in chronic childhood illness. *Journal of Pediatric Psychology, 6,* 211–228.

Eccles, J. S., Midgley, C., Wigfield, A., Buchanan, C. M., Reuman, D., Flanagan, C., & Mac Iver, D. (1993). Development during adolescence: The impact of stage-environment fit on young adolescents' experiences in schools and in families. *American Psychologist, 48*(2), 90–101.

Egan, M., & Delaat, M. D. (1994). Considering spirituality in occupational therapy practice. *Canadian Journal of Occupational Therapy, 61*(2), 95–101.

Epstein, S. (1990). The self-concept, the traumatic neurosis, and the structure of personality. In D. Ozer, J. M. Healy, Jr., & A. J. Stewart (Eds.), *Perspectives on personality* (Vol. 3). Greenwich, CT: JAI Press.

Erikson, E. (1963). *Childhood and society.* New York: Norton.

Faulks, S. (1997). *The fatal Englishman.* London: Vintage.

Festinger, L. (1957). *A theory of cognitive dissonance.* Stanford, CA: Stanford University Press.

Frolick, V. (1999). *Fire into ice: Charles Fipke and the great diamond hunt.* Vancouver, BC: Raincoast Books.

Fulford, R. (1999, May 1). The power of ritual: Reinventing ceremony in a secular time. *The Globe and Mail,* p. D9.

Garmezy, N. (1983). Stressors of childhood. In N. Garmezy & M. Rutter (Eds.), *Stress, coping, and development in children* (pp. 43–84). New York: McGraw-Hill.

Garmezy, N. (1991). Resilience and vulnerability to adverse developmental outcomes associated with poverty. *American Behavioral Scientist, 34,* 416–430.

Goode, E. (1999, February 27). The best years of our lives. *The Globe and Mail,* p. D5.

Gotlib, I. H., & Wheaton, B. (1997). Trajectories and turning points over the life course: Concepts and themes. In I. H. Gotlib & B. Wheaton (Eds.), *Stress and adversity over the life course* (pp. 1–28). Cambridge, UK: Cambridge University Press.

Griffin, D. R. (Ed.). (1988). *Spirituality and society: Postmodern vision.* Albany: State University of New York Press.

Harter, S. (1982). The perceived competence scale for children. *Child Development, 53,* 87–97.

Harter, S. (1983). Developmental perspectives on the self. In P. H. Mussen (Ed.), *Handbook of child psychology* (pp. 275–385). New York: Wiley.

Headey, B. & Wearing, A. (1989). Personality, life events, and subjective well-being: Toward a dynamic equilibrium model. *Journal of Personality and Social Psychology, 57,* 731–739.

Hechtman, L. (1991). Resilience and vulnerability in long term outcome of attention deficit hyperactive disorder. *Canadian Journal of Psychiatry, 36,* 415–421.

Hegi, U. (1997). *Stones from the river.* New York: Simon & Schuster.

Hinkle, L. E. (1973). The concept of "stress" in the biological and social sciences. *Science, Medicine, and Man, 1*(1), 31–48.

Hobbs, N., Perrin, J.M., & Ireys, H.T. (1985). *Chronically ill children and their families.* San Francisco: Jossey-Bass.

Humphreys, K., & Rappaport, J. (1994). Researching self-help/mutual aid groups and organizations: Many roads, one journey. *Applied and Preventive Psychology, 3,* 217–231.

Hupcey, J.E. (1998). Social support: Assessing conceptual coherence. *Qualitative Health Research, 8*(3), 304–318.

Ishiguro, K. (1990). *The remains of the day.* Toronto: Penguin Books Canada.

Izard, C.E. (1971). *The face of emotion.* New York: Appleton-Century-Crofts.

James, W. (1956). "Is life worth living?" In *The will to believe and other essays in popular philosophy.* New York: Dover.

Janoff-Bulman, R. (1992). *Shattered assumptions: Towards a new psychology of trauma.* New York: The Free Press.

Kaschak, E. (1992). Making meaning. In E. Kaschak, *Engendered lives: A new psychology of women's experience* (pp. 9–36). New York: Basic Books.

Kelly, J.R. (1983). *Leisure identities and interactions.* London: Allen and Unwin.

Klinger, E. (1977). *Meaning and void: Inner experience and incentives in people's lives.* Minneapolis: University of Minnesota Press.

Knoll, K. (1999, May 8). The man who moils for diamonds. *The Globe and Mail,* p. D12.

Lacey, L. (1999, March 8). Director peered into dark side of humanity. *The Globe and Mail,* p. C5.

Lambert, N.M. (1988). Adolescent outcomes for hyperactive children: Perspectives on general and specific patterns of childhood risk for adolescent educational, social, and mental health problems. *American Psychologist, 43,* 786–799.

Lazarus, R.S., & Folkman, S. (1984). *Stress, appraisal, and coping.* New York: Springer.

Levinson, D.J. (with Darrow, C.N., Klein, E.B., Levinson, M.H., & McKee, B.) (1978). *The seasons of a man's life.* New York: Knopf.

Levinson, D.J. (1986). A conception of adult development. *American Psychologist, 41,* 3–13.

Mandelbaum, D.G. (1973). The study of life history: Gandhi. *Current Anthropology, 14,* 177–206.

Martin, L.L., Tesser, A., & McIntosh, W.D. (1993). Wanting but not having: The effects of unattained goals on thoughts and feelings. In D.M. Wegner & J.W. Pennebaker (Eds.), *Handbook of mental control. Century psychology series* (pp. 552–572). Upper Saddle River, NJ: Prentice-Hall.

Martin, T. (2000, April 29). Playing the market changes Eddy's life. *The Globe and Mail,* p. N5.

Masten, A.S., Best, K.M., & Garmezy, N. (1990). Resilience and development: Contributions from the study of children who overcome adversity. *Development and Psychopathology, 2,* 425–444.

Mathews, G. (1996). *What makes life worth living?: How Japanese and Americans make sense of their worlds.* Berkeley: University of California Press.

Meyer, A. (1957). *Psychobiology: A science of man.* Springfield, IL: Charles C Thomas.

Mickleburgh, R. (2002, March 22). Was TV star's disease born of B.C. virus? *The Globe and Mail,* pp. A1, A11.

Moritsugu, K. (1999). *Old flames.* Erin, ON: Porcupine's Quill.

Murphy, L., & Moriarty, A. (1976). *Vulnerability, coping, and growth from infancy to adolescence.* New Haven, CT: Yale University Press.

Niester, A. (1999, April 17). A chip off the old Bachman. *The Globe and Mail,* p. C17.

Parkes, C.M. (1971). Psycho-social transitions: A field for study. *Social Science & Medicine, 2*(5), 101–115.

Peck, M.S. (1978). *The road less traveled.* New York: Simon & Schuster.

Pellegrini, D.S. (1990). Psychosocial risk and protective factors in childhood. *Journal of Developmental and Behavioral Pediatrics, 11,* 201–209.

Posner, M (1999, May 1). A pop phenomenon who prefers to sing opera. *The Globe and Mail,* p. C24.

Rosenbluth, V. (1997). *Keeping family stories alive: Discovering and recording the stories and reflections of a lifetime* (2nd ed.). Point Roberts, WA: Hartley & Marks.

Rutter, M. (1985). Resilience in the face of diversity: Protective factors and resistance to psychiatric disorder. *British Journal of Psychiatry, 147,* 598–611.

Rutter, M. (1987). Psychosocial resilience and protective mechanisms. *American Journal of Orthopsychiatry, 57,* 316–331.

Rutter, M. (1990). Psychosocial resilience and protective mechanisms. In J. Rolf, A.S. Masten, D. Cicchetti, K.H. Neuchterlein, & S. Weintraub (Eds.), *Risk and protective factors in the development of psychopathology* (pp. 181–214). Cambridge, UK: Cambridge University Press.

Sacks, O. (1995). *An anthropologist on Mars: Seven paradoxical tales.* Toronto: Random House Canada.

Sandidge, R.L., & Ward, A.C. (1999). Reframing. In J.F. Gardner & S. Nudler (Eds.), *Quality performance in human services: Leadership values, and vision* (pp. 201–221). Baltimore: Paul H. Brookes.

Schwandt, T. (1994). Constructivist, interpretivist approaches to human inquiry. In N.K. Denzin & Y.S. Lincoln (Eds.), *Handbook of qualitative research* (pp. 118–137). Thousand Oaks, CA: Sage.

Shaver, P., Schwartz, J., Kirson, D., & O'Connor, C. (1987). Emotion knowledge: Further exploration of a prototype approach. *Journal of Personality and Social Psychology, 52,* 1061–1086.

Sheehy, G. (1977). *Passages: Predictable crises of adult life.* New York: Bantam Books.

Sheehy, G. (1982). *Pathfinders.* New York: Bantam Books.

Sherry, N. (1996). *The life of Graham Greene* (Vol. 2). New York: Penguin.

Shumaker, S. A., & Brownell, A. (1984). Toward a theory of social support: Closing conceptual gaps. *Journal of Social Issues, 40,* 11–36.

Singer, G. H. S., & Powers, L. E. (1993). Contributing to resilience in families: An overview. G.H.S. Singer & L. E. Powers (Eds.), *Families, disability, and empowerment: Active coping skills and strategies for family interventions* (pp. 1–25). Baltimore: Paul H. Brookes.

Singing praises of recreation. (2000, February 29). *Focus on ability: A partnership marketing supplement. The Globe and Mail,* p. C5.

Sinnema, G. (1991). Resilience among children with special health-care needs and among their families. *Pediatric Annals, 20,* 483–486.

Starr, P., & Heiserman, K. (1977). Acceptance of disability by teenagers with oral-facial clefts. *Rehabilitation Counseling Bulletin, 28,* 198–201.

Tennen, H., & Affleck, G. (1998). Personality and transformation in the face of adversity. In R. G. Tedeschi, C. L. Park, & L. G. Calhoun (Eds.), *Posttraumatic growth: Positive changes in the aftermath of crisis* (pp. 65–98). Mahwah, NJ: Lawrence Erlbaum.

Terkel, S. (1972). *Working.* New York: Avon Books.

Treloar, L. L. (1999). Spiritual care: Assessment and intervention. *Journal of Christian Nursing, 16*(2), 15–18.

Turnbull, A. P., & Turnbull, H. R. (2001). *Families, professionals, and exceptionality: Collaborating for empowerment* (4th ed.). Upper Saddle River, NJ: Prentice-Hall.

Urbanowski, R., & Vargo, J. (1994). Spirituality, daily practice, and the occupational performance model. *Canadian Journal of Occupational Therapy, 61*(2), 88–94.

Watson, J. (1979). *Nursing: The philosophy and science of caring.* Boston: Little, Brown and Company Press.

Watson, J. (1985). *Nursing: The philosophy and science of caring.* Boulder: Colorado Associated University Press.

Weiss, G., & Hechtman, L. T. (1993). *Hyperactive children grown up: ADHD in children, adolescents, and adults* (2nd ed.). New York: Guilford Press.

Werner, E. E., & Smith, R. S. (1977). *Kauai's children come of age.* Honolulu: University of Hawaii Press.

Werner, E. E., & Smith, R. S. (1989). *Vulnerable, but invincible: A longitudinal study of resilient children and youth.* New York: Adams-Banister-Cox.

Wethington, E., Cooper, H., & Holmes, C. S. (1997). Turning points in midlife. In I. H. Gotlib & B. Wheaton (Eds.), *Stress and adversity over the life course* (pp. 215–231). Cambridge, UK: Cambridge University Press.

Whyte, W. H., Jr. (1957). *The organization man.* New York: Simon & Schuster.

Wright, L. R. (2000, June 10). Why we write mystery novels. *The Globe and Mail,*
    p. D17.
Wyman, P. A., Sandler, I., Wolchik, S., & Nelson, K. (2000). Resilience as cumu-
    lative competence promotion and stress protection: Theory and interven-
    tion. In D. Cicchetti, J. Rappaport, I. Sandler, & R. P. Weissberg (Eds.), *The
    promotion of wellness in children and adolescents* (pp. 133–184). Wash-
    ington, D.C.: Child Welfare League of America Press.

Chapter 3

THE RESILIENT SELF—WHAT HELPS AND WHAT HINDERS?

Colleen Willoughby, Elizabeth G. Brown, Gillian A. King, Jacqueline Specht, and Linda K. Smith

Reading through the previous chapter on turning points makes it evident that each person in our study experienced personal triumphs and struggles throughout their life's journey. One common theme that resonates through each person's life story is the ability to cope with life's setbacks and keep going. This reflects the notion of the *resilient self.*

The academic literature on resilience deals with the factors and processes that keep us going when faced with the challenges of life. This literature indicates that people with chronic conditions or disabilities are at greater risk for behavioral and emotional problems such as aggression, conflicts with peers, hyperactivity, depression, anxiety, and isolation from others (Brooks, 1994; Lavigne & Faier-Routman, 1992). Yet only a small proportion of adults with disabilities experience these serious problems. Why is this? We want to know *why* so we can understand *how* to work toward ensuring that all of us—those with and those without disabilities—can be protected from the risks we will undoubtedly encounter during our life courses.

Webster's Dictionary defines *resilience* as "an ability to recover from or adjust easily to change or misfortune." Some of the people in our study may question this definition. They may feel that the adjustment was not always "easy." Nonetheless, they bounced back from many negative events and continued on with their lives. When we say that each person demonstrated an ability to cope, this is not meant to imply that somehow the participants were a select sample of extraordinarily resilient individuals or that they did not experience struggles or difficulties. Not everyone fared well in the face of adversity but, over time, the majority of the participants were able to interpret their experiences in a positive way that allowed them to learn from their experiences and move on in their lives. The resolution to their turning points may not have been complete. In fact, resolution to life crises can be mixed with some continuing distress (Tedeschi & Calhoun, 1995). We also do not mean to leave the impression that people with disabilities—or people in general—will do well if left to cope on their own. On the contrary, participants' stories indicated that support from others was crucial at turning points in their lives, as we will see in this chapter. The key point we want to make is that psychological growth is a common outcome of turning points in life, not the exception (Calhoun & Tedeschi, 1998), which indicates the resilience of human nature.

We experience a sense of inner strength when we realize that we possess the resources to cope with whatever challenges life sends our way. Who would not want this quality for themselves or for their children? The question is where does resilience come from? How do we foster resilience for ourselves and for others we love?

This chapter will examine how the people in our study—as individuals in relation with others and the larger world—developed resilience. The chapter outlines the helpful factors mentioned by participants and considers the processes that lead to a resilient self. We examine how personal competencies and ways of thinking are related to resilience and how social support contributes to resilience. We also consider a third major category of helpful factors, which consists of people's philosophies of living and the lessons they have learned from life. The information contained in this chapter suggests things we can do to bolster our own resilience. Since we all face adversity at some point in our lives, we can learn from listening to the stories of other people who have reflected on the *what* and the *how* of their successful negotiation of life's challenges.

To help put the wealth of insight and wisdom people shared with us into a manageable format, we have adopted a particular framework—a way of categorizing things. We could have presented the findings in a number of different ways. We could have used Uri Bronfenbrenner's (1979) ecological framework of self, family, and environment, which has been used extensively by childhood resilience researchers to group factors thought to offer protection from life stresses (e.g., Garmezy, 1983; Wyman, Sandler, Wolchik, & Nelson, 2000). As mentioned in chapter 1, Norman Garmezy, a professor at the University of Minnesota, has reviewed factors that encourage people's resilience in life. He groups the factors into the following categories: personal characteristics, supportive families, and supportive community context (Garmezy, 1983). Personal characteristics that foster resilience include effective problem-solving skills, good coping abilities, and a positive view of ourselves. Supportive families have low conflict, good communication among family members, and parent(s) that generally function well. A supportive community context means that we have a group of friends, peers, or other unrelated adults who promote our ability to cope with life's challenges. This may also include our participation in groups such as clubs and senior citizens' centers.

Similarly, Peter Wyman, Irwin Sandler, Sharlene Wolchik, and Kathleen Nelson (2000) consider these groupings of ecological factors to reflect different types of resources available to people, including person-level characteristics (e.g., beliefs about self-worth and control), characteristics of the family, and community resources, such as social support. These frameworks outline types of protective factors but do not deal with the ways in which these factors enhance people's adjustment.

There is a growing interest in explaining how people adapt by considering general developmental processes that contribute to well-being (e.g., Masten & Coatsworth, 1998). These general processes include mechanisms that facilitate children's mastery or protect children from stressful cognitive and emotional effects (Wyman et al., 2000). We wanted to follow this approach in this chapter and push thinking forward by linking factors found to be important in our study to particular mechanisms or processes that involve the self. Researchers have done well in outlining personal resilience factors. What is lacking is an integrated understanding of the mechanisms underlying other protective factors—particularly social support (Ryff & Singer, 2000).

In this chapter, we adopt a *self* framework in which the focus is on how the support of family, friends, and other people contributes to resilience on the level of the individual. This is why we refer to *the resilient self* in the title of this chapter. We begin by presenting a brief history on how the self has been viewed, and then define the three components of the *self* framework: self-concept, self-esteem, and self-efficacy. We then outline the personal resilience factors found to be important to study participants at crucial turning points in their lives, using the *self* framework to present this material. The topic of social support is then considered, which was the major helpful factor cited by study participants. How do social ties buffer the effects of stress? What is the meaning of social support for people who receive it? We outline the mechanisms that explain how social support helps individuals to cope, adjust, and bounce back from adverse experiences, using examples from the interviews to illustrate various points.

A BRIEF HISTORY OF ASPECTS OF THE SELF

First of all, what is the self? We frequently talk about "myself," "yourself," "herself," and so on, but the self is a fairly abstract concept to understand. This simple exercise may help clarify what the self is. Pretend you are going on the television game show *Jeopardy*. The producer needs a short biography for Alex Trebek to read. How would you describe yourself? The adjectives and qualities that you would use in your biography constitute the self. The self therefore is the collection of beliefs, knowledge, feelings, and characteristics that we as individuals ascribe to our own person (Harter, 1983).

It is helpful to adopt a distinction offered by psychologist William James more than a century ago. In 1890, James began a tradition of separating two important aspects of the self—*I* and *me*. In his classic work, *The Principles of Psychology* (1890), William James differentiated between self as an active agent (I—who does), and self as the object of one's knowledge (me—who understands myself). The *me* is often called the *self-concept* and consists of all the ideas that the individual forms to label or define the self.

Two social psychologists, Charles Cooley (1964) and George Mead (1934) elaborated on William James's idea of describing the self as an object. Cooley (1964) introduced the notion of the *looking-glass self,* in which ideas about the self were seen to originate through interactions with others. The idea that the self developed solely through social interaction became known as the interactionist perspective. Mead (1934) added to the interactionist viewpoint by indicating that it is our efforts to grasp what others expect of us, and to act accordingly, that makes the self a social object.

Susan Harter, a professor of psychology at the University of Denver, also differentiates between the *self as subject* and the *self as object,* using a developmental perspective. She has provided an extensive review of the literature on the self undergoing developmental changes (Harter, 1983). Through this review, Harter was able to formulate a new framework for self theory, illustrating developmental changes in the self. She argues that the development of the self can only be fully understood through consideration of the self as a subject. According to Harter's model, the self is an active agent, represented by the concept of *I,* rather than a passive object, represented by the concept of *me*. Thus, according to Harter's theory, our concept of ourselves evolves through our participation in life experiences.

The main point of this historical review is that self-conception is fundamentally social in nature. The traditions of symbolic interactionism and the *looking-glass self,* and more recent research on the *interpersonal self* (Markus & Cross, 1990), all propose that we understand ourselves through our interactions with other people (Ryff & Singer, 2000).

A SELF FRAMEWORK (SELF-CONCEPT, SELF-ESTEEM, AND SELF-EFFICACY)

Three terms are commonly used to describe the functions of the self: self-concept, self-esteem, and self-efficacy. It is helpful to explain these functions because we will use them as a framework to understand what study participants found helpful and hindering when faced with challenges in life.

Self-concept is the description we attach to ourselves. As Norman Garmezy (1983) said, self-concept refers to our perception of our personal characteristics—who we are. Our self-concept represents the beliefs, ideas, and attitudes we have about ourselves and is based on the roles we play (e.g., lover, wife, husband, adventurer) and the attributes we possess (e.g., good coping skills, effective problem-solving abilities). Morris Rosenberg, a sociologist at the University of Maryland, described self-concept as a body of knowledge that people possess about themselves (Rosenberg, 1986). It is helpful to conceptualize self-concept as a form of self-understanding—what we know about ourselves.

Self-esteem (sometimes referred to as *self-worth*) refers to the overall value that we place on ourselves as individuals or our general feeling of our worthiness (Crocker & Major, 1989; Harter, 1989). Many researchers, including Susan Harter (1986), believe that our sense of self-esteem is created by our competencies, relative to others, and the support we get from other people. Self-concept, therefore, refers to how we describe ourselves, whereas self-esteem refers to how we evaluate ourselves compared to others. According to Norman Garmezy (1983), our families and communities play an important role in nurturing self-esteem. Having healthy self-esteem can help us successfully negotiate the challenges of our lives. This is one of the protective processes outlined by Michael Rutter (1987), as seen in chapter 2.

The third important function of the self is *self-efficacy.* Albert Bandura (1982), a psychology professor at Stanford University, describes self-efficacy as our estimation of how well we can carry out the actions necessary to deal with life events. Our sense of self-efficacy will vary depending on the activity. We can think of self-efficacy as our perception of how well we can meet the demands of our environment or the daily challenges we face. For example, you might believe you will pass a university exam or that you will get to work on time. These beliefs indicate your perception of your ability to control aspects of your environment (such as finding time to study or negotiating traffic) and achieve the goals you desire (namely passing the exam and getting to work on time).

We will now use these aspects of the self (self-concept, self-esteem, and self-efficacy) to examine participants' descriptions of what helped and what hindered them as they adapted to turning points in their lives. We will then consider how social support is beneficial through its effects on these three aspects of the self.

SELF-CONCEPT—HOW WE UNDERSTAND OURSELVES

Self-concept refers to our perceptions of our personal characteristics. Our self-understanding involves ascribing relatively stable traits or attributes to ourselves (Wyman et al., 2000). Individuals experiencing post-traumatic growth may experience changes in how they perceive themselves, and this is often shown in the labels they use to describe themselves (Tedeschi, Park, & Calhoun, 1998).

Many helpful factors described by people in our study focused on their personal characteristics. These factors included the usefulness of receiving a diagnosis, the traits of perseverance and a sense of humor, and spiritual beliefs.

Receiving a Diagnosis

Receiving a diagnosis was particularly important for individuals with attention deficit disorder (ADD). Many people with learning disabilities encounter failure early in life—when they enter school and are without a peer group of other individuals with a learning disability to share the experience (Spekman, Goldberg, & Herman, 1993). Prior to receiving a diagnosis, these children and young adults may attribute their lack of success in school to a lack of intelligence. When they compare their skills to those of their peers without learning disabilities, they may feel different—not as smart. This phenomenon reflects Cooley's *looking-glass self,* where your feelings about yourself arise from the comparisons you make between yourself and others.

Rick, a 34-year-old student who lives alone, describes how he felt when he was diagnosed with ADD: "Well, it felt good to finally know what was wrong with me. I'm not alone in the world. I'm not the only one that has this."

Rick also describes how attending a meeting at a learning disability association helped him: "It was different because I had never met anybody else that had it. . . . They were talking about their lives, right, and I was saying, 'Hey that sounds like me.' "

Diagnosis and membership in a group for individuals with learning disabilities helped to reduce Rick's feelings of isolation and helped him to understand what was "wrong" with him.

Perseverance

Perseverance has been described as "stubbornness with a purpose." Frank, who has attention deficit hyperactivity disorder (ADHD), describes his own belief in his ability to reach his goals. He recognizes the characteristics of his personality that will stand him in good stead throughout his life course.

> To get through things basically for me it is perseverance. I have great perseverance that I will work extremely hard at something to accomplish it. Sometimes I don't work as smart as I would like. I rush into things but I think that is just my hyperactivity. I get kind of anxious and I will try to do everything instead of slowing myself down and doing things. But you know I am a hard worker, I persevere, I just work hard at things, and that is kind of what has got me through everything. Just plugging away. I always sort of relate to that tortoise who basically beats the hare in the long term. I always see myself as a tortoise. I am not too fast on the mark but I get things done.

It appears that Frank has learned from an early age that he needs to work extremely hard to achieve his goals. He perceives that this ability to persevere works to his advantage because it enables him to complete the tasks he sets out to do, even if it does take him longer than others.

Sense of Humor

Grace, who has spina bifida, indicates that her sense of humor helped her get through the stresses of life. She speaks of the sense of humor that her family shares and how this sustained her through many trials, including a kidney operation.

> There is such a humor [that] runs through our family and it stood us in good stead so many times. In fact, we often deal with each other on a humorous basis—I cannot imagine facing anything without that. It is so strong between us and it's been passed on to my brother's children as well. They're very, very much a part of that. It is lovely.
>
> It's what gets us through and it's a very embracing thing. You know I was saying to my brother about something the other day, "Could you at least be nice to me?" and he said, "If I was nice to you, you'd think I didn't like you!" (*Laughter*) And he's right! It's the humor that carries us through. As I say, it's been that way since I can remember. There's tenderness about it, that carries us through and it speaks volumes. So actually, we have our serious talks, but they're in that context.
>
> When we're really upset or facing crises, we're not having serious talks, but we're saying volumes in the humor that is going back and forth. And that's something that you can't learn. It's either there or it's not. But it's vital. It's a big component for us.

Grace was sustained by the humor her family used as a coping strategy.

Spiritual Beliefs

For several people, spiritual faith was instrumental in giving them perspective on life and helping them cope. Ellen Idler, from Rutgers University in New Jersey, writes on the concept of self and its relation to spirituality (1995). She divides the self-concept into the physical and the nonphysical self. The nonphysical sense of self includes our perceptions about how smart we are; our appreciation for music, literature, and other art forms; and our spirituality. She discusses this sense of nonphysical self as a helpful factor because this division of the self into components allows people with disabilities to see themselves as separate from their "failing bodies." In a study of individuals from a rehabilitation clinic that dealt with pain in the musculoskeletal system, she found that people who rated themselves as strongly religious and/or spiritual possessed a healthy concept of self. She found that spirituality was strong especially after a sudden illness or injury, as we've seen in the turning point experiences of participants shared in chapter 2.

A strong sense of spirituality also was evident as a helping factor in the stories people shared with us. Trudy, age 39, has ADD, is married and has children. She provides an arresting analogy of stepping-stones to describe how her faith helped her to cope during difficult times.

> Life is a big ocean and I guess, you know, I don't know how this is for other people, but again because of my Christianity, because of my belief in the Lord, it's like you stand on a rock—you're standing on these big cement blocks or inlaid things and you're always standing there. And then at different times the Lord puts down another cement block and then you step on that. So it's like that's what I think of—stepping-stones. I'm always provided with another step, but I can go on and I never step into the water. I never drown, but I can go on to speak because of what I've gone through.

Trudy refers back to this analogy when she explains how she coped with the death of her father and her son's illness. Her spiritual beliefs provided her with strength and a perspective to deal with otherwise overwhelming life events.

> But no one, not any one—the most put together person—can't do things on their own. That's why, that's what a spiritual relationship with the Lord is all about.
> I think that's where I get my stepping-stone part. I walk through life; it's like walking through life blindfolded. It's like reading a book. You can go to the end of the book and read it. Well, do you know what's going to happen in 10 years in your life? No, we can't read the ending of our book. So for me it's like the Lord's writing my book, but he's placing my stepping-stones. So I tie my stepping-stones very much to my faith.

Trudy sees her spiritual relationship with God as being her most important way of coping. Her faith gives her the confidence that she can deal with whatever challenges come her way. She does not expect or even hope that everything will be positive in the future. She simply accepts that both joy and sorrow are likely ahead of her and trusts that her faith in God will continue to guide her journey.

In addition to helping people cope, spiritual beliefs may be considered a helpful factor in that such beliefs can shape people's views of disability by providing a purpose for life. Linda Treloar, a nurse, conducted a research study examining the spiritual beliefs of adults with disabilities and their family members (Treloar, 1999). She found that religious belief systems, whether formalized or personal, are an important stabilizing force for people with disabilities. Spiritual beliefs provide assistance with coping and help establish meaning related to having a disability. These beliefs can

lead to various positive outcomes: accepting a disability, rising above limitations, and discovering new things about oneself (Gourgey, 1993; Schaefer, 1995). Loretta doRozario, an occupational therapist from Australia,
discusses spirituality as helping in the journey of separation from *self* back
to the understanding of *true self* (i.e., understanding the meaning for our
purpose in life) (doRozario, 1994).

Both Karen (aged 37, who has cerebral palsy, lives alone, and works
part-time) and Dan (aged 34, and who, like Karen, has cerebral palsy, lives
alone, and works part-time), described their spiritual beliefs as giving
them a reason for living and helping them to understand their purpose in
life. Karen explained:

> [I] personally believe that each person is put on earth for a special purpose
> and that God has different jobs for different people. And mine, I don't know
> what I would label it, but it's different than other people. I get to meet and
> talk to many, many groups of people that I would never get the opportunity
> to if I was able-bodied.
>
> There are many people who cannot speak for themselves who are dis-
> abled and I always try to be sort of a spokesperson—not because I want
> myself all over the paper, or whatever, [but] because I feel that I have a
> responsibility to help them. To help...people...with disabilities and to try
> to make their world a better place for even myself.

In a similar way, Dan described the effect of his spiritual philosophy on
his view of life: "I've always realized there has been a reason why I am on
earth like I am...It has just sort of helped me to put my life in perspective."

For Karen and Dan, spirituality seems to be at the heart of their description of helpful factors because it provides meaning in their lives. The
meaning and impact of spirituality can affect the everyday activities in
which we participate (Urbanowski & Vargo, 1994) and the values that
guide our lives (Egan & Delaat, 1994).

The discussion of spiritual beliefs by people in this study is not surprising. Henry McCarthy, from the Department of Rehabilitation Counseling
at the Louisiana State Medical Center, reported that 90 percent of Americans have never doubted the existence of God, 80 percent believe that God
works miracles, and 80 percent believe that prayer or meditation can lead
to a miraculous cure of disease (McCarthy, 1995). Although it is often not
something we discuss in public, many of us clearly think a lot about spirituality in private. Certainly, for people in this study, spiritual beliefs were
a major source of resilience—the ability to manage critical life events.

The Canadian Association of Occupational Therapists (1997) has developed and endorsed a model of occupational performance (which refers to all the activities that one performs in life), that includes mental, physical, sociocultural, and spiritual concerns. Psychologists also see the need to treat the whole person in therapy sessions. Very few practitioners, however, address spiritual beliefs in their daily practice (McCarthy, 1995), perhaps because people are uncomfortable discussing such issues. However, it is important to remember that while a lot of religious people are spiritual, the terms *religious* and *spiritual* are not synonymous.

As discussed in chapter 2, spirituality can, in its simplest form, be how we live our lives (Muldoon & King, 1991). According to Mary Egan and M. Denise Delaat, both occupational therapists, the spirit can be viewed as "our truest selves which we attempt to express in all of our actions" (Egan & Delaat, 1994, p. 96). They suggest that the spirit is the essence of the individual that connects with the self, others, and the rest of creation. This very connection of individuals with themselves and others relates back to Norman Garmezy's idea of resilience involving the individual, family, and others. Clearly, through spirituality we can develop a concept of ourselves that fosters relationships with others. This relationship, in turn, may be helpful in promoting resiliency for an individual.

SELF-ESTEEM—VALUING AND ACCEPTING OURSELVES

According to Rutter (1987), one of the protective processes operating at turning points in life involves events that foster the development of self-esteem. Our self-esteem—our feeling of self-worth—is developed in part through our relationships with others, such as our families, friends, and peers, and in part through how we see our competencies (i.e., how we view our strengths and abilities) (Harter, 1983). If those we care about give us the message that we are valuable and loved, then this can translate into a belief in ourselves that can help us bounce back from the challenges we face. We also develop beliefs in our abilities that can enhance our self-esteem. Accordingly, the following section deals with participants' belief in themselves and in their abilities.

Belief in Oneself and One's Abilities

One helpful factor frequently described by participants was the importance of believing in yourself: "I started feeling that I could make a difference." One participant suggested that anyone with a disability will lack self-confidence and that this would make believing in themselves more difficult. Intuitively, many of us would agree with this notion, believing that the loss of skills associated with a disability (or possessing different skills from one's peers) would erode a person's sense of self-esteem. However, research on the self-esteem of individuals with disabilities repeatedly finds that their overall feelings of self-esteem are not significantly different from the self-esteem of individuals without disabilities (Willoughby, King, & Polatajko, 1996). It appears that it is our perception of how well we can perform the tasks that are most important to us that is most related to our self-esteem (Harter, 1986; Specht, King, & Francis, 1998). If a specific dimension of our self-concept is low but devalued by us, it likely will not reduce our overall self-esteem. For example, if Jennifer perceives that she has poor athletic competence but athletic skills are not important to her, then her self-esteem (how she evaluates herself) will not be affected.

When we believe in ourselves, we can stand strong in our own *boots*. These boots keep us rooted in what we know to be true about our strengths and our sense of self. When we believe in ourselves, we can pursue our dreams and hopes with the confidence of a solid foundation. Should we falter, or doubt ourselves, we can always return to our solid sense of ourselves.

It is interesting that while people in our study felt that believing in and relying on themselves was an important helpful factor, so was the ability to express themselves and to ask for help. One participant said, "It is alright to reach out to people when you are feeling down." As another participant phrased it, "Life could be a lot better if you just take and ask." Perhaps, once independence and a healthy self-concept are established, asking for assistance does not threaten our sense of ourselves. Once we recognize what our skills and competencies are, and accept our strengths as well as our limitations, we may not perceive requesting help from others as a sign of weakness in us. Therefore, our sense of self—who we are—can remain intact.

The ability to reframe events (i.e., turn a negative situation into a positive one) was another type of belief seen as a helpful factor by people in the study. Helen, aged 39 and who has ADD, explained the usefulness of this ability. She calls it "making lemonade out of lemons." Helen says, "I know...one of the main lessons that I've learned in life [is] that it doesn't matter what you're protecting or taking care of. To produce a certain outcome you can't always control those things. You have to be flexible and you have to roll with the punches, and you have to make lemonade out of lemons. That's some of the lessons I learned."

Similarly, both Grace and Neil explain how they used another type of ability—how to harness their anger—to help them deal with frustrating situations. Grace, who is 51, notes, "I have learned to recognize my anger reaches a point where it becomes motivation. I have learned how to set goals. I have learned how to equip myself with what I need to move on."

In a similar manner Neil, age 36, describes his philosophy when looking back to decisions he made when he was 18. "I always found the best change in my life always came out of that deep-seated anger, knowing there was something wrong and knowing that the only way to do anything about it was to launch into a positive mode and try and do things. To lobby people to try and get things changed. But I would say on the whole I tend to be an optimist for all my pessimism."

Grace and Neil have learned through experience to use their frustration and anger to make changes that turn negative situations into positive ones. The changes they make are related to both personal (self) characteristics (i.e., learning new skills) and removing external barriers around them.

SELF-EFFICACY—AM I COMPETENT?

The aspects of the self we've considered so far deal with self-concept (Who am I?) and self-esteem (Am I worthy?). This section deals with the notion of self-efficacy (Am I competent?). According to Albert Bandura (1982), self-efficacy refers to our own judgment about how well we are able to carry out the actions necessary to deal with life events. People with a strong sense of self-efficacy feel they can be successful. They feel competent. They believe they have the ability to be effective in certain types of situations.

Efficacy refers to having the power to have an effect, so *self-efficacy* refers to our personal sense of power to have the consequences or effects that we desire. Being efficacious means acting or exerting power, causing things to happen, having an impact on the world, and being capable of making changes in our lives, influencing others, and attaining what we want. A high sense of self-efficacy is considered to be very helpful because it helps us deal with difficulties in life.

Most of us feel competent in some areas of our lives, and not in others. For example, we can feel competent at our jobs but not socially competent. We can feel ill at ease at parties or social gatherings, and experience difficulty in making friends, yet feel remarkably poised and confident in our work environment. Some of us enjoy being with others, feel comfortable in meeting new people and making new friends, yet doubt our ability to do a good job at work. So, self-efficacy is specific to a particular type of activity. Social self-efficacy reflects our judgment about whether we are capable of carrying out the social tasks that underlie successful relations with others. We can also feel competent in sports or recreational activities such as hiking, painting, or scuba diving.

The term *self-efficacy* is frequently confused with *self-esteem* (Willoughby, King, & Polatajko, 1996). An important difference between the two is that our perceptions of our efficacy vary depending on the activity in question. Self-esteem, on the other hand, refers to a relatively stable way in which we view ourselves. Competence grows as we successfully master challenges and learn new skills. Self-efficacy, therefore, changes more often than does our overall sense of self-worth.

Learning a New Activity or Skill

Multiple skill sets are involved in mastering an activity in a way that leads to a sense of self-efficacy. We first must have a vision of what we want to do or achieve. We then need to plan how we are going to accomplish that goal and ensure that all the necessary resources and supports are in place to learn the new activity. We attempt the activity, evaluate the outcome, and then need to try it again. This process continues until mastery has occurred, or failure—or boredom.

Learning to drive a car is a good example of how a person learns to master an activity or skill. First, you decide, at some point in your life, that you want to learn to drive. It becomes a goal for you. At that point, you likely will seek some training (we hope), either from a family member or from a professional. Your first experiences, especially if you are learning to drive a standard, may be a little rough. The important thing is not to give up. Other people can help here by encouraging you and believing you will succeed. When you ultimately get your driver's license, you likely will experience a feeling of competence and a sense of pride.

This example of learning to drive illustrates the kinds of factors that are important in mastering new skills and therefore in developing a sense of self-efficacy. These factors include personal characteristics, such as having a strong desire or motivation to get a driver's license. Without this strong desire and persistence, experiencing difficulties in learning to drive might make you decide to give up. Certain physical and cognitive abilities also are required, which allow you to do things like shift gears, work the brake, and make navigational decisions. Other factors include the support of various people: the person training you, friends, and family members who provide instructional guidance and tips, emotional support ("You can do it"), and practical assistance, like loaning you a car to practice on and driving you to lessons. Things that might prevent you from learning to drive are lack of physical ability or lack of self-confidence. Negative mind-sets or self-statements ("I'm not going to get this"; "I know I'm not going to be able to do this") may also play a role, as might having little opportunity to practice.

Let's consider what the participants in our study said about self-efficacy: what it felt like to them, what consequences it had for them, and, most important, the things that helped them acquire a sense of self-efficacy and the things that hindered this.

What Does Self-Efficacy Feel Like?

When people talked about self-efficacy, they talked about feeling a sense of accomplishment, a sense of pride, and feeling good about themselves.

Frank, who has ADHD, talks about a number of activities that led to feelings of self-efficacy—feelings of accomplishment and pride.

> I had another incident where I felt good about myself as an individual. I think it was grade five or six where I made the ski team at the ski club. I made the first ski team where my older brother made the second ski team, and the reason I made it was because they needed a consistent younger skier in the first team. So that made me feel really good about myself.
>
> I remember one year I won the regatta championship. My dad was so pleased with me. You feel you've accomplished something. It's ego. You know that you did something well.

As Frank talked about his experience in mastering these leisure activities, what he describes is a sense of self-efficacy.

> That period of time showed me that I could do things—that I could accomplish things if I put my mind to it, if I worked hard at it. I knew that I had to work harder but I knew that I could accomplish things.
>
> You know with the ski team it was that I wasn't the fastest down the hill but I was the most consistent down the hill. I always finished the race. I always got a point. I was never in the top five but I was consistent. I skied the courses. I did the work in school to make me be consistent and then I

could challenge, in an average manner, everyone else. So I felt instead of being in my own world, I felt part of the regular world.

From his leisure and school activities, Frank realized he could do well, despite his disability, if he worked hard. Moreover, his sense of competency gave him access to the "regular world." He said that taking part in regular activities made him feel like he belonged, didn't stand out, and was "just a plain individual."

Cory, Trudy, and Scott all talked about what it felt like to have a low sense of self-efficacy with respect to schoolwork due to having ADD. Cory shares how it felt to be thought of as stupid. This perception made him give up hope. Cory says, "I thought, well, I'm cooked. This is it. It is over and people called me stupid and stuff and I guess I am. I will have to live with it. There was just no hope. I have tried and it doesn't work. That was around 14 or 15 and then I went through that year kind of just partying and stuff like that."

Trudy had the same type of experience of feeling stupid while she was growing up. Other people told her she had "trains instead of brains."

> In the sixties and seventies you had to be, everybody was in a box and you had to learn the square method. If you learned in a round way you couldn't fit in that square.... I think very much I was that kind of person.... I learned differently.
>
> I grew up learning I could not do anything for myself. Nothing I thought of or decided was good. All my thoughts were dumb because I had "trains instead of brains."

Scott, who ended up completing college, talks about how having ADD made it difficult for him to study: "Now that I look back at it and see the difficulties with ADD and the differences with Ritalin and without, I recognize more now why my marks were the way they were. If you can't sit down and concentrate to study, you are screwed."

For the people with ADD in our study, their lower sense of self-efficacy was related to not being able to achieve good marks at school and to feeling unintelligent. This is a fairly typical experience for people with ADD.

Why Is It Important to Develop a Strong Sense of Self-Efficacy?

High self-efficacy helps us tackle challenges in life. When we believe that we can do things and reach the goals we set for ourselves, then we are more effective in doing so. Lack of belief in our abilities can undermine our efforts. We can lose hope and give up rather than persist. High self-efficacy gives us the confidence that we can overcome barriers, so that we don't throw in the towel or throw up our hands in dismay. Work by Michael Rutter (1985) indicates that high self-efficacy is an important protective factor that gives us the conviction that we can successfully deal with adverse life events.

The experiences of Karen, who was a Paralympic athlete, show why it is important to be an active participant in life. Karen learned many things from her Paralympic experiences. She learned about similarities and differences between people and that she could achieve.

> It [was] extremely unique. You see people from countries all over the world. You see people that are similar to you, [people] who have more abilities than you have [but] who do less with it. You see all kinds. The spectrum is tremendous.
>
> [The experience of going to the Paralympics] really showed me what I could do. I came home with one gold, two silver, and 2 bronze.... And that kind of turned my life because I realized that I could do other things in life—I could be involved athletically to keep in shape.
>
> The turning point was being able to be a Paralympic athlete. Really the medal is all part of that, but the medal hangs on a wall in a corner somewhere. That medal part is not important. The important part was learning that I was something, [that] I could do something. And the opportunities that I have had because of that—those events are so numerous that I couldn't begin to cover them all.

The Things That Help Us Gain a Sense of Self-Efficacy

A number of factors help us gain a sense of high self-efficacy. These include things about us, such as our persistence or belief in ourselves. The support of other people, as shown through encouragement, mentoring, or providing role models, also is important. Most important, perhaps, are opportunities in our environment to try out new skills. Medications and devices also help us to participate in day-to-day events and activities.

First, let's consider persistence. In a research study conducted by two authors of this book and several colleagues, we examined the factors that predicted persistence in adolescents who had physical disabilities (King, Shultz, Steel, Gilpin, & Cathers, 1993). The most important predictor was social self-efficacy. Thus, persistence was associated with a strong sense of self-efficacy.

Karen's experience with the Paralympics gave her many opportunities to speak to young people. A key message in her speaking engagements is the importance of being persistent and of being in control of your own destiny.

> I love it because [I] get to talk to these kids about what I have done and they turn around and see what they can do in their life. It helps to encourage them to go after their own dreams. Just to realize that you don't have to have a perfect life or body to be somebody. You make or break your own destiny.
>
> [A key message is] that they can do anything if they try. And not to let people stop them. If I had stopped because people told me I couldn't do it, I would have been out of the game a long time ago.

The importance of role models in shaping attitudes, interests, and aspirations is generally acknowledged. Exposure to role models is also considered important in the development of self-efficacy and self-esteem. A 1995 study by Laurie Powers of Dartmouth Medical School, and her colleagues Jo-Ann Sowers and Tuck Stevens, found that youth with disabilities who were exposed to mentors had higher levels of self-efficacy and self-confidence than youth who were not exposed to such models (Powers, Sowers, & Stevens, 1995).

The importance of role models is shown in the following quote from Dan, who is 34 and has cerebral palsy. He realized that he could live on his own by observing the accomplishments of someone else with a disability.

> At the time, my brother was going to school with a fellow that was in a wheelchair. He had been on his own, and he's a lot worse off than I am. So I went up to see him, and [when] I saw this guy for the first time, I thought to myself, "Hell, if this guy can do it on his own with support care, if I get in the right situation, I can live on my own. [I realized that] if he could live on his own with support care, I could live on my own with a little bit.

Thus, role models can help us see possibilities and embrace visions for our futures. For people with physical disabilities, living on their own and establishing independence can be a key challenge.

The availability of opportunities to acquire and try out new skills is an extremely important factor in determining self-efficacy. When opportunities are not there, people cannot participate, skills and abilities are not acquired or strengthened, and it is impossible to develop a sense of self-efficacy or competence.

Participation is therefore necessary for the development of competence. Participation has tremendous impact on the quality of people's lives. It is the context in which people form friendships, develop skills and competencies, express creativity, achieve mental and physical health, and determine meaning and purpose in life (Fidler & Fidler, 1978; King et al., 2003).

As children, we all need opportunities for successful social experiences with peers. To develop competence at activities, we need to be in situations where there is an optimal degree of challenge, where we can define the boundaries of our competence by experiencing failure, and where we are reinforced for attempting to succeed (Bandura, 1992). These experiences allow us to develop realistic expectations for our performance and to see improvement in our skills when we persevere. These are important lessons that lead to a sense of self-efficacy.

An excellent example of how participation—doing—leads to self-efficacy is shown in Loreena's scuba diving experiences. Loreena has spina bifida.

> When you are down there [underwater] you know who has the advantage in diving—deaf people—because they can sign and communicate much easier than you and I can.
>
> It was a learning experience because I was the first person with a disability that the company taught how to dive. It was a whole new learning process for everybody.
>
> For me, diving is something that I thoroughly enjoy. It is a sport that I can participate in and I won't give it up until I have to.
>
> My greatest accomplishment [has been] learning how to dive.

Bernie, who also has spina bifida, talks about the importance of opportunities for people with disabilities. Such opportunities allow people to gain skills and thereby feel good about themselves.

> Having grown up with physical disabilities and never [being able to] achieve, I would have just loved someplace where I could have had a fair playing field. I never had that opportunity....If I could have had a level playing ground—to be out there playing games where I could win occasionally—I could start to build some self-concept and feel good about [myself].

Medications and devices also help us to engage in activities. Grace gives an example of how a device, a power wheelchair, helped her to participate.

> The first time [I used my wheelchair] was with a girlfriend of mine who is a confirmed shopaholic. She had often avoided going shopping with me and knew it really hurt me. I would love to shop with her, but she just could not

deal with it, she was going to spend hours hanging around me while I would sit down, move on and so on and so forth. She was the first person to go shopping with me once I had the wheelchair. She had no problem taking it in and out of the car and so on and so forth. I had a ball with it. I kept right up with her. I spent a pile of money too, got this and this and this. [It's a] major disaster if I now don't go shopping in the wheelchair or the scooter because I am so comfortable I can outstay the best of them now.

[When I got the wheelchair], my participation came right back out. I could go shopping with my girlfriends. I could do my entire Christmas shopping by myself without feeling absolutely exhausted and so on, and [do] day trips. One of the same male friends who has been very supportive was the first to say, "Okay, let's spend a weekend at Niagara Falls and look at stuff you have never looked at before because you couldn't access [it] with your crutches."

The Things that Hinder Us in Gaining a Sense of Self-Efficacy

Many of the things that hinder the development of self-efficacy are the opposite of the helping factors we have just considered. Due to physical limitations and others' negative attitudes, people with disabilities, particularly visible disabilities such as cerebral palsy and spina bifida, may not have a chance to experience the sorts of mastery experiences that Mihaly Csikszentmihalyi (1990) talks about. These are the types of experiences that lead to a sense of *flow*. Lack of opportunity for skill development through lowered participation, therefore, is an important hindering factor.

Other people's lack of belief in our abilities is also an important hindering factor, as shown in chapter 2. It is often not enough to attempt to improve a child's level of competence through training and to provide sufficient opportunities for the child to practice newly learned skills at home or at school. Our work on social skills training for children with physical disabilities has indicated that the beliefs and assumptions of classmates, teachers, and other community members often need to change as well (King et al., 1997).

In conclusion, self-efficacy is an important aspect of how we view ourselves, as shown in the quotes of participants. The key helpful factor is having an opportunity to participate, and the key hindering factor is other people's negative attitudes, which limit participation. People with disabilities want what all of us want for ourselves and our children: the opportunity to reach our true potential through active participation in our worlds.

SOCIAL SUPPORT—SELF-AWARENESS, SELF-ACCEPTANCE, AND SELF-EFFICACY THROUGH RELATIONSHIPS WITH FAMILY, FRIENDS, AND COMMUNITY

I've learned to know myself through support.

—Grace, a participant in the study

Social support refers to a category of protective factors that deal with social relationships and ties to others (Ryff & Singer, 2000). What makes us resilient is a combination of ourselves—as reflected in our self-concept, self-esteem, and sense of self-efficacy—and our social environment.

Theories of social support focus on the importance of human connection. Social support is a complex and multifaceted construct, and there has been a great deal of debate over how to define and measure it (Wortman & Dunkel-Schetter, 1987). In general, there has been a movement away from seeing social support as a unitary construct and toward identifying particular components or kinds of support, which overlap considerably (Wortman & Dunkel-Schetter, 1987). The more inclusive definitions define social support in ways that reflect the three paths to meaning discussed in chapter 2. For example, Kahn and Antonucci (1980) define *social support* as interpersonal relations that involve the expression of positive affect (belonging), the provision of tangible assistance (doing), and the affirmation or endorsement of a person's beliefs (understanding).

Social support also refers to the mechanisms by which interpersonal relationships protect people from distress, but little attention has been paid to identifying precisely how social support operates (Wortman & Dunkel-Schetter, 1987). What is it about social support that helps a person to be resilient? Does social support influence how people initially interpret a potentially problematic situation, or does it offer protection through enhancing people's coping strategies or bolstering their self-esteem? Does social support provide practical assistance that helps to resolve a problem, or does it influence an individual's motivation to do something about a situation? Social support likely has beneficial effects in all these ways—through providing practical assistance, by affecting a person's motivation and behavior, and by influencing aspects of the self.

According to Thoits (1985), social support bolsters aspects of the self by providing various types of support—emotional support, practical or tangible support, and informational support. It therefore appears that supportive relationships contribute to resilience through mechanisms that involve the three aspects of the self that we have been considering. Social support can provide a sense of belonging and intimacy (emotional support), thereby enhancing self-esteem (Berkman, 1995; Wortman & Dunkel-Schetter, 1987). Social support can help individuals feel competent, thereby enhancing self-efficacy (Berkman, 1995). And social support can provide information that increases the accuracy of self-perception, thereby strengthening a person's self-concept.

Social support, therefore, provides us with various messages that relate to the three paths to meaning described in chapter 2. People receive a message of social acceptance through expressions of caring and concern (Baumeister & Leary, 1995), which contributes to self-acceptance (a sense of belonging). People receive a message that they are "believed in" or considered to be competent through social comparison and information that clarifies the meaning of their behavior or others' behavior, which contributes to self-efficacy (doing). People receive a message about who they are or what they truly believe in, which contributes to self-awareness (understanding).

Some researchers have described support from others as a *convoy* that accompanies us on our life journey (e.g., Kahn & Antonucci, 1981). The larger groups of which we are a part—our friends, family, and community—affect our development as people throughout life. The convoys of social support that friends, family, and community provide can help or hinder us at different junctures in our lives (Antonucci & Akiymama, 1995).

Research studies have indicated that we have two types of relationships in our lives—formal relationships and informal ones (Dunst, Trivette, & Deal, 1988). These categories of formal versus informal relationships are not always distinct. Rather, they evolve and change over time.

Informal contexts for support include relationships with our families and friends. Formal contexts include relationships with professionals and community ties (e.g., clubs, religious organizations, and self-help groups). Neither formal nor informal relationships are inherently supportive, but they can take on a supportive character. We decide if we find our relationships supportive. This perception is influenced by our own personal ideas and cultural ideas of what constitutes support.

In the next part of the chapter, we will look at formal and informal types of support. We'll describe what support looked and felt like for the people in our study, and will examine how supportive relationships affected participants' self-esteem. People who were part of our study spoke eloquently about the importance and usefulness of supportive relationships at key turning points in their lives. These relationships helped to foster their resilience in the face of challenges in life.

The 15 people who were part of our study spoke about support from others to a great extent—over 134 times in the course of their interviews. They described key players in their life dramas who were helpful to them in times of challenge. Most often these people were mothers, fathers, friends, teachers, and/or counselors. It did not seem to matter who the relationship was with or the number of relationships the person had. For the promotion of a person's self-esteem, what was important was that at least one relationship—one person—provided support. When one person believed in, valued, encouraged, or listened to them, this made a significant difference, as we shall see. This sense of support helped people get through their turning points. It fostered their self-esteem and resilience in the face of challenges.

The Importance of Support

To be loved is to be given great power.
—Janet Aitken Kidd, horsewoman

A minister at a funeral service for a remarkable woman (who had been, among other things, a mother of eight children) described the best gift a mother can give her children as "roots and wings." Family is one of the most basic contexts for relationships. Family is the site of our earliest and often most enduring relationships. Relationships with family members have a fundamental influence on us. Family relationships shape our attitudes, outlooks, motivations, strategies for achievement, and ways of coping with challenges. Family relationships and experiences deeply affect our competence and sense of belonging, which in turn contributes to our self-esteem, and thereby our resilience and sense of well-being in life.

The families of people in our study were often described as supports that helped them develop strong self-esteem and resilience in the face of challenges. Neil, Grace, and Frank all described their family roots, which formed a solid foundation for them to grow and develop. Family support gave each of them wings to help them soar to desired heights in their lives.

Frank, who has attention deficit disorder, was helped during elementary school by his special education teacher (discussed in chapter 2). His mother also played a big role in supporting him throughout his life.

> A psychologist said that I wouldn't proceed to high school—that I wouldn't graduate from high school because I had in grade 3 gone backwards. And it was my mother who basically said, "Listen this is a smart individual who just needs the right help and the right direction," and again she played my

advocate. She fought for what I needed and once she knew more of what I needed, she lobbied for that from the school board and from the principal.

She believed in me and it is that sense of family—that they were there for me, that they really stood by me.

I don't think that I would be where I am now if it wasn't for her...I needed that help at that particular time.

Frank's mom believed in her son's abilities. The combination of her belief and the special education teacher's assistance encouraged and stimulated Frank's intellect and belief in his own skills, thereby enhancing his self-esteem. Frank now has a master's degree and works full-time in a field he enjoys.

Neil, who has children of his own, recalls the role his parents played when he was a child and other children with cerebral palsy were being placed in institutions.

I had strong parents. Most parents then either put the child in an institution or kept the child under lock and key. For its safety I guess. My parents were the exact opposite....When I [was] four, it was time to go to school....Now everybody told us that there is a special school....My mother didn't listen and enrolled me into a regular school—a two-story school and the kindergarten level began on the second floor. So they had to make arrangements to carry me up and down stairs to go the bathroom, which was in the basement of the school. And she did that and made sure I got educated. Which is far more than a lot of other people would do.

Neil went on to complete a university degree. For both Frank and Neil, their mothers' belief in them contributed to their academic success.

Grace's family also had faith in her ability and potential, which was very encouraging to her. As a 51-year-old woman with spina bifida, Grace describes her family as the important root from which her life has taken wing.

From the very starting point, my parents were very family committed. First and foremost, they treated me as a loved and valued child. There was a terrific emphasis on independence and adaptation from day one. That has been my root, my basis. They allowed me the physical freedom to explore my own abilities and they encouraged the mental stimulation because that struck them as very important as there were going to be limitations and they didn't know what, so the provision was there for lots of mental stimulation.

You have to understand [that] when I was born, little was known about spina bifida and the survival rate was very, very low. And I had an excellent surgeon who just dealt with my parents from day one, who basically told them, "We'll work through this together and don't you dare not have other children. It would be the worst thing you could do for her." So they did....They didn't sacrifice the other two [children] for me. And that was a hard balance to strike. Both my parents have said at different times, "You were a very willful, strong, beguiling child and it was very, very easy to fall into the trap of you know, you're special," and they fought it very hard.

Somebody else has pointed out to me, actually many people pointed out to me, [that] my parents were way ahead of their time. They really were. They always wanted to have a family and that came first and they dealt with the glitches.

They just used to encourage me....First of all, they would never put an emphasis on looks, not for any of us, and, again, would very much encourage me to be sociable and to have other things to offer.

Now as adults, my siblings, my parents, and I don't live in each other's pockets. We all have very independent and very full lives and actually can go months without seeing each other. Not without talking to each other, but without seeing each other. But you put a celebration or a crisis down and there's nobody missing. I think that speaks volumes.

When Grace went through a divorce and her life seemed to shatter, it was the support of her family that sustained her. Her brother was one of the many people who helped her through the crisis by encouraging her when her faith in herself wavered.

I lent on him for hours...He is a great person for helping one to figure out what is going to be done....He taught me something that has stayed with me forever. I didn't know what to do when he asked me, and so he suggested that I needed to commit some goals to paper. My initial response to that was..."I am sitting here pouring out my life to you and how miserable it is and how angry I am and you want me to write some goals down!" He stuck with me through that and he said, "You do it on three different pieces of paper. The first set of goals documents everything you have achieved in your life until now. The second is containing your goals for the next ...month, the next six months, but don't go beyond a year. The third one is your five-year goal."

I took him seriously and I sat down with it and what I had achieved actually started to make me feel better there and then. And I began to realize the purpose of the sequence he suggested.

It has had an incredible impact on me. It's made me do a number of things. It's made me look back and see how I handle crisis. It has given me a very clear picture of where I have been and where I might like to be going....That was one of the most helpful things that my brother had put towards me.

Grace's brother therefore supported her through the crisis with practical assistance. He suggested how she could cope and deal with the situation. As a result of this support, Grace developed a good sense of her past and future.

Grace, Neil, and Frank all gained "strong roots and wings" from their families, which sustained them in times of crisis. The positive feedback and strategies they received from family members fostered positive feelings about themselves. Family relationships, however, are complex. Relationships in the family aren't supportive all the time. Sometimes these relationships have periods when the support lags behind the optimum or desired level. This doesn't mean that a person's family is not, in general, supportive. It just means that relationships are inherently human—they can be inconsistent and imperfect.

Helen speaks about the lack of support she received at one point in her relationship with her mother. She describes her mother's response to the challenges that having attention deficit disorder posed for her when she was studying for her university degree.

> I had some real concerns about writing one exam at nine in the morning and one exam at two. I only had two [exams]. There were no mid-terms for either of these exams, so I don't know what the professor really wanted. That is really risky. Putting them on the same day is insane because I am a write-off after an exam. My mother couldn't understand that. She thought, "Well, why can't you just focus on the fact that you are going to have a month of holidays?" I said, "Well that is how I started this conversation, and I am glad, but can't you see how that would be a problem for me, mom?" And she said, "No." She didn't understand that. She couldn't see how badly I am affected by exams. She has no concept and yet I have been telling her all along. I mean that is the whole reason why I went and found out about ADD because of the problems I've had. Now [exams] have become extremely stressful for me. It is pretty basic. I would think that someone would understand that if they had any concept because she has read the books. But no, she doesn't understand. So I ended up the conversation by saying something like, "Yeah well, I will just focus on the fact that I am getting a month off."

Despite this incident, Helen succeeded in her school endeavors. She describes her "stubborn personality" as the factor that allowed her to conquer challenges in her path to an education. She sought help with studying techniques, got extra exam time, and was successful in her studies.

Helen provides a good example of how lack of support in a particular moment doesn't necessarily result in low self-esteem or lack of resilience.

If this lack of support had been repeated on many occasions, then perhaps its cumulative effect would have reduced Helen's self-esteem.

The Importance of Friends

Through the eyes of our friends we learn to see ourselves
Through the love of our friends we learn to love ourselves
Through the caring of our friends we learn what it means to love our-
    selves completely.

                            —From a tapestry—author unknown

Although our family plays a substantial supportive role in our lives, friends also play an important role. Friendships are based on reciprocity and an acceptance that each friend is an equal in the relationship (Freeman & Kasari, 1998). This can mean that requesting help from friends may be easier than requesting help from a boss or colleague because of the voluntary and reciprocal nature of the relationship. Certainly, friendships can contribute much to our quality of life and play a major role in bolstering our sense of well-being (Shalock, 2000). In our study, people described friendships that sustained them and helped them at difficult times in their lives.

Alisha, who has a university degree and works full-time, recognizes the importance and value of supportive friendships.

> When my life is really, really stressful or really, really down, it is [Joanne] that I call. I don't have to explain anything. She knows me well and she supports me.... Some of my other friends, when I go to them for support, they like to make me look like I am unstable. They try to sort of paint a picture in my mind that it is not good to be down. [Joanne] has never ever done that. Never, ever. She always pushes me up because it is like when you are down you can beat yourself up all by yourself. You don't need somebody else helping you [to]. [Joanne] never does that. Never has, never did, never will. She has always been my support when I needed her.

Joanne's constant support was critical to Alisha when Alisha was striving to secure a job that would end her financial reliance on a disability pension.

Loreena, who is 36 years old and has spina bifida, also has learned the importance of support from friends. She describes the comfort and understanding her friend provides:

> I'm really comfortable with him and I've never felt that comfortable with anybody, but it's because he has spina bifida and he can understand where I

am coming from. He understands the emotions that come with explaining to someone that you have this disability and this is what I can't do and this is what I can do and going through that whole rigmarole with someone. He totally understands and that's nice, and that's an exciting feeling that someone else out there can understand.

Loreena and Alisha each know the value and importance of friendship. Their relationships have buoyed and sustained them during challenging times. These relationships have taught them the importance of having someone to support them.

Support from friends can make realizing our dreams feel within reach. As Dan, who is 34 and has cerebral palsy, said, "It is like feeling two feet taller when you are with friends who support you—who believe in you."

Social Support from Community Players

We each have family and many of us have friends. These relationships can be supportive and enrich our self-esteem. However, we don't live in a vacuum with only our family and friends. The broader context of our community influences our self-esteem and resilience. Important community players in our lives include counselors, people who provide services, and teachers.

Neil found meaningful support from a counselor. Neil, who has cerebral palsy, was at a juncture in his life where he was unsure which career path to take. The counselor asked Neil to describe his hopes and dreams.

> I have always wanted to go to school. I have always wanted to go to university. That has been a dream. I want to know history. He said he knew this guy in a wheelchair, he went to [college] and he got his degree. I happened to ask, "Who is it?" And he told me and I said, "Oh I know him. I went to high school with him." And he said, "Well, go to university. Don't listen to those people. Do what you want to do. Get ahead." And that is when I started to pull myself out.

The counselor's belief in Neil's ability helped him to believe in himself and encouraged him to pursue his dreams.

Cory, who struggled with attention deficit disorder and drug and alcohol abuse, describes the importance of meeting someone at a social service agency who believed in him. The man he met described his own life challenges and believed that if he could overcome these obstacles, so could Cory. "I left there believing that somebody cared and that somebody did something with their life, the way I wanted to. I started to believe there were still more answers and maybe I wasn't all alone."

This encounter gave Cory hope. The hope was founded on the example of another person surmounting obstacles in life and believing that Cory could also do so. Hearing this man's story assured Cory that he was not alone. His challenges were not unique or impossible to address.

Trudy is a mother of two who, like Cory, has attention deficit disorder. For Trudy, the diagnosis of the disorder by a supportive professional gave her a fresh perspective on the challenges she had encountered during her life course.

> After hearing that, it was like you have reason to feel tired, to feel frustrated, to feel like pulling out your hair, but you are not a failure. That was just wonderful.
>
> Being diagnosed, it put everything in perspective....I felt for the first time that I could walk with my head high and proud....I'm an interesting and unique individual.

The person who diagnosed Trudy was supportive because she did not blame or judge Trudy. Rather, she offered an explanation for some of Trudy's struggles. Trudy had been haunted by desperate feelings.

> I felt I was drowning. I felt I was out all by myself and there on that phone call was someone [who] threw me the life rope so I wasn't alone....They took the time to listen and they're caring. I felt cared for. I felt they didn't push me off...and that just makes all the world of difference....It's the support, it's the genuine caring and listening that I felt. But it was the treatment of the whole family....You know they would go the long mile....They listened and they never pushed me off.

The person who listened to Trudy helped her realize she was not alone. This realization encouraged her and was helpful to her.

Frank speaks about the support of a teacher who increased his self-confidence at a critical time in his childhood.

> She provided me with the education, with the exercises to help me feel good about myself but also to challenge me in a way that I could learn....I think that it did definitely affect my self-confidence, it was much better.
>
> [We had a trampoline in this special education class that provided] me with something that made me feel special....I was in this class not just because I had a learning disability, but it showed other people that we were

special in some way. And that made me feel special [and] that then helped my self-confidence and made me feel better about myself.

Teachers and other professionals were supportive in their relationships with study participants. For Frank, Trudy, Cory, and Neil, these supportive relationships helped them manage the challenges of their lives and maintain positive feelings about themselves.

The Essence of Support

As we have seen, one of the most important factors that protects us from adversity or poor outcomes in life is the extent to which we have close and supportive personal relationships with others. As we have seen from the stories of people in the study, it only requires one supportive adult to help protect us from possible adverse outcomes.

Mary-Lou Ellerton, of the School of Nursing at Dalhousie University, has researched the topic of social support. Along with colleagues, she has defined support as "interactions with family, friends, peers, and health professionals that communicate information, esteem, aid, or emotional help" (Ellerton, Stewart, Ritchie, & Hirth, 1996, p. 19). Katherine Wolkow (1999), a psychiatrist at the Hospital for Sick Children in Toronto, asserts that children who experience the presence of a caring and warm adult in their formative years are protected to a greater extent from possible poor outcomes (e.g., violent behavior, poor school performance, or low self-esteem) than children who do not have a caring adult in their lives. She states:

> When even one caring adult unconditionally accepts a young person and communicates a belief in his or her potential, a sense of acceptance is fostered in the child which in turn leads to an increase in self-esteem and self-confidence. The inner strength that a caring adult nurtures in a child buffers him or her in the face of adverse circumstances, and leads the child toward more favorable life outcomes. (Wolkow, 1999, p. 2)

Supportive relationships and their effects are influential and important throughout life—when we are children, adolescents, and adults. Julie Wall, Katherine Covell, and Peter MacIntyre from the Psychology Department of the University College of Cape Breton, studied 260 students in grades 9–12 to look at the relationships among support, perceptions of future opportunity, and career aspirations and expectations (Wall, Covell, & MacIntyre, 1999). They found that when students are satisfied with at least one support, they are more optimistic about their lives, believe they have more control over their future and present, and believe they have opportunity for careers and education. When adolescents have low levels of support from others, they may see their access or ability to pursue future opportunities in education and career as limited. Similarly, in our study, support from others was a critical helpful factor in the lives of participants, both as children and later in life. As seen in chapter 1, study participants also reported generally high levels of overall satisfaction with their lives and felt that their chronic conditions did not significantly influence their life quality.

When support is effective, it is powerful. Supportive relationships help us feel valued, esteemed, and loved. Supportive people sustain us in times of challenge, celebrate with us when we have successes, encourage us to achieve our goals, listen to our feelings, value us for who we are and who we are yet to be, and believe in our strengths but know our weaknesses. Sometimes support from others, although well intended, can be detrimental. Good intentions may result in being overprotective of others, which can hinder the development of the skills and abilities necessary to master life events.

Unsupportive Social Interactions

Researchers have tended to focus on how social interactions help, and they have tended to ignore the negative aspects of interpersonal interactions (Wortman & Dunkel-Schetter, 1987). Unsupportive social interactions include those that are purposefully unhelpful and those that are well-meaning. According to Camille Wortman and Christine Dunkel-Schetter (1987), when people experience life crises, others' attempts to help often are judged to be unsupportive. Holly Peters-Golden (1982) reported that 72 percent of cancer patients in her study felt that they were misunderstood by people with whom they came in contact, which led them to feel isolated and alone.

How do well-meaning interactions turn into unhelpful ones? Interviews with cancer patients have determined what is helpful and not helpful to people experiencing stressful life events (Dakof & Taylor, 1990; Wortman & Dunkel-Schetter, 1979). First, it is important to note that people with cancer require an appreciable amount of social support. Their assumptions and beliefs about themselves and the world are called into question, they are unsure about whether their reactions to their illness are reasonable and normal, and they are faced with the need to make many complex decisions (Wortman & Dunkel-Schetter, 1979). Family and friends can provide help in all these areas but, for various reasons, may not do so in satisfactory or effective ways.

Wortman and Dunkel-Schetter (1979) considered the effects of having cancer on people's interpersonal relationships. People with cancer often reported experiences of rejection, withdrawal, and difficulties communicating with family and friends, which affected their self-esteem and emotional adjustment. Family, friends, and acquaintances seem to believe that they need to act in an optimistic and cheerful way toward someone with a chronic illness, when in fact these responses, as well as physical avoidance and avoidance of open discussion of the person's situation, are unintentionally damaging.

So, how can one help someone with a chronic illness? The most helpful type of support is emotional support (Dakof & Taylor, 1990). Cancer patients whose needs for support are met have been found to have higher postoperative levels of self-esteem and self-efficacy than patients who do not feel adequately supported (Wortman & Dunkel-Schetter, 1979).

What does not help? Absent or misguided emotional support is unhelpful, especially from intimate others. Unsupportive behaviors include expressing too much worry or pessimism and, on the other hand, expressing too little concern, empathy, or affection (Dakof & Taylor, 1990). It also does not help to avoid the topic of illness or to tell someone what they should do. Well-meaning advice, such as "You should cheer up and think about all the wonderful things in your life" or "It could be a lot worse," may be interpreted as criticism. It appears that an important feature of help is that it enhances rather than detracts from a person's sense of self-control and does not undermine his or her self-esteem.

These notions also are relevant to people with disabilities, who may experience unsupportive interactions and feel misunderstood. Due to feelings of social awkwardness, people may avoid people with disabilities or behave in an overly cheerful manner. It is important to listen to issues they are concerned about, not to minimize or trivialize their worries, and, above all, to try to understand their situation.

PHILOSOPHIES OF LIVING: LESSONS LEARNED FROM LIFE

Throughout the participants' discussions of what helped them on their life journeys, one significant theme emerged—the discovery of an ability to accept themselves. Grace, at age 51, explains her approach to living.

Now I am at full maturity I am able to look back and see there are no regrets, although there are some aches in my heart which are part of the fabric of life. And as I look forward, I know there will be other disappointments but on balance many, many more horizons to conquer or reach. That is a part of my lifetime thinking, that there will always be disappointments and setbacks but there is still so much more to go.

I find it interesting that my peers have now reached the age where body parts are breaking down and some have difficulty accepting this. I don't. I have long ago, or always, had to face the periodic hospital stays and the setbacks and the limitations. Now I view them as an inconvenience but an integral part of the life I have always lived.... So many people are having difficulty with diminished capacity, if you will, or interventions and I am not. I don't know any different. I don't like them any more than anyone else does, but they have been a part of me always on a periodic basis.

There are those who think very much like I do: hey, there is a whole lot more to go and we are just going to take full advantage of it. Interestingly, there are those—and I am amazed at those that have reached this age who are saying this: "This is it, we have had the bulk of it we are winding down now," and I find this just unbelievable. That is the thinking I can't relate to and I think that is interesting. I am the one with the long-term disability and it would never, never occur to me to say "Okay, this is the point, I have had a really good time, on balance it has been great but it's now time to kick back and let it be." That part does rather amaze me, that there is still that mind-set among some people who reach this age.

For Grace, the experience of living with her disability and the inconvenience associated with it have helped her foster an attitude of acceptance. Grace has never been able to take her physical health for granted. Consequently, her self-concept—her understanding of who she is—has not been threatened by the loss of physical abilities associated with aging.

Grace is not fearful of the future but anticipates the challenges to come, knowing from experience that she possesses the inner (self) and outer (support from others) resources to deal with these challenges. Grace later explained that it is this attitude that has kept her alive: "I have made some adaptations and accepted them and I also accept there will be more. There will have to be more because I don't plan on rolling over and dying yet."

At the end of her interview, Grace elaborated on her life philosophy as she discussed her life's course.

I don't know where it is going. I don't want to know. I just look forward to it.

I don't want to control [it] because then I won't be surprised. Actually somebody once put it to me that if we knew there would be no surprises...[then] we would shy away from the bad stuff, which is true.

I mean I really would rather not know when the bad stuff is coming because I feel better with it when it just lands in my lap and I don't want to know the good stuff in advance either. If you know every single day or every single year, what you are going to be facing, where is your challenge?

It is very tempting to say, "Oh let there be no more bad things," but it is not very realistic. I think the best you can say is that I would be able to get through them.

Grace emphasized the importance of living in the present and not worrying about the future. Again, it appeared that Grace was able to do this because she believed that she had the coping skills (in herself and with the support of others) to deal with whatever came her way.

Loreena (who is 36 years old and has spina bifida) described how she learned to accept her disability as part of her self.

I think that you have to meet the disability, you learn to live with your disability and accept it. It's a long drawn-out process, but I have to say when you're born with it, it takes a long time, but I can imagine anybody who wasn't disabled and all of a sudden they become disabled, it must be really, really difficult. They must go through an awful denial period.

Loreena felt that she had to learn to accept her disability herself before she could expect others to accept her. She also illustrates an attitude of self-acceptance when she shares her personal definition of success.

I'm proud of what I've accomplished. To me the definition of success used to be that I'm going to be the president of a company some day and then I realized that I didn't fit in the corporate world; that's not the meaning of success. To me success is achieving what you want to achieve and when you achieve it, that's the meaning of success. No, it's not somebody else's definition anymore, it's your own. When you're proud of something you've done, that's success.

To arrive at this definition of success, Loreena had to discover who she really was and what was important to her. Loreena relinquished the idea of establishing who she is by comparing herself to others. She decided to live up to her own standards rather than focusing on impressing others. Undoubtedly, it must take a healthy self-concept, good self-esteem, and a strong sense of self-efficacy to be able to manage the pressures and expectations society imposes on us.

WHAT ARE THE MOST IMPORTANT HELPFUL FACTORS?

In conclusion, we have seen that the most important helpful factors mentioned by participants are social support from family, friends, and community members; personality traits such as determination or persistence; and spiritual beliefs. Other factors that assist in the development of a healthy self-concept, strong self-esteem, and a sense of self-efficacy include receiving a diagnosis that helps people make sense of their experiences, having a sense of humor, believing in themselves, having opportunities to try out new skills, and the availability of appropriate and effective medications and devices. How does this list of factors fit with what the literature says?

In 1979, Michael Rutter, writing about protective factors for disadvantaged children, said:

> The scanty evidence so far available suggests that when the findings are all in, the explanation will probably include the patterning of stresses, individual differences caused by both constitutional and experiential factors, compensating experiences outside the home, the development of self-esteem, the scope and range of available opportunities, an appropriate degree of environmental structure and control, the availability of personal bonds and intimate relationships, and the acquisition of coping skills. (p. 70)

All of these factors mentioned by Michael Rutter were found to be important themes in the turning point experiences shared by participants in our study. His predictions therefore appear to be correct, not only for children living in adverse conditions such as poverty, but also for adults with disabilities looking back on their lives. Participants' experiences, therefore, strongly support the set of key factors outlined by Michael Rutter (1979) and other later researchers (e.g., Luthar, 1991; Masten, Best, & Garmezy, 1990; Smokowski, Reynolds, & Bezruczko, 1999). In summary, these common protective factors are: a positive outlook, high self-esteem, perseverance, supportive relationships within the family, having meaningful activity in life, and having a strong social network, including peers and nonrelated adults. Spiritual beliefs, the use of medications and devices, and receiving a diagnosis appear to be helpful factors that are particularly important—or unique to—individuals with disabilities.

It is not enough, however, to accept ourselves, to believe in our abilities and strengths, to possess effective coping strategies, and to experience support from others. The attitudes, assumptions, and beliefs of the main culture are also factors that influence our resilience in the face of challenges in life.

Bob Rae, former premier of the Province of Ontario, Canada, wrote a book *The Three Questions: Prosperity and the Public Good* (Rae, 1998). He wrote about a rabbi named Hillel who asked three questions, in Babylon, over two thousand years ago: "If I am not for myself, who is for me? But if I am only for myself, what am I? And if not now, when?" These questions make it clear that we each have responsibility to ourselves and to others. We are all intricately linked as part of humanity. Bob Rae states that society should recognize individual success and demonstrate an organized capacity for social compassion. This is the community level of support that is so necessary for resilience, which goes beyond strengths within the individual and support from family and friends.

The next chapter explores specific recommendations and advice from people in our study. Much of what people recommended focused on community members' attitudes, assumptions, and beliefs—the larger context to which we belong.

REFERENCES

Antonucci, T., & Akiyama, H. (1995). Convoys of social relations: Family and friendships in a life span context. In R. Bleiszner & V. Bedford (Eds.), *Handbook of aging and the family.* Westport, CT: Greenwood Press.

Bandura, A. (1982). Self-efficacy mechanism in human agency. *American Psychologist, 37,* 122–147.

Bandura, A. (1992). Self-efficacy mechanism in psychobiologic functioning. In R. Schwarzer (Ed.), *Self-efficacy: Thought control of action* (pp. 355–394). Washington, DC: Hemisphere Publishing Co.

Baumeister, R. F., & Leary, M. R. (1995). The need to belong: Desire for interpersonal attachments as a fundamental human motivation. *Psychological Bulletin, 117*(3), 497–529.

Berkman, L. F. (1995). The role of social relations in health promotion. *Psychosomatic Medicine, 57,* 245–254.

Bronfenbrenner, U. (1979). *The ecology of human development: Experiments by nature and design.* Cambridge, MA: Harvard University Press.

Brooks, R. B. (1994). Children at risk: Fostering resilience and hope. *American Journal of Orthopsychiatry, 64,* 545–553.

Calhoun, L. G., & Tedeschi, R. G. (1998). Posttraumatic growth: Future directions. In R. G. Tedeschi, C. L. Park, & L. G. Calhoun (Eds.), *Posttraumatic growth: Positive changes in the aftermath of crisis* (pp. 215–238). Mahwah, NJ: Lawrence Erlbaum.

Canadian Association of Occupational Therapists. (1997). *Enabling occupation: An occupational therapy perspective.* Ottawa: CAOT Publications ACE.

Columbo, J. R. (1991). *The dictionary of Canadian quotations.* Toronto: Stoddart.

Cooley, C. H. (1964). *Human nature and the social order.* New York: Free Press.

Crocker, J., & Major, B. (1989). Social stigma and self-esteem: The self-protective properties of stigma. *Psychological Review, 96,* 608–630.

Csikszentmihalyi, M. (1990). *Flow: The psychology of optimal experience.* New York: Harper & Row.

Dakof, G. A., & Taylor, S. E. (1990). Victims' perceptions of social support: What is helpful from whom? *Journal of Personality and Social Psychology, 58*(1), 80–89.

doRozario, L. (1994). Ritual, meaning and transcendence: The role of occupation in modern life. *Journal of Occupational Science: Australia, 1*(3), 46–53.

Dunst, C., Trivette, D., & Deal, A. (1988). *Enabling & empowering families: Principles & guidelines for practice.* Cambridge, MA: Brookline Books.

Egan, M., & Delaat, M. D. (1994). Considering spirituality in occupational therapy practice. *Canadian Journal of Occupational Therapy, 61*(2), 95–101.

Ellerton, M., Stewart, M. J., Ritchie, J. A., & Hirth, A. M. (1996). Social support in children with a chronic condition. *Canadian Journal of Nursing Research, 28*(4), 15–36.

Fidler, G. S., & Fidler, J. W. (1978). Doing and becoming: Purposeful action and self-actualization. *American Journal of Occupational Therapy, 32,* 305–310.

Freeman, S. F. N., & Kasari, C. (1998). Friendships in children with developmental disabilities. *Early Education and Development, 9,* 341–355.

Garmezy, N. (1983). Stressors of childhood. In N. Garmezy & M. Rutter (Eds.), *Stress, coping, and development in children* (pp. 43–84). New York: McGraw-Hill.

Gourgey, C. (1993). From weakness to strength: A spiritual response to disability. *Journal of Religion in Disability and Rehabilitation, 1,* 69–80.

Harter, S. (1983). Developmental perspectives on the self. In P. H. Mussen (Ed.), *Handbook of child psychology* (pp. 275–385). New York: Wiley.

Harter, S. (1986). Processes underlying the construction, maintenance, and enhancement of the self-concept in children. In J. Suls & A. G. Greenwald (Eds.), *Psychological perspectives on the self* (Vol. 3, pp. 136–182). Hillsdale, NJ: Erlbaum.

Harter, S. (1989). Causes, correlates, and the functional role of global self-worth: A life-span perspective. In J. Kolligian & R. Sternberg (Eds.), *Perceptions of competence and incompetence across the life-span* (pp. 67–102). New Haven, CT: Yale University Press.

Idler, E. L. (1995). Religion, health, and nonphysical senses of self. *Social Forces, 74,* 683-704.

James, W. (1890). *The principles of psychology.* New York: Henry Holt and Company.

Kahn, R.L., & Antonucci, T. (1980). Convoys over the life course: Attachment, roles and social support. In P.B. Baltes & O. Brim (Eds.), *Life-span development and behavior* (Vol. 3, pp. 254–286). Boston: Lexington Press.

Kahn, R.L., & Antonucci, T.C. (1981). Convoys of social support: A life course approach. In S.B. Kiesler, J.N. Morgan, & V.K. Oppenheimer (Eds.), *Aging and social change* (pp. 383–402). New York: Academic Press.

King, G., Law, M., King, S., Rosenbaum, P., Kertoy, M., & Young. N. (2003). A conceptual model of the factors affecting the recreation and leisure participation of children with disabilities. *Physical & Occupational Therapy in Pediatrics, 23*(1), 63–90.

King, G.A., Shultz, I.Z., Steel, K., Gilpin, M., & Cathers, T. (1993). Self-evaluation and self-concept of adolescents with physical disabilities. *American Journal of Occupational Therapy, 47,* 132–140.

King, G., Specht, J., Schultz, I., Warr-Leeper, G., Redekop, W., & Risebrough, N. (1997). Social skills training for withdrawn unpopular children with physical disabilities: A preliminary evaluation. *Rehabilitation Psychology, 42,* 47–60.

Lavigne, J.V., & Faier-Routman, J. (1992). Psychological adjustment to pediatric physical disorders: A meta-analytic review. *Journal of Pediatric Psychology, 17,* 33–157.

Luthar, S.S. (1991). Vulnerability and resilience: A study of high-risk adolescents. *Child Development, 62,* 600–616.

Markus, H.R., & Cross, S. (1990). The interpersonal self. In L. Pervin (Ed.), *Handbook of personality theory and research* (pp. 576–608). New York: Guilford.

Masten, A.S., Best, K.M., & Garmezy, N. (1990). Resilience and development: Contributions from the study of children who overcome adversity. *Development and Psychopathology, 2,* 425–444.

Masten, A.S., & Coatsworth, J.D. (1998). The development of competence in favorable and unfavorable environments: Lessons from research on successful children. *American Psychologist, 53,* 205–220.

McCarthy, H. (1995). Understanding and reversing rehabilitation counseling's neglect of spirituality. *Rehabilitation Education, 9*(2), 187–199.

Mead, G.H. (1934). *Mind, self, and society.* Chicago: University of Chicago Press.

Muldoon, M.H., & King, J.N. (1991). A spirituality for the long haul: Response to chronic illness. *Journal of Religion and Health, 30,* 99–108.

Peters-Golden, H. (1982). Breast cancer: Varied perceptions of social support in the illness experience. *Social Science and Medicine, 16,* 483–491.

Powers, L.E., Sowers, J., & Stevens, T. (1995). An exploratory randomized study of the impact of mentoring on the self-efficacy and community-based knowledge of adolescents with severe physical challenges. *Journal of Rehabilitation, 61*(1), 33–41.

Rae, B. (1998). *The three questions: Prosperity and the public good.* Toronto: Viking.

Rosenberg, M. (1986). Self-concept from middle childhood through adolescence: In J. Suls & A. G. Greenwald (Eds.), *Psychological perspectives on the self* (pp. 107–135). Hillsdale, NJ: Erlbaum.

Rutter, M. (1979). Protective factors in children's responses to stress and disadvantage. In M. W. Kent & J. E. Rolf (Eds.), *Primary prevention of psychopathology (Vol. 3), Social competence in children* (pp. 49–74). Hanover, NH: University Press of New England.

Rutter, M. (1985). Resilience in the face of adversity: Protective factors and resistance to psychiatric disorder. *British Journal of Psychiatry, 147,* 598–611.

Rutter, M. (1987). Psychosocial resilience and protective mechanisms. *American Journal of Orthopsychiatry, 57,* 316–331.

Ryff, C. D., & Singer, B. (2000). Interpersonal flourishing: A positive health agenda for the new millennium. *Personality and Social Psychology Review, 4*(1), 30–44.

Schaefer, K. M. (1995). Women living in paradox: Loss and discovery in chronic illness. *Holistic Nursing Practice, 9,* 63–74.

Shalock, R. L. (2000). Three decades of quality of life. *Focus on autism and other developmental disabilities, 15,* 116–127.

Smokowski, P. R., Reynolds, A. J., & Bezruczko, N. (1999). Resilience and protective factors in adolescence: An autobiographical perspective from disadvantaged youth. *Journal of School Psychology, 37,* 25–448.

Specht, J., King, G., & Francis, P. (1998). A preliminary study of strategies for maintaining self-esteem in adolescents with physical disabilities. *Canadian Journal of Rehabilitation, 11,* 103–110.

Spekman, N. J., Goldberg, R. J., & Herman, K. L. (1993). An exploration of risk and resilience in the lives of individuals with learning disabilities. *Learning Disabilities: Research & Practice, 8,* 11–18.

Tedeschi, R. G., & Calhoun, L. G. (1995). *Trauma and transformation: Growing in the aftermath of suffering.* Thousand Oaks, CA: Sage.

Tedeschi, R. G., Park, C. L., & Calhoun, L. G. (1998). Posttraumatic growth: Conceptual issues. In R. G. Tedeschi, C. L. Park, & L. G. Calhoun (Eds.), *Posttraumatic growth: Positive changes in the aftermath of crisis* (pp. 1–22). Mahwah, NJ: Lawrence Erlbaum.

Thoits, P. A. (1985). Social support and psychological well-being: Theoretical possibilities. In I. G. Sarason & B. R. Sarason (Eds.), *Social support: Theory, research and application* (pp. 51–72). Boston: Nijhoff.

Treloar, L. L. (1999). Spiritual care: Assessment and intervention. *Journal of Christian Nursing, 16*(2), 15–18.

Urbanowski, R., & Vargo, J. (1994). Spirituality, daily practice, and the occupational performance model. *Canadian Journal of Occupational Therapy, 61*(2), 88–94.

Wall, J., Covell, K., & MacIntyre, P. D. (1999). Implications of social supports for adolescents' education and career aspirations. *Canadian Journal of Behavioral Science, 31,* 63–71.

Willoughby, C., King, G., & Polatajko, H. (1996). A therapist's guide to children's self-esteem. *American Journal of Occupational Therapy, 50,* 124–132.

Wolkow, K. (1999). Just one adult can make a difference. *The Hospital for Sick Children Journal, 1*(1), 1–2.

Wortman, C. B., & Dunkel-Schetter, C. (1979). Interpersonal relationships and cancer: A theoretical analysis. *Journal of Social Issues, 35*(1), 120–155.

Wortman, C. B., & Dunkel-Schetter, C. (1987). Conceptual and methodological issues in the study of social support. In A. Baum & J. E. Singer (Eds.), *Handbook of psychology and health,* (Volume V: *Stress*) (pp. 63–108). Hillsdale, NJ: Erlbaum.

Wyman, P. A., Sandler, I., Wolchik, S., & Nelson, K. (2000). Resilience as cumulative competence promotion and stress protection: Theory and intervention. In D. Cicchetti, J. Rappaport, I. Sandler, & R. P. Weissberg (Eds.), *The promotion of wellness in children and adolescents* (pp. 133–184). Washington, D.C.: Child Welfare League of America Press.

Chapter 4

"CHORAL MUSIC" FOR COMMUNITY CHANGE

*Elizabeth MacKinnon, Elizabeth G. Brown,
Janice Miller Polgar, and Lisa Havens*

A single voice can be clear, engaging, and focused. It can entrance the heart and mind. The participants of this study spoke as individual voices, each with a specific message. Each of them anticipated that his or her participation would ensure that learning, realization, and change would happen for those who heard their stories. They wanted to tell their stories so that thinkers, decision makers, care providers, and people in their neighborhoods and communities would listen and then realize that improvements could be made. They wanted the sharing of their life stories to have meaning and impact. They wanted their song to be heard and acted upon. Although they sang as individuals, a chorus of themes and ideas emerged.

This chapter is about their recommendations for change. It is a call for action. It gives meaning to the collective suggestions made by the participants. Some suggestions were very specific. Others were conceptual or philosophical. Yet there were common scores throughout the commentaries.

Throughout this chapter, we use a music metaphor to describe the voices of single participants and the common themes that emerged. You, the reader, are the audience in this metaphor. As a member of the audience, you can listen to the choruses' words and lines, along with the musical accompaniment. The chorus wants you, the reader, to listen with your heart and mind. But more important, they want you to act upon their ideas so that their stories truly make a difference.

Often when we are asked to remember the words of a song, we remember the chorus lines. These are the lines that are repeated over and over again between the verses of the song. In this chapter, there is a chorus. It relates to how the participants want to be involved in their communities and society. It is about *community belonging*. The *Concise Oxford Dictionary* defines *belong* as "to be a member of (club, household, grade of society, etc.), be resident in or connected with." *Community* is defined as "joint ownership or liability; state of being shared or held in common; fellowship; organized political, municipal or social body; body of people living in same locality; the public."

Therefore, *community belonging* is about being connected to a group, whether defined by political, geographic, social, or other parameters. The participants strongly indicated their desire to be recognized as individuals connected with and participating in society. Each person sang this chorus about community belonging in his or her own way. There were different words and harmonics but when put together the voices were clear about a need to participate and relate with others in the world.

Rebecca Renwick and Ivan Brown are researchers in the area of rehabilitation and health promotion. They define *community belonging* as embodying "the connections people have with resources typically available to members of their community and society. This includes information about and access to sources of adequate income, employment, educational and recreational programs, health and social services, and community events and activities" (Renwick & Brown, 1996, p. 83). In the following verses about health, education, and employment, participants clearly indicate their desire for this type of community belonging. The connections that are typically available to other members of society have not always been available to them. The themes of connections, interactions, and relationships emerge. Each of the participants has a different impression, image, or definition of what *community* means, but they all want to actively participate in their own sense of community.

Brian Peck, a sociological writer, said that if we are to use the word *community* meaningfully "we must restrict it to a group of individuals who have learned to communicate honestly with each other, whose relationships go deeper than their masks of composure and who have developed some significant commitment to rejoice together, mourn together and to delight in each other, make others' conditions their own" (1987, p. 59). Peck's words about communication, relationships, and commitment are themes that are interwoven throughout the suggestions in this chapter. They illuminate the way to true community belonging.

The suggestions in this chapter came from several aspects of our research. First, they were directly derived from the interview transcripts themselves. As part of the research process, we assigned a code to each part of the transcripts where a participant said that something "should" happen. We felt that the word *should* indicated a need for some type of action. Through the use of a specialized computer software program, we were able to retrieve all of the *should* comments for review. We considered these to be the participants' main recommendations. We also wanted to verify these recommendations at the member checking sessions. At these sessions, a cross-section of participants was asked to review and check the overall themes emerging from the research. While doing so, they made further *should* comments. These comments also are included in the recommendations that follow. As well, a general review of the transcripts was done to identify any *nonshould* statements that were clearly suggestions for change or improvement. At the end of the study, participants were asked to answer a questionnaire that focused on recommendations only. The comments from the questionnaire were collected and reviewed. The three sources from which the recommendations emerged provided consistent suggestions, ideas, and themes, so that the chorus and the verses for change were clear.

This chapter is organized by verse. The first verse you are about to hear focuses on societal awareness relative to the participation of individuals with disabilities. It focuses on their lives within the larger context of community and society. Later on in this chapter, you will hear verses about health, education, and employment. Throughout these verses you will hear the chorus about community belonging. Health, education, and employment are service systems that need refinement and enhancement so that the participants and you, the listeners, can truly live and belong within your community. Suggestions for changes are presented in this order to reflect the sequence in which a developing child typically encounters the various service systems (from health to education to employment). The next verse of the chapter provides wisdom and advice for those who are living with disabilities and provides a simple directive for promoting change. The "choral finale" is the final verse. It is a final challenge to all of us who have listened. It challenges us to applaud but then to move from our seats and take action within our own communities so that societal changes can occur at the grassroots level to ensure that everyone can *belong*.

Sometimes messages come from surprising sources. One such message was seen on the back of a T-shirt worn by a gentleman pushing his wife in her wheelchair up the aisle of a church. His T-shirt read: "While we can't think ourselves into new ways of living, we can *live* ourselves into new ways of thinking." It is a call to reshape our thinking into living. Action can lead to new ways of thinking.

GETTING TO KNOW YOU—SOCIETAL VERSE

In the musical score for *The King and I,* there is a well-known song in which the chorus repeats, "Getting to know you, getting to know all about you." These words describe succinctly what the study participants want society to do. Robert Murphy, a noted anthropologist and author of *The Body Silent,* related to this by saying that "No matter who we are or how we got into our unenviable situation, the able bodied treat the physically handicapped in much the same way. Disability is defined by society and is given meaning by culture: it is a social malady" (1987, p. 4). When contemplating this thought, it is obvious that community belonging is minimized for people with disabilities.

A social malady or illness inhibits connections between people. One participant suggested that to change this, members of society must "get to know the individuals with disabilities as people." Another participant said, "I think it is important for everybody to be part of the community and to be out with people. I mean people are important to everybody, whether they think so or not—to have contact [is important]."

These comments illustrate that, to break down societal assumptions and stereotypes about disability, all members of society (i.e., all of us) need to get to know what individuals with disabilities like, dislike, enjoy, find distasteful, value or abhor, and find interesting or boring. Such connections form the heart of human relations. We need to do this in order to create a healthy, collaborative, and caring society.

One participant, when describing the development of a relationship with friends that was based on getting to know her as a person, said: "I got more than I bargained for. I got more than people that cared. I got a couple that really cared about me and loved me as a person." She felt valued, respected, needed, and as she put it "at home." She belonged, first as a person, and then as someone with a disability. Her use of the word *love* is not insignificant. It indicates the deep emotional connection underlying the relationship she developed with this couple.

Howard D. Schwartz, a sociologist from Radford University in Virginia, noted that society needs "to refrain from viewing all disabled people as occupying a unitary social status" (1988, p. 39). It is interesting that Western society strongly upholds the rights of the individual. These rights are so highly valued that we have converted them into laws and constitutions. We praise individualism and strongly recognize individual accomplishments and efforts. And yet we also classify and categorize people, with what we think are common characteristics, into tidy social units. Hence the term, *the disabled*. This classification promotes the development of stereotypes. As a result of this process, we develop myths about the needs, wishes, and perspectives of people who happen to fall into this category. This is done in spite of research that may note the contrary.

A participant in the study said, "We put too much emphasis on people being perfect and we are all different. We all learn differently and do different things." The "perfection stereotype," particularly on the physical level, blinds us to recognizing people as individuals. We see the physical or cognitive difference first, link it to our mythology or way of classifying people, and make assumptions and inferences about people. Yet on a personal level, we despise this type of thinking when it affects how others see *us*. No one wants to have one characteristic define them. For individuals with disabilities, their disability—whether visible or invisible—is not the *only* defining aspect of who they are. A man in the study said, "People with disabilities are just like everyone else—the best way to educate others is to have people with disabilities in the workplace, social settings, etc." By doing so, the disability fades into the background on an interpersonal level and, eventually, on a societal level.

Harlan Hahn, a political scientist from the University of Southern California, proposed that many of our societal attitudes toward individuals with disabilities could be derived from "aesthetic" and "existential" anxiety (1988). *Aesthetic anxiety* refers to fears that people have when they encounter an appearance that is either markedly different from the usual human form or includes unappealing traits. *Existential anxiety* refers to the threat of potential loss of functional capabilities by the nondisabled person. Hahn wrote that "In a society that appears to prize liberty more than equality and that tends to equate freedom with personal autonomy rather than with the opportunity to exercise meaningful choice, the apprehensions aroused by functional restrictions resulting from a disability often seem overwhelming" (1988, p. 43). Robert Murphy makes the same point when he writes: "The greatest impediment to a person's taking full part in society are not his physical flaws but rather the tissue of myths, fears, and misunderstandings that society attaches to them" (1987, p. 113).

Considering Hahn and Murphy's thoughts, anxiety and fear could be the overriding reasons why society and its members do not always recognize the person first. If we allow ourselves to get to know a person, then fear subsides because we understand. Stephen Covey, a popular speaker and writer, wrote in his book the *Seven Habits of Highly Effective Families:* "Isn't it interesting: When you understand, you don't judge.... Wisdom comes from understanding. Without it, people act unwisely. Yet from their own frame of reference, what they are doing makes perfect sense. The reason we judge is that it protects us. We don't have to deal with the person, we can just deal with the label" (1997, p. 208). So classification protects us. And yet in order to belong, we need to be understood.

The participants in this study want to be understood so that they can connect with society. Supporting this, Covey also wrote: "The deepest hunger of the human heart is to be understood, for understanding implicitly affirms, validates, recognizes, and appreciates the intrinsic worth of another. When you really listen to another person, you acknowledge and respond to the most insistent need" (1997, p. 213). The challenge then is to seek to understand so that we can wash away the fear that limits individuals with disabilities from truly belonging to society. Remember the T-shirt worn by the gentleman in church: we need to *live* new ways of thinking. This is one way we can do that.

Each of us has a vision of what our society is and should become. When we asked participants about their vision, one person noted that they wanted, "a more humanistic and cooperative society in which every individual participates, first as a human being, and second where differences are incorporated or celebrated as the norm." This vision contains many components. *Humanistic* relates to a societal focus on the needs of people. *Cooperative* refers to the helpful interaction between individuals. *Participates* refers to active involvement. The reference to *human being* indicates individual identity. *Differences are celebrated as the norm* highlights the need for individual respect and acknowledgment. This vision speaks to the need to understand people as people first, appreciating their uniquenesses and differences. Support for this vision came from another participant who said, "[Members of society] have to understand that everyone is different." Since this is a vision, it is obviously not yet a reality. The challenge then is to change perspectives and attitudes to allow this vision to emerge as a societal reality.

This type of change implies a need to communicate openly. As one young man in the study said, "The biggest change wanted is to talk directly to me as a person and not to someone else." To get to know someone, there is a need to interact. Obviously, this young man has experienced noninteraction—someone has ignored his presence and spoken to someone else on his behalf rather than to him directly. Through interaction, communication emerges.

Communication requires an exchange that includes perceiving, listening, interpreting, and expressing. The interplay between communication and interaction facilitates the development of a relationship. Relationships, in turn, form the foundations of partnerships, families, neighborhoods, communities, and societies. Rules and codes of behavior have evolved from these relationships. To develop the vision of a humanistic and cooperative society, individuals need to communicate. By avoiding such communication, we prevent interaction and relationships from forming. Hence, we again do not recognize the individual.

A gentleman in the study suggested that to improve the communication gap "Parents should allow children when in public to ask the disabled [person] questions about their disability. The children are just curious and most of us are willing to answer their questions. This will help the children understand and be at ease." By providing such an opportunity for exchange, we allow our children to understand individual differences, while reducing personal and societal anxiety.

Starting at the individual level, we can shape children, families, neighborhoods, and communities so that individuals with disabilities are recognized as individuals who contribute to, participate in, and are involved at all levels of society. By getting to know them as individuals, we can relish the development of a community and a society that promotes and facilitates everyone's participation.

Carl Rogers, a psychologist, wrote in his book *On Becoming a Person* that "I have found it of enormous value when I can permit myself to understand another person" (1961, p. 18). The key word here is *permit*. We need to individually and collectively permit ourselves to make that connection. Stephen Covey wrote that "If I were to summarize in one sentence the single most important principle I have learned in the field of interpersonal relations, it would be this: Seek first to understand, then to be understood. This principle is the key to effective interpersonal communications" (1989, p. 237). If this is true on an individual level, how much truer could it be for society?

In the context of each of our societal roles, we have a strong need to be needed. We need to feel that what we do and say has meaning and significance to someone other than ourselves. We need to be valued and cared about. We also want to value and care for others. This is part of the reciprocal connection between individuals and society. It is an exchange of belonging. One must give as well as get. Individuals with disabilities want to participate in this exchange. By promoting such a direction, we can move toward the humanistic, cooperative society that one of the participants envisioned for all. We can all belong to our small and larger communities.

HEALTH VERSE

It is not an understatement to say that we enter the health system at the moment we are conceived. The health system generally is the first societal system that we encounter in life. Prenatally, at birth, immediately following birth, and through the first few years of life, there is frequent contact with the health system. Each of the participants in the study had stories and reflections about their interactions with this system. Some of these experiences were extremely positive; some were tragic. An example of a tragic situation described by one participant dealt with a period of hospitalization as a child. She said:

> I was in hospital for about a week and the nurses and doctors were very, very cruel to me. They wouldn't help feed me, they wouldn't let my parents stay. I was just left in a crib.... I couldn't eat because I couldn't get fed and it was just awful. I remembered the doctors saying if I wanted to go home I better smarten up and eat. And I've always had a fear of hospitals since that point.

From all the shared stories, one message emerged repeatedly about this major service system. It was specifically directed toward those who provide service and care. It was simply put by one member of the study: "Listen, listen, listen."

Listening is a simple word, but it is not a simple activity. According to Raymond Ross, a professor of communication at Wayne State University, "Listening may be defined as a conscious cognitive effort involving primarily the sense of hearing (reinforced by other senses) and leading to interpretation and understanding" (1974, p. 35). So listening is more than just hearing. Hearing and the other senses are the conduits for communicated messages. The key element of listening is interpretation and understanding. Again Stephen Covey's thoughts on listening can guide health care providers. He notes that "Really listening to get inside another person's mind and heart is called 'empathic' listening. It's listening with empathy. It's trying to see the world through someone else's eyes" (1997, p. 222).

Several participants indicated the need for such empathic listening. One said: "Listen to them. They know their bodies far more intimately than you can possibly understand." Another said: "I wished so often doctors and specialists could come and live with me for a week and watch me for a week and then they would know what I am talking about." A third said: "Look at the whole person, not at simply a case study with symptoms." Obviously, from these comments, the participants had not always encountered empathetic listening. They want to be heard as individuals.

Communication appears to lie at the base of the participants' concerns in that it reflects a need for exchange. One person involved in the study said, "Sensitivity training is a must. Talk to the person and include them in the decision [about] health procedures. Don't assume a lack of intelligence exists because of a disability." This comment reflects a need to exchange information and to make decisions cooperatively.

Robert Murphy indicates from his own experience with the health system that "The full subjective states of the patients are of little concern in the medical model of disability, which holds that the problem arises wholly from some anatomic or physiological disorder and is correctable by standard modes of therapy—drugs, surgery, radiation, or whatever. What goes on inside the patient's head is another matter" (1987, p. 88). Many of the participants would agree with his perspective. They often felt that communication was a one-way adventure in the health system. They were expected to listen and concur. And yet they could not expect the same in exchange. They often did not feel recognized or valued in their interactions with health care providers. Hence their call for "empathic" listening from the health system.

Jennifer York, Beverly Rainforth, and Winnie Dunn (1990), who have backgrounds in the applied health sciences, suggest that health care providers should work from Robert and Martha Perske's (1988) *people first orientation*. With a people first orientation as a fundamental principle underlying service design, there is a belief "that each individual who happens to have a disability is first and foremost a person. Furthermore, each person is an individual with unique interests, assets, and difficulties" (York, Rainforth, & Dunn, 1990, p. 157). This is a call to design a service system based on putting the needs of the individual first. Such a health system would respond to people rather than primarily focusing on their physical, cognitive, social, or emotional differences. To help incorporate this recommendation, participants suggested that service providers should: "Know the individual—invite his or her thoughts on what is needed or wanted." They also said, "Listen to the person." One person specifically said, "I think the most instrumental thing is to realize that it [should be] the early... [education] of educators, of doctors, of all realms of personnel to listen carefully..." The listening message is a very clear aspect of the health care verse.

For those who are engaged in the pediatric sector of health, such messages support the need to design and implement services that are focused on the child and family. This orientation to service is referred to as *family-centered care* (Rosenbaum, King, Law, King, & Evans, 1998). This type of care is based on the expressed needs, desires, and valued outcomes of the child and family. It is a model of service delivery that encourages the child and family to direct and individualize their care and service planning. Through such a process, children and their families are encouraged to identify their strengths and capabilities, preferences, and desires, as well as the barriers that interfere with their accomplishment of goals.

Thames Valley Children's Centre is a rehabilitation center in the southwestern region of Ontario, Canada. This center has developed a Life Needs Model of Service Delivery that outlines the needs of children with disabilities, their families, and communities (King et al., 2002). This service delivery model integrates current thinking about family-centered service into a developmental model of services that addresses different needs over time. The purpose of such a system of service "is for children to develop into individuals who are satisfied with their level of participation in their communities and therefore with the quality of their life" (King et al., 2002, p. 65). The vision arising from such a system "is one of true participation and integration, where environmental supports, positive community attitudes, and strengths of individuals converge to support people in pursuing their goals and reaching their potential" (King et al., 2002, p. 65).

Such a service model necessitates empathic listening. Within this process, children need to be actively heard. This means that adult service providers have to try to listen from the perspective of the child. This task is difficult in a world where decisions are often made by adults on behalf of children. It also raises the possibility of conflict between parents and their children. Nonetheless, to encourage the development and growth of children's self-esteem and self-efficacy, it is important that children be heard, regarded, and valued. It is in childhood that identity and perspective grow. This is also the time when children learn how to shape relationships. Health care should be about listening, interacting, and relating. It is important that children with disabilities learn to maneuver and cope within the health system because it is a system that they will encounter throughout their lives. Health care providers dealing with children need to be able to demonstrate empathic listening, communicative exchange, and mutual regard so that children learn how a cooperative, humanistic, and supportive system can work.

Physicians were often mentioned by participants as playing an important role in their lives. This is understandable, given the medical needs of many participants. A specific message was directed to physicians who participated in the early stages of some of the participants' lives. It was a message about expectations. Several participants said that physicians minimized expectations for them during the early stages of their lives. One participant said, "A lot of doctors didn't know what I could do." The remarks made by physicians to study participants when they were children often left an impression that lasted a lifetime. One participant said that physicians need to be very sensitive to the impact of their words upon children. Such words can form attitudes and perceptions of self at an early age.

Linked to the various myths held about the nature of disability are assumptions about quality of life. Quality of life is the ultimate goal of a model of service delivery based on life needs. According to Lindström and Köhler (1991), quality of life reflects a holistic view of health encompassing experience in: the personal sphere including self-esteem, self-concept, and abilities; the interpersonal sphere of relationships; and the external sphere including achievement of employment or other meaningful occupation, receiving an education, and living independently. From the aesthetic and existential fears about disability that Harlan Hahn (1988) has noted often come perceptions, stereotypes, and judgments about the quality of life that individuals with disabilities experience.

Rebecca Renwick, Ivan Brown, and Mark Nagler, from the University of Toronto, have written a book on the connection between the fields of health promotion and rehabilitation, as they relate to quality of life issues (Renwick, Brown, & Nagler, 1996). Some people may find this an unusual relationship because health promotion and rehabilitation are often seen at opposite ends of the health care spectrum. The authors wrote the book because, as they state, "The most striking area of commonality between the two fields is their shared overarching goal: to improve quality of life within the lives of people and groups of people with and without disabilities" (p. 10). Their book is "not about judging the value of lives but rather about how we can enhance the quality of each person's life. A major theme running throughout the book is the fundamental importance of listening to and acting on people's own judgments about quality" (Baker, 1996, p. xiv). Again the word *listening* is heard. One of the participants in this study stated clearly: "We want the same quality of life as everyone else." Another said that, if they were educating others, they "would stress [the] quality of life issue—quality time with family and friends." Quality of life is a personal perspective. Society's role is to appreciate, honor, and respect these perspectives. The participants in this study want that to happen now and in the future.

So this verse about health concludes amid messages about the importance of listening and recognizing the individual as a person. It is a call to provide health services based on these two premises so that quality of life can occur at the personal, interpersonal, and societal levels.

EDUCATION VERSE

Education refers to the process of formal learning through a system that is determined, monitored, and often operated by the government. It is generally the next major system that the growing child encounters after the health system. Unlike health, a person's experience with education is usually time-defined, since graduation is usually predetermined either by age criteria or curriculum completion.

Participants in the study were asked to comment on their educational experiences. Their thoughts were based on their own experiences and on their knowledge of the present educational system. In this verse about education, they highlighted accessibility and inclusion. They considered these to be basic elements for belonging in the school setting.

Accessibility and inclusion refer to physical and social aspects of participation that affect entrance and connection within the educational system. Despite advocacy, changes in legislation, and public education about physical access to buildings, the participants noted that there were still barriers to some educational facilities. One of the youngest participants commented that her "neighborhood school was not accessible." In her situation, her father did the renovations to make the school accessible. He did so by building a ramp and installing grab bars in the bathroom. These are basic adaptations that, fortunately, are now showing up in public buildings due to building code requirements. Physical access continues to improve as society comes to understand its benefits for all. Creating physical access means that individuals with disabilities can participate.

Social access and inclusion were defined by the participants as the ability to develop interactive connections within the school community. One participant expressed his concern about this when he said, "Make sure that all school activities are fully accessible." He was referring to physical and social access to school activities. Another participant commented, "Help educate students on disabilities so that the individual with the disability is accepted."

Acceptance refers to being considered part of the school community. Gwyneth Ferguson Matthews (1983) wrote about this type of acceptance in her book *Voices from the Shadows*. Matthews is a woman who became a paraplegic during her university years. Matthews suggests that one simple way to facilitate acceptance is to share with students all facets of living with disability. She wrote that "Once they know the facts, they're usually pretty good about disabilities" (p. 52).

One woman involved in our study indicated that she experienced this type of acceptance at school because of the support she received from her classmates and teachers. This support included being pushed in her wheelchair between classes by friends. Friends also shared notes with her. In high school she felt the same type of support.

Acceptance involves recognizing each individual student for who they are within the social context of school. Paul Wehman wrote in his book *Life Beyond the Classroom: Transition Strategies for Young People with Disabilities* that:

> Fostering greater inclusion of individuals with disabilities during the school year rests on two premises: [First] if society is for everybody, then schools should be for everyone. Therefore the first measure of a school should be the extent to which it can serve all of its students. [Second] schools are responsible, not only for the education that students receive, but also for what students are prepared to do once they graduate: that is schools are responsible for providing services in ways that ensure their graduates' success." (1996, p. 25)

Returning to our musical metaphor, school is the practice hall for society. Within the context of the educational system, children learn about academic subjects but, more important, they learn about social rules and boundaries. They learn about relationships and how these form the foundation blocks for social roles. They learn about authority, regulation, reputation, and bureaucracy. They learn about success, prejudice, values, and stereotypes. They learn about the "fairness" of justice and judgment. Within this enclosed chamber, they experiment, fail, progress, and learn. Evolution from this practice hall merges them into adult society.

School is the nurturing environment for societal values and perspectives. It is a critical forum in which attitudes are formed. It is in this setting that adults (teachers) and other children shape perspectives about people with disabilities. As Gary Clark, from the University of Kansas, and Oliver Kolstoe, from the University of Northern Colorado, state in their book *Career Development and Transition Education for Adolescents with Dis-*

abilities, "Educators must recognize the school's formal role in personal-social development...so social learning activities in the company of peers, particularly at school, are important" (1994, p. 49). It is evident that school plays a critical role in the development of people's perspectives about an inclusive society.

Educators have a critical role in the formulation of an inclusive society. To assist educators with these directions, the participants made some specific suggestions. They particularly emphasized the need for teachers to recognize and adapt to different learning abilities. One participant said: "Don't keep the child out of the class but realize that their needs may differ from other students." Another said, "Tell all students everyone learns in a different way and [at] a different...[pace]." A third said, "Treat them the same as other students when possible but, if they can't learn one way, be willing to adapt to a different method that suits them."

Statements such as these point to a need to be flexible in approaching the learning process. To help with this flexibility, one participant said, "I think the teachers should have been forewarned a bit about who I was and what I could or I couldn't do." She felt that this would have eased the teacher's apprehension when the teacher first met her in the classroom. One young man with a chronic physical disability said that he encountered a teacher who was very uncomfortable with him in her class. However, "Once she got to know me, she wasn't scared of me and she was willing to get to know me as a person." He felt that she was one of the best teachers he ever had.

The "getting to know me" theme, which participants hope society learns to do as a whole, also emerged in their comments about the educational system. As in the health system, the participants identified a need for educators to listen to their individual needs and to respond in ways that respect and acknowledge their individual characteristics. Recognizing learning differences highlights and values the person first. The overall tone of these comments is that differences in learning should be appreciated in everyone. As one participant said, "It is not difficult to teach from a workbook or run off ditto sheets: it is more challenging to individualize every student's program according to what each needs for his or her age and skill level." This is a challenge for educators and parents because this is also a call for support.

One of the participants credited his educational success to the educational support he had received. His school recognized his particular need for educational support and pursued a volunteer tutoring option to assist him: "After Christmas, they got one of the high school teacher's wives to come in as a tutor." He truly appreciated this support, since it allowed him to succeed academically.

Tangible, specific, and flexible support is needed to facilitate individual learning processes. Creative alternatives may need to be pursued to ensure success. Gwyneth Ferguson Matthews supported this notion of success when she wrote about her belief that children with disabilities "have the same potential as able-bodied youngsters, and that with full integration of the schools, accessible buildings, improved transportation, and specialist tutors [i.e., support], they can succeed as completely and convincingly" (1983, p. 60).

Support was viewed as a precursor to success when considering the transition role that the education system plays. This role involves the preparation and graduation of students into the employment system. One woman in the study said that the point of graduation was "when life got to be a bit scary and frustrating." The support she had felt from the education system ended and she did not experience any transition planning into adult life. Fortunately for her, a significant person stepped into her life and facilitated her moving into the employment sector. Many participants echoed what another participant said: "Include career exploration and decisions in [the] curriculum so that graduates have knowledge of the path." Several called for the development of meaningful and realistic vocational skills. The inclusion of vocational possibilities and options was seen as a necessary role for the education system.

The need to be prepared for tomorrow's workforce extended specifically into the area of providing needed equipment for students with disabilities. One participant who had experience using computers early on in her educational experience said: "It was awesome. I could do more." Another participant said, "Obtain the very latest in computer equipment with disabled modifications." The range of technological options is enormous and includes commercially available alternative access systems, electronic communications, and adaptive software. These options are seen as tools for leveling the employment playing field. This is especially important in a competitive workforce where computer literacy is becoming a basic skill requirement. By learning these skills within the practice hall of the school system, students can experiment, fail, try again, and succeed in developing their employment readiness. This educational experience will enhance their ability to use technology effectively and efficiently in their employment careers.

This verse about education echoes the importance of support as a helpful factor in participants' lives, as shown in chapter 3. It highlights the need for support to facilitate people's access and inclusion in the educational system so that their transition into the adult world is smooth and leads to meaningful occupation. Again, there is a call to understand the personal needs of the individual in the context of the school system, with a vision of their future kept in mind. By recognizing these needs, students with disabilities can be accepted, acknowledged, and become participating members of their schools. What a wonderful opportunity this provides for their preparation and transition into adult society.

MONEY MAKES THE WORLD GO AROUND OR DOES IT?—EMPLOYMENT VERSE

Gail Fawcett, author of *Living with Disability in Canada: An Economic Portrait,* noted from her analysis of the Canadian 1991 Health and Activity Limitation Survey that "the level of education attained by persons with disabilities has a strong effect on their participation in the paid labor force" (1996, p. 32). The data indicated that people who attained the highest level of education (university) participated in the labor force at almost double the rate of those with the lowest level (primary school). She drew the conclusion that higher education appears to be one of the most valuable mechanisms available to mitigate the difficulty that people with disabilities encounter when they try to enter and remain in the paid workforce. This type of data echoes the perspective of the participants that the educational system needs to prepare young people for the employment sector.

Employment involves the ability to care for oneself through productive activities that result in financial compensation. To obtain employment, people need to have skills that the market wants to buy. In light of this marketability idea, two of the participants made the following comments: "Train them in suitable areas where there will be work that they can do" and "Job training, co-op, short-term placement, mentoring, job shadowing [are needed]."

Participants' comments indicate that there is a need for practical training and experiential learning that can be transported into the labor force. The issue of employment readiness, or "transition," must be considered as part of the educational process.

In 1994, the Council for Exceptional Children's Division on Career Development and Transition in the United States defined *transition* as "a change in status from behaving primarily as a student to assuming emergent adult roles in the community. These roles include employment, participating in post-secondary education, maintaining a home, becoming appropriately involved in the community and experiencing satisfactory personal and social relationships" (Halpern, 1994, p. 117). This definition articulately defines the essence of community belonging.

Emergence into the employment sector is a natural social process by which individuals connect with their community. It is the adult focus of community connection because we often define ourselves by our employment. According to Paul Wehman:

> The ability to be employed is important for many reasons. First, working in competitive employment provides an opportunity to receive wages and benefits that may lead to greater independence and mobility in the community at large. Second, being productive on a daily basis in a meaningful vocation is critically important to one's self-esteem and dignity. Third, establishing new friendships and networks of social support in the community is almost always facilitated by having a job within a career path. (1996, p. 9)

So employment is about doing meaningful tasks, in the context of a network of relationships, that provide financial self-sufficiency. Note the connection here between what employment can provide and the three paths of acquiring meaning in life—doing, belonging, and understanding—that were discussed in chapter 2.

Employment is not just about having a job. It is not just about money, although financial security is a critical issue. Employment is a vital aspect of community connection. When someone is unemployed, there is a disconnection. Individuals with disabilities often realize that the employment sector is another system that disconnects them from belonging in their community. Gail Fawcett (1996) noted that individuals with disabilities had an employment participation rate in 1991 of about 56 percent in Canada. That means that about 44 percent of individuals with disabilities were not participating in the paid workforce.

In her report, Fawcett noted some of the factors that led to this low participation rate in employment. These factors included education, gender, the nature and severity of a person's disability, his or her age, living arrangements, accommodations, and other people's attitudinal perspectives. Of particular interest are Fawcett's comments about the link between employment and poverty. She reported that "Adults with disabilities are much more likely to be poor than those without disabilities. In 1991, 21.9 percent of adults (aged 15 years and older) with disabilities were living in poverty compared to 12.6 percent of adults without disabilities....It is evident that full-time employment in the paid labor market greatly decreases the chances of living in poverty for persons with disabilities" (1996, p. 130). There is no doubt then that financial well-being is directly linked to employment. There is also no doubt that poverty is a major life stress for individuals with disabilities. This is compounded by the structure of social assistance plans. One gentleman identified this frustration when he said, "It's a frustrating situation to be in. You're stuck and society gives X amount of dollars, which is far below poverty, and you are expected to live on that and not try to get ahead at all. You can't have savings, you can't have inheritance, and you can't own anything of value and I think that's very degrading and inhumane."

This gentleman does not feel that the society he lives in provides him with opportunities for employment that allow him to grow. He obviously does not feel valued and he definitely does not feel a connection with his community.

Another participant commented that "You should be allowed to own or buy a life insurance policy." Although this is a specific comment relating to life insurance, it points to people's need to be able to plan financially for the future. It appears from some of the comments made by the participants that social assistance systems take meager care of the present day and do not allow for the unforeseen or the future. These systems seem to inhibit the ability of an individual with a disability to develop any financial security from other sources. This perpetuates insecurity about the future.

Fawcett (1996) reported that individuals who derive their financial support from social assistance sources may find that their odds of living in poverty can vary widely depending on the program. Some participants felt trapped by the social assistance system because, if they pursued employment, then their benefits were cut. One study participant said: "Most of us wanted to be able to keep our pension and supplement it for a couple or three thousand dollars a year and feel like we are contributing something to our families. That's what I would dearly like to do."

There appears to be a need for compromise and negotiation based on the employability, income supplementation, and living needs of the individual with a disability. These living needs may include transportation costs, assistive devices, and medical or therapeutic expenses. A specific written suggestion from one of the participants was this: "Disability pensions should continue on for a while once you start working (e.g., transportation)." This assistance would ensure a financial base during the transition into employment. This might be an important process to assist those entering the workforce for the first time. It would minimize the perspective, stated by a study participant, that "The current system is a deterrent to work." From this vantage point, existing Canadian social assistance programs do not breach the gap of community belonging; rather, they maintain it. These programs foster poverty and dependence. They continue the cycle of keeping people with disabilities outside of society.

Employment is therefore not just about financial support. Financial support is the tool that allows individuals to connect with others and to develop relationships. For some, financial support is the vehicle to community belonging. Money allows us to be both a consumer and a participant. In *Cabaret,* there is a chorus line with the words: "Money makes the world go 'round, the world go 'round, the world go 'round. Money makes the world go 'round." There is a fair amount of truth in this chorus. To participate as adults in society, people need to have the financial capability to feed and care for themselves. Thus, money makes the world go around people. But it also lets people into the world. Employment, therefore, provides the route to community belonging. Our participants want the opportunity to participate in the employment sector so that they are members of society, so that they, too, can engage in the world.

DREAM THE IMPOSSIBLE DREAM—PERSONAL WISDOM VERSE

Throughout the interviews, participants provided words of wisdom based on their knowledge and life experiences. They wanted to share some of their personal wisdom with those who are younger than they are and who are living with disabilities. One common song emerged in their interviews: Speak up and go after what you want. In the musical *The Man from LaMancha,* there is a song *The Impossible Dream.* It is a song that challenges listeners to pursue their dreams, to go after what they want regardless of the obstacles. The study participants offer the same advice to others with disabilities. They suggest that young people pursue their dreams and ambitions. One person said, "Speak loudly. Be as clear as possible if you want [things to happen]." This is a call to advocate, to express one's needs clearly and succinctly.

Young people may need support in developing their ability to assert themselves since, as Paul Wehman says, "Self-advocacy is grounded in the roots of freedom, choice, and self-determination" (1996, p. 39). He also states: "The goal of self-advocacy is very important for people with disabilities as they: fight for the best service to which they are entitled, gain information and knowledge about financial entitlement that they may be eligible to receive..., and gain awareness of community happenings that could affect them" (1996, p. 39). This means advocating for the right to belong to the community group, the classroom, the recreational group, the neighborhood, and the political party.

Complacency will not promote belonging. Change will come about only through effort and perseverance. One participant said, "Encourage them (young people with disabilities) to advocate because no one else will do it for you and, if you want to get somewhere, you have to let your voice be known." Another man said more pointedly, "Force change to happen." The message of this verse is "Make it happen." Go after what you want, recognize your expectations, and pursue them. Impossible dreams have to be pursued in order for them to be possibilities.

CHORAL FINALE

This brings us to the conclusion of the verses. It is hoped that the participants' voices were heard both individually and collectively throughout this chapter. Their recommendations centered around the need for understanding and support. The recommendations related to people's need to connect to the community and to be active participants in it. But they also dealt with the need for members of society to recognize people as individuals with special and unique needs, issues, and concerns. The recommendations are about belonging as active, participatory individuals within our communities.

Through participants' comments, one can see that there are practical, tangible processes and systems that need to be changed and enhanced. Within the systems, there is a need for an emotional understanding that will facilitate interaction, communication, and relationships. These relationships include familial, neighborly, educational, community, and societal relationships.

John Lord, who wrote a book about personal empowerment for individuals with disabilities during transitions, said, "Of all the factors that were identified as being helpful, people support was mentioned most often. In fact, everyone [in his work] identified at least one person as being important to their personal empowerment" (1991, p. 30). Lord identified three types of people support: moral support, practical support, and mentoring support. These are the types of support that many of the participants in our study either had experienced or were searching for. Such support depends on interaction, communication, and relationships. Lord found that "the importance of relationships between the individual and a support person...emerged as a common element" (1991, p. 40). One of the overarching themes arising from our study is the importance of relationships between the individual and his or her family, neighbors, and community.

As seen in chapter 3, support from others was identified by participants as one of the most important helpful factors at critical periods in their lives.

We have seen the theme of "belonging" again and again in the chapters of this book. We have discussed "belonging" as a way in which life takes on meaning (chapter 2), as a way in which we develop self-esteem (chapter 3), and now as the ultimate aim of advocacy for and by individuals with disabilities (i.e., belonging on a community level).

A number of themes arose in John Lord's (1991) work that indicate the centrality of supportive relationships. They include a deep respect shown by participants when referring to a person who was helpful; a strong sense of being valued by supportive people; a sense of mutuality and collaboration in the relationship; and the belief (for a few people) that the discovery of their own capabilities and potential occurred through the relationship with others. Lord's work points to the certainty that connections between people matter, whether on an individual or a societal level. His work focuses on the relationships with supportive individuals, but could not the same thing be said about a supportive community? A deep respect would be noted by the participants for members of the health community, if they listened and helped. A strong sense of being valued would be felt if employment opportunities were readily available. A sense of mutuality and collaboration would be perceived in the social and educational relationships experienced by the participants. And lastly, the participants would feel that their capabilities and potential were recognized and that they were fully participating members of their community. It is our belief in each other that brings about the power of change.

The song has ended. There were five verses—about society, health, education, employment, and personal wisdom—interspersed with a chorus that sang about community belonging. Common verse themes included participation, inclusion, interaction, communication, connections, and relationships. Now the applause begins. This applause will not come from our hands but will come from the result of our daily actions, our attitudes, and our words. We need to work toward building communities that recognize people for their abilities, potential, and contributions. We need to foster dreams of possibilities. We need to interact, communicate, and relate to each other individually and communally. As one participant said, "This is a time of change and, if an appropriate plan is designed, people with disabilities can move ahead and get the equality they deserve. Use the themes, suggestions, and comments from the study to start the plan." Could there be a clearer mission for the audience? Remember the man with the T-shirt in church sitting beside his wife in the wheelchair?

REFERENCES

Baker, J. D. (1996). Introduction. In R. Renwick, I. Brown, & M. Nagler (Eds.), *Quality of life in health promotion and rehabilitation: Conceptual approaches, issues, and applications* (pp. xiii–xv). Thousand Oaks, CA: Sage Publications.

Clark, G. M., & Kolstoe, O. P. (1994). *Career development and transition education for adolescents with disabilities* (2nd ed.). Needham Heights, MA: Allyn and Bacon.

Covey, S. R. (1997). *Seven habits of highly effective families.* New York: Golden Books.

Covey, S. R. (1989). *The seven habits of highly effective people.* London: Simon & Schuster UK Ltd.

Fawcett, G. (1996). *Living with disability in Canada: An economic portrait.* Hull, QC: Human Resources Development Canada.

Hahn, H. (1988). The politics of physical differences: Disability and discrimination. *Journal of Social Issues, 44*(1), 39–47.

Halpern, A. (1994). The transition of youths with disabilities to adult life: A position statement of the Division on Career Development and Transition, Council for Exceptional Children. *Career Development of Exceptional Individuals, 17*(2), 115–124.

King, G., Tucker, M. A., Baldwin, P., Lowry, K., LaPorta, J., & Martens, L. (2002). A Life Needs Model of pediatric service delivery: Services to support community participation and quality of life for children and youth with disabilities. *Physical & Occupational Therapy in Pediatrics, 22*(2), 53–77.

Lindström, B., & Köhler, L. (1991). Youth, disability, and quality of life. *Pediatrician, 18,* 121–128.

Lord, J. (1991). Lives in transition: The process of personal empowerment. Hull, QC: Disabled Persons Participation Program.

Matthews, G. F. (1983). *Voices from the shadows.* Oshawa, ON: The Women's Press.

Murphy, R. (1987). *The body silent.* New York: Henry Holt and Company.

Peck, B. (1987). *A different drum: Community making and peace.* New York: Simon & Schuster.

Perske, R., & Perske, M. (1988). *Circles of friends.* Nashville: Abingdon Press.

Renwick, R., & Brown, I. (1996). The Centre for Health Promotion's conceptual approach to quality of life: Being, belonging, and becoming. In R. Renwick, I. Brown, & M. Nagler (Eds.), *Quality of life in health promotion and rehabilitation: Conceptual approaches, issues, and applications* (pp. 75–88). Thousand Oaks, CA: Sage Publications.

Renwick, R., Brown, I., & Nagler, M. (Eds.). (1996). *Quality of life in health promotion and rehabilitation: Conceptual approaches, issues, and applications.* Thousand Oaks, CA: Sage Publications.

Rogers, C. (1961). *On becoming a person: A therapist's view of psychotherapy.* Boston: Houghton Mifflin.

Rosenbaum, P., King, S., Law, M., King, G., & Evans, J. (1998). Family-centred service: A conceptual framework and research review. *Physical & Occupational Therapy in Pediatrics, 18,* 1–20.

Ross, R.S. (1974). *Speech communication: Fundamentals and practice.* Englewood Cliffs, NJ: Prentice-Hall.

Schwartz, H.D. (Fall, 1988). Further thoughts on a "Sociology of acceptance for disabled people." *Social Policy, 19*(2), 36–39.

Wehman, P. (1996). *Life beyond the classroom: Transition strategies for young people with disabilities* (2nd ed.). Baltimore: Paul H. Brookes Publishing Inc.

York, J., Rainforth, B., & Dunn, W. (1990). Training needs of physical and occupational therapists who provide services to children and youth with severe disabilities. In A. Kaiser & C. McWhorter (Eds.), *Preparing personnel to work with persons with severe disabilities* (pp. 153–180). Baltimore: Paul H. Brookes Publishing Co.

Chapter 5

TYING IT ALL TOGETHER: FRAMES OF REFERENCE AND MEANING IN LIFE

Gillian A. King

The most important things in life are not things.

—Anonymous

What are the most important things in life? This chapter builds on the idea that people may value different things, but reach conclusions about what they value in common ways—these are the three ways in which we determine meaning in life. We create meaning through our interconnections with others (belonging), taking part in activities (doing), and seeking to understand our own natures and the world around us (understanding). These fundamental ways of establishing meaning have been seen repeatedly in the chapters of this book.

Have you ever wondered:

- Why absence can make the heart grow fonder?
- Why we often come to love the things we suffer for?
- Why saying "I don't care" can really help distance you from something bothering you?
- Why having a pet is often a wonderful thing?
- Why winning a lottery does not lead to happiness?
- Whether "love and understanding are the best answers I've heard yet?" [from a song "Love and Understanding" by Blue Rodeo, Keelor & Cuddy (1988, 1989)]
- Why is it better to have loved and lost than never to have loved at all?
- Whether a reevaluation of life necessarily involves pain and disruption?

This chapter will answer these questions. The main focus, though, is to tie together the key messages in this book about meaning and resilience in life, as revealed through the turning points, key helpful and hindering factors, and recommendations of individuals with disabilities.

Unlike meaning in life, this chapter has a beginning, a middle, and an end. To start, we will return to the Möbius strip analogy for life experience introduced in chapter 2 and show how the three strands of meaning in this visual model are intricately connected. The helpful and hindering factors that lead to resilience in life and the recommendations discussed in chapters 3 and 4 will be tied to this model of meaning in life experience.

What evidence is there for three ways of establishing and maintaining meaning? This chapter will examine frames of reference used in psychology, social work, nursing, occupational therapy, and the other rehabilitation sciences to see what evidence there is for the three paths of belonging, doing, and understanding. The chapter also will consider other types of evidence that are not based on theory, including practical knowledge. It is important to remember that the three aspects of meaning were uncovered by considering the turning point experiences shared by study participants (discussed in chapter 2). We will see that these three different types of evidence—theoretical, empirical, and qualitative—all point to the existence of three ways of establishing meaning in life.

The chapter will explore how different professional disciplines (and theoretical perspectives within these disciplines) emphasize the primacy of one or more of the three aspects of meaning in their explanations of various life experiences. Connections will be made to numerous frames of reference (theoretical perspectives) dealing with life experiences of various types. These types of life experiences include basic ways of processing information about the world, individual differences in ways of experiencing the world, types or functions of caregiving, and determinants of quality of life, health, or well-being. By discussing the three aspects of meaning in various contexts, this chapter will show that the three aspects are fundamental. It also will demonstrate the wide applicability, utility, and unifying power of a model of the meaning of life experiences.

The chapter will end by considering how we can live our lives in ways that lead to resilience and optimize a sense of meaning. The message provided by this book's exploration of resilience in the lives of people who happen to have disabilities is that all of us can benefit from engaging in multiple roles and endeavors. Diverse ways of belonging, doing, and understanding ourselves and the world lead to resilience and bring a sense of meaning in life. By developing a wide set of interests and participating in an array of work, leisure, and social activities, we can develop sustaining and growth-enhancing relationships, obtain a sense of contribution to and interconnection with the larger world, and develop a complex and resilient sense of ourselves. Participation in life is the key. As the study participants have shown us, we participate in life by committing ourselves to important relationships with other people, pursuing meaningful activities, and investing our energies in seeking to understand ourselves and our world.

KEY THEMES ABOUT TURNING POINTS AND RESILIENCE

What have we discovered so far? We know the nature of turning points and how they unfold—what triggers them, what resolves them, what meaning and direction comes out of them, and how these meanings are similar from one person to another. Our exploration of turning points has shown that people's lives are in continual transformation and that people successfully adapt to many turning points in life. As well, we have learned that there are three fundamental paths by which we create meaning in life—through belonging, doing, and understanding.

We also discovered three protective processes involved in turning points that appear not to have been explicitly described before in the literature on risk and resilience. Perhaps this is because we were interested in adults with chronic disabilities, whereas other researchers have focused on adults with chronic illnesses or children facing environmental adversity, such as poverty, abuse, or neglect. As well, other researchers have not explicitly asked people to consider the feelings, thoughts, and experiences that lead up to and follow from turning points. Another contributing factor may have been our interest in the positive and protective effects of turning points, whereas others have focused more on negative effects and vulnerability factors.

First, we found strong evidence that people create new understandings or beliefs about life that involve turning a loss into a gain (the process of *transcending*). This is the idea of seeing the *positive learning* arising from a situation. When we come to see some event that was initially experienced as a loss in terms of its benefits, then a loss is turned into a gain. Through this process of reframing, we make sense of our experiences and then are able to have hope for our futures and go on. Without hope, life can become meaningless.

Second, we found that turning points can involve recognizing something new about oneself—such as an interest or a strength or a desire for further education—that can take a person's life in a new direction (the process of *self-understanding*). Third, we found that life can head in a new direction when people relinquish a hope or come to terms with something in their lives (the process of *accommodating*). For example, some participants in our study saw the benefit of better mobility after they decided to use a power wheelchair and give up the goal of walking. Turning points therefore can involve symbolic losses, like the loss of dreams or the loss of physical function, and are resolved when these losses are accepted and the benefits of the new situation are realized.

The life experiences of people with disabilities therefore have provided new insights into the processes by which turning points begin and end. We believe that the reframing of loss of dreams and/or physical function can be an important turning point for many people, not only those with disabilities. Such turning points will occur for many of us as we go on in life. Studies of turning points are few and have tended to go no further than studying adjustment to midlife. Because some people with disabilities may deal with issues of symbolic loss and gain earlier on in life, these processes have become starkly apparent in the present study. In chapter 3, Grace talks about how accepting her disability has been a benefit in her approach to aging. While her friends struggle to find a positive way to cope with their increasing physical limitations, Grace has already come to terms with the idea of having a physical limitation.

We have learned that we need to focus on the gain—the positive—in all things. *Transcendence* refers to going beyond the limits, to climbing over. When we transcend a life crisis, this means we have created a partial replacement for something that was lost. We turn adversity into a strength by constructive action and commitment to a new beginning. This approach to life can be thought of as an attitude of lifelong learning, which is grounded in the assumption that stress and change are expected parts of life. When we are humble about ourselves and our understanding of life, then there is always something to gain from the things that happen in our lives. This is a choice we can make about how to live our lives.

What have we learned about resilience? Chapter 3 took a detailed look at the nature of the factors contributing to a "resilient self," and thereby to meaning. The emphasis was on specific helpful experiences, rather than on the meaning of these experiences. That chapter considered the things about us as people, the aspects of our relationships with others, and the things in our communities that were seen as helpful or hindering factors by the people who took part in the study. By tying these helpful and hindering factors to what is known about resilience, chapter 3 highlighted the key things associated with positive outcomes for people in life. The key message here was the importance of personality traits such as determination, the social support of others, and spiritual beliefs.

Of the many helpful factors, social support was the most important and widely mentioned by participants. Similarly, the most powerful hindering factor reported by participants was negative, limiting attitudes of others in the community. The social support of others therefore is key to transcending life crises and climbing over barriers.

How do these findings tie into the major recommendations made in chapter 4? The major recommendations made by people with disabilities concerned being listened to, the need to educate people about disability by getting to know people with disabilities on a person level, and the importance of advocacy to bring about community participation and belonging. We must reduce erroneous information and combat myths, stereotypes, and ways of thinking that limit people's participation, and thereby their opportunity to attain or create meaning in life. As children, we are limited in how we can participate when we are not able to play with others. As adults, we are limited in our participation when we are not able to join groups of various kinds or be exposed to a wide circle of different types of people, and when we are not able to have the education we desire or get the jobs for which we are skilled. Limited participation can mean that we are limited in our potential to build relationships, to attain meaning through doing, and to develop a complex, full understanding of ourselves and our abilities.

A MODEL OF LIFE EXPERIENCE

> Things cannot exist and be known apart from active connection with other things.
>   — John Dewey, *Experience and Nature*

In chapter 2, a Möbius strip was introduced as an analogy for the continuity and interconnectedness of life experience. A Möbius strip is a two-dimensional shape that has only one surface. The strip therefore has no beginning and no end. A braided Möbius strip was used to show how the three strands of meaning in life are intertwined with one another and circle back on themselves in a seamless whole with no beginning and no end. The beginning of any experience is simply where we choose to start on the strip. This is because many things come before any experience, and these things create the meaning of that experience. For example, how we deal with a failure experience, such as not getting a job we want or a partner we desire, is determined by our personality and sense of self-worth, by our previous experiences with failure (whether they turned out alright in the end or not), the support (or lack of support) we received from others while going through these experiences, and the meaning of success and failure within our broader culture.

We're going to put the analogy aside for a moment and consider a model of the meaning of life experiences (King, in press). A model is simply a device or framework that is used to communicate key ideas about something—in this case, life experience. A model helps us understand complex ideas by presenting them in a simpler form. We propose that meaning in life is acquired and created through the three paths of belonging, doing, and understanding, and that all aspects of how humans perceive their experiences reflect a basic and fundamental three-way distinction that is related, on different levels, to these three paths. Table 5.1 shows how three levels of experience (the micro level of perception, the middle level at which we experience everyday events, and the macro level of meaning in life) can be interrelated using this basic three-way distinction.

Let's expand on the Möbius strip analogy. Think about the strip as having four levels, going from smallest to largest. Starting at the smallest level, there are fibers, then threads, then the braided strands, and, finally, the Möbius strip as a whole.

The fibers are experience or function on the psychological level—the cognitive, affective, and behavioral levels of experience. The threads are the phenomena that we seek to explain through theory; these are composed of the cognitive, affective, and behavioral aspects of experience. The strands are the aspects of meaning—belonging, doing, and understanding—which are braided or intertwined with one another. The Möbius strip as a whole represents the interconnectedness of the strands of mean-

Table 5.1
A Model of Life Experience

Levels of Experience	Three Fundamental Elements		
Psychological or Perceptual Level	Cognition (thoughts)	Affect (emotions or feelings)	Behavior
Phenomenological Level	Multiple phenomena composed of the 3 components of cognition, affect, and behavior		
Level of Meaning	Understanding	Belonging	Doing

ing into a single entity. Because the Möbius strip has no beginning and no end, it nicely portrays the idea that there is no true beginning or end to how we acquire meaning in life. Rather, meaning is determined by the continuous and complex interplay between the strands.

It is beneficial to see both the parts of the Möbius strip and their unification into a whole. We can see this in a cross-sectional view of the Möbius strip, which shows how the different levels are connected to one another (see Figure 5.1). According to psychologist Ellyn Kaschak (1992), multiple meanings emanate from all levels of experience and we should not consider any one aspect of experience as preceding or causing the others. Life is like a long braid, a helix of ideas and experiences.

On the fiber level are cognition, affect, and behavior, which are transformed into different yet related concepts on the thread level (the phenomenon level). All phenomena are composed of the components of cognition, affect, and behavior. For instance, when we talk about phenomena concerning ourselves, such as self-esteem or mastery, these experiences of ourselves are formed from our interactions with the world on all the levels of experience—our cognitions or understandings, our evaluations of events, and our behaviors.

The thread level, the level of phenomena—our lived experience—is the mucky level. There are literally hundreds of phenomena examined in social

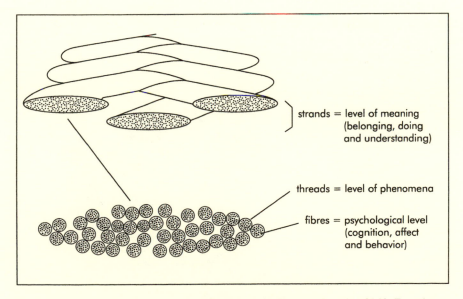

Figure 5.1 Cross-sectional View of the Möbius Strip Showing Levels of Life Experience

work, occupational therapy, physical therapy, speech and language pathology, nursing, and psychology, including topics such as occupational performance, self-concept, group behavior, role acquisition, attitude formation and change, caregiving, and leadership. Many different theories are used to explain these phenomena and lots of jargon is used to describe them.

How can we show a phenomenon using our visual model? We can do this by drawing lines on the Möbius strip that cut the flow of life experience into a "chunk in time." Figure 5.2 shows two boxes, representing phenomena, that differ in the overlap of the strands of meaning. Theories or descriptions of phenomena emphasize particular aspects of meaning in a temporal, causal pattern. That is, theories attempt to account for one aspect of meaning (although they use different terms for this) by showing how this aspect is caused by another aspect. For instance, the box on the left in the Figure 5.2 shows Mihaly Csikszentmihalyi's (1990) phenomenon of *flow,* in which absorbing, challenging types of activities (a particular thread of the *doing* strand) create—or lead to—self-understanding. The box on the right shows Susan Harter's (1983) theory of self-esteem, in which the approval of others (a thread of the *belonging* strand) and people's own judgments about their competence in key domains (a thread of *doing*) combine to create self-esteem (a component of *self-understanding*). Of course, this chunking of life experience into something that begins and

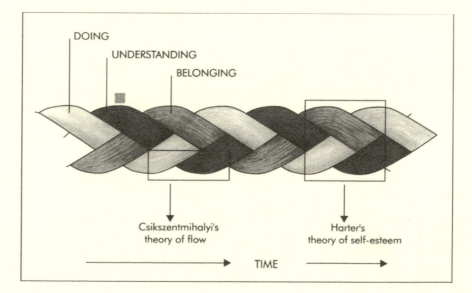

Figure 5.2 Showing Temporal Phenomena (Theory) Using the Möbius Strip

ends and in which one strand causes another is illusory. When we take a bigger perspective and consider meaning in life, we realize that the strands continually intertwine to create overall meaning.

The life experience model, therefore, portrays life experience as simple on the psychological level (three functions—thoughts, feelings, and behaviors—represented by three types of fibers in our Möbius strip analogy), complex on the phenomenon level (multiple threads), and simple again on the level of meaning (three strands).

Throughout life, different aspects of meaning become more important at particular times while others fade into the background. During adolescence, for instance, belonging to a group of peers may be paramount. Later on, getting good marks and achieving (doing) may be the *raison d'être* for those of us who go to college or university. In midlife, some people reevaluate their lives and seek new creative endeavors to optimize their self-growth (understanding). These changes throughout life can be portrayed by the placement of the strands relative to one another—their position on the top or bottom of the braided strip.

As we've seen, life events and experiences can create a friction between a person and his or her environment that is experienced as a turning point—a change in life's direction. These turning points are represented by the crossings in the braid—where life's meaning undergoes a major change. Some of us will have a life represented by a relatively smooth or loosely braided Möbius strip, because we have had few turning points. Others will have a tightly braided life experience due to more frequent changes in meaning associated with a greater number of changes in life direction. Individual differences in life experience, therefore, can be portrayed by the tightness or looseness in the braiding of the Möbius strip.

The analogy also allows us to see that the usefulness of the three strands differs across people. For some of us, the *doing* strand is much thicker than the other strands. This will be the case when some activity—work, hobby, sport, or volunteer activity—is so important and meaningful to us that it becomes one of our *key life structures,* to use Daniel Levinson's (1986) term. The sizes of the three strands in the strip, therefore, can be made bigger or smaller relative to one another to show individual differences in preferred ways of engaging in the world.

Let's consider some of the intriguing properties of the Möbius strip that can be applied to life experience. We've already considered one of the strip's interesting features—the fact that it has no beginning and no end, and therefore can be used to symbolize continuity in life experience. A second property of the strip is seen when you attempt to divide the strip in two by cutting it around the middle. What you actually get is a single strip, not two separate strips. As shown by the following limerick, the strip remains one thing when cut in half.

> A mathematician confided
> That a Möbius band is one-sided
> And you'll get quite a laugh
> If you cut one in half
> For it stays in one piece when divided.

This second property of the Möbius strip illustrates that the separateness of the strands of meaning is, in some sense, an illusion. Although the strands of meaning in life can be discussed as separate, they are intricately connected to one another. The three strands are really one thing—meaning of life experience—because the three meanings cannot really be disentangled for us in terms of our day-to-day lives.

> We cannot live only for ourselves. A thousand fibers connect us with our fellow men; and among those fibers, as sympathetic threads, our actions run as causes, and they come back to us as effects. (Herman Melville (1819–1891) American writer)

EVIDENCE FOR THE THREE STANDS OF MEANING: INTEGRATING DISCIPLINARY PERSPECTIVES ABOUT WHAT IS IMPORTANT IN LIFE

Ellyn Kaschak, in *Making Meaning* (1992), says we typically divide experience into different levels or chunks. The most commonly used frameworks (ways of categorizing the world) are the individual, interpersonal, and societal levels of experience, and the cognitive, affective, and behavioral levels of experience. There is overwhelming evidence of the use of these and similar frameworks to divide life experience into three primary aspects.

We will use the framework we are most enamored of—aspects of meaning in life—to tie together the most common theoretical perspectives of the various disciplines concerned with life experiences on the different levels of abstraction (from processing information to establishing meaning in life). From all kinds of disciplines and perspectives we will see, again and again, the importance of the three concepts of belonging, doing, and understanding. Despite differences in preferred explanatory concepts, there is a powerful consensus across many theories and frames of reference, and in our own understandings of experience as reflected in popular thought. By placing the three aspects of life experience we have been discussing into a rich array of contexts, we hope to provide a vivid and convincing demonstration of the all-encompassing nature of these aspects of meaning. We also hope to shed light on both the utility and limitations of disciplinary perspectives.

We first need to consider what a *discipline* is. *Disciplines* refer to branches of knowledge or areas of study that make certain assumptions and thereby direct our attention to phenomena in particular ways. These prescribed ways of looking at things help us to understand the phenomena we are interested in. These prescribed viewpoints are called various things: disciplinary perspectives, theories, or frames of reference. These terms are similar to a point of view, context, or paradigm.

Students studying a particular discipline are trained, through the use of theories or frames of reference, to focus their attention in particular ways and on particular things. According to Dennis Salebey, author of *The Strengths Perspective in Social Work Practice* (1992), every model of clinical practice has an ideological core comprised of fundamental assumptions about what is and fundamental values about what should be. The different disciplines such as social work, psychology, and occupational therapy therefore differ in where they draw the line between the things of interest (the foreground) and the things that are less important (the background).

Theories or frames of reference are simply frameworks or bounded contexts that provide understanding and a sense of coherence or order to our thoughts. Disciplines such as psychology, sociology, or occupational therapy have favorite frameworks, paradigms, and ways of approaching the world. Like stereotypes, frames of reference are useful because they allow us to investigate phenomena on a level of detail that would not be possible otherwise, resulting in a rich understanding of a topic. As with stereotypes, however, frameworks can limit our understanding on a broader level. Like blinders on a horse that keep the horse focused on the road ahead, frameworks can be intellectual blinders that keep us focused on something, but limit broader insights or understandings. They can make us fit observations of life into preconceived views in ways that can be constraining and sometimes are destructive to ourselves and others.

Like any framework, our model of life experience has both utility and limitations. Part of establishing its usefulness is to look at its consensus and coherence. These are the two major *epistemic values,* that is, the things that make scientific claims valid. Yvonna Lincoln and Egon Guba, authors of *Naturalistic Inquiry* (1985), state that consensus occurs when independent investigators, starting with different assumptions and examining different phenomena in different ways, reach the same conclusion. Consensus implies that a phenomenon is robust. A robust phenomenon shows up again and again; there is strong evidence for the same conclusion. So, group agreement (consensus) is one way of determining truth. Note that consensus is not always a good way of determining truth: It was once commonly believed that the earth was flat. Another way of establishing truth is coherence. Something is coherent when it makes sense, when all the bits fit together into a logical, integrated, understandable, and consistent whole (Schwandt, 1994).

Truth is coherence within a system.
— Mary Hesse, cited by Lincoln & Guba, 1985, p. 91

What evidence is there in the literature for a consensus that there are three aspects of meaning in life and that they form a coherent system? This is where the various frames of reference from the psychological, sociological, and applied health science disciplines come in. These disciplinary frames of reference differ in their level of analysis (e.g., self, self in social context, self in broader community context), in the phenomena of interest, and in the aspects of meaning that they see as primary. The professional disciplines put different emphasis on the primacy and causal role of the three aspects of life meaning in their explanations of various life experiences. That is, they truncate the stream of life experience differently. For example, theories of empowerment (e.g., Dunst, Trivette, Davis, & Cornwell, 1988) look at how empowerment (a component of *doing*) leads to a sense of personal competence and control (*understanding*) or to a sense of community (*belonging*). Theories of leisure (e.g., Crawford & Godbey, 1987) look at how participation in leisure activities (*doing*) leads to the development of identity (*understanding*).

It is interesting to see how this difference in disciplinary focus results in one discipline's dependent variable being another discipline's independent variable. For example, physical therapists working in the area of childhood disability put primary emphasis on how to optimize a child's physical mobility. Rather than seeing mobility as a dependent variable (the crucial thing to be examined), occupational therapists may view mobility as one of many independent variables that affect a different dependent variable of interest, such as children's participation in the community. As another example, nurses may view resilience as an important independent variable influencing a key area of nursing interest and theory—health promotion by parents within the family context—whereas psychologists may choose to examine resilience as a dependent variable.

Theoretical perspectives simply consider one aspect of life experience (a term in a temporal order) to be primary and go from there. In reality, according to John Dewey (1958), the last term in any sequential order may be an initial term in another sequential order. This is the idea that one person's (or discipline's) beginning can be another's end point—beginnings are endings too.

Despite the different emphases on the causal sequence of the aspects of meaning, there is lots of evidence for three aspects of meaning in the various disciplines of knowledge that seek to understand and explain the human condition. From all kinds of disciplines and perspectives we see the importance of these three concepts. They appear from a psychological perspective (theories of attitudes, motivation, and personality), the applied health science perspective (theories and frames of reference used in occupational therapy and nursing), and the sociological or cultural anthropological perspective.

Table 5.2 groups selected theories or frames of reference according to a micro to macro focus, ranging from how we process information, to individual differences in ways of experiencing the world, to the types or functions of caregiving, and, lastly, to the meaning of life events or the determinants of quality of life, health, or well-being. The right side of the table gives the names for the three key concepts that are used by the theory or frame of reference. When they are fundamental ways of processing the world, they are called *functions, feelings, needs,* or *components.* When they are seen as individual differences, they are called *preferences, domains,* or *criteria.* When they concern the meaning of life events, they are called *dimensions* or *aspects.*

The 32 theories and frames of reference in this table point to the existence of three fundamental concepts, which are related, on various levels of analysis, to the three aspects of meaning in life. What these three concepts are called (for example, functions, behaviors, needs, or strands of meaning) and how they are worded (as outcomes—nouns—reflecting functions or individual differences, or as actions or processes—verbs—reflecting behaviors, needs, or ways of acquiring meaning) depends on the phenomenon the researcher is interested in trying to explain and the framework he or she adopts to do so.

Table 5.2
Mapping Selected Frames of Reference onto Three Strands of Life Experience

Theory or Frame of Reference	The Three Key Concepts		
	Belonging	Doing	Understanding Self & World
A. Fundamental ways of processing or experiencing the world			
Components of attitudes (Rajecki, 1982; Triandis, 1971)	affect	behavior	cognition
Basic mental activities (Arendt, 1978)	judging (feeling)	willing	thinking
Innate psychological needs (Connell & Wellborn, 1990; Deci & Ryan, 1985)	interpersonal relatedness	competence	self-determination (autonomy)
Fundamental human needs (Maslow, 1970)	affiliation (love-belongingness)	achievement	self-actualization
Fundamental psychological functions or aspects of experience (Perls, 1973)	emotion (affect)	actions (behavior or motivation)	thought (cognition)
B. Individual differences in ways of experiencing the world			
Aspects of a sense of coherence (Antonovsky, 1987)	emotional sense (meaningfulness)	manageability	comprehensibility
Domains of children s adjustment (Cowan, Cowan, Schulz, & Heming, 1994)	social	academic	emotional and behavioral
Domains of competence (Harter, 1982)	social	physical	cognitive
Elements of competence (Adler, 1982)	interactional functioning	performance of major social roles	self-concept
Domains of motivation (Kagan, 1972)	affiliation orientation	achievement orientation	uncertainty orientation
Competencies for scientific inquiry (Abreu, Peloquin, & Ottenbacher, 1998)	attitudes	skills	knowledge
Domains of intrinsic aspirations (Kasser & Ryan, 1993, 1996)	affiliation	community feeling	self-acceptance or self-actualization
Types of coping skills (Schaefer & Moos, 1992)	emotion-focused (managing emotional reactions)	problem-focused (seeking information and taking action)	appraisal-focused (efforts to define, interpret, and understand a situation)
C. Types or functions of caregiving and social support			
Goals of nursing care (Watson, 1985)	psychological support (feeling accepted)	stress management (feeling capable of functioning)	self-fulfillment (feeling understood)
Types of resources leading to social support (Jacobson, 1986)	emotional	material	cognitive

166

Table 5.2 (*continued*)

Main goals or values of rehabilitation (Wax, 1972)	interaction	mastery (achievement)	development of inner resources
Types of support for disadvantaged youth (Smokowski, Reynolds, & Bezruczko, 1999)	emotional support	motivational support	informational support
Functions of social support (Thoits, 1985)	socioemotional aid	instrumental aid	informational aid

D. Meaning of life events or determinants of quality of life, health, or well-being

Commitment to types of goals in 3 spheres of life (Klinger, 1977)	intimacy	identity	understanding
Ways of investing the self in spheres of life (Mathews, 1996)	commitment to family or group	roles & activities in daily life (commitment to work)	knowing oneself (commitment to self-realization)
Performance components in a model of occupational behavior (Kielhofner, 1985)	belonging	doing	understanding
Prompts to psychological turning points (Clausen, 1993)	relationships (attachment)	life events and role transitions (involvement)	view of self (reflection)
Components of quality of life (Raphael, Brown, Renwick, & Rootman, 1996)	belonging	becoming	being
Aspects of quality of life (Naess, 1987)	human relations	activity	self-esteem
Aspects of health (Pender, 1987)	satisfying relationships with others	goal-directed behavior	actualization of human potential
Aspects of community integration after brain injury (Willer, Linn, & Allen, 1996)	loving (integration into a social network)	doing (integration in productive activities)	living (integration into the home environment)
Categories of positive life outcomes (Schaefer & Moos, 1992)	social resources (e.g., social support)	coping skills (e.g., problem-solving, help-seeking)	personal resources (e.g., self-understanding, self-awareness)
Needs associated with quality of life (Campbell, Converse, & Rodgers, 1976)	social recognition (feeling of identification with community)	achievement (sense of satisfaction with work)	self-actualization (sense of fulfillment of one s potential)
Aspects of quality of life (Allardt, 1975)	loving	having	being
Aspects of the subjective experience of aging (Stewart & Ostrove, 1998)	generativity	feelings of confident power (efficacy)	identity certainty

167

Let's consider examples of how the three key concepts called belonging, doing, and understanding have been used in discussions of various phenomena. We'll start with *fundamental ways of processing or experiencing the world* (section A in the table). Attitude theorists have consistently suggested that there are three components of attitudes: affect (which corresponds to belonging), behavior (doing), and cognition (understanding) (Rajecki, 1982; Triandis, 1971). Arendt (1978) discussed three basic mental activities—judging or feeling (belonging), willing (doing), and thinking (understanding). Abraham Maslow (1970) discusses three basic human needs (the need for affiliation, the need for achievement, and the need for self-actualization).

Let's consider some examples dealing with *individual differences* (section B). Antonovsky (1987) proposed three aspects of a sense of coherence or resilience: emotional sense (corresponding to belonging), manageability (doing), and comprehensibility (understanding). Many researchers, including Philip Cowan, Carolyn Pape Cowan, and their colleagues, have talked about the existence of three key domains of children's adjustment during the early and middle childhood years. These are children's social competence, their academic performance, and their emotional and behavioral functioning (Cowan, Cowan, Schulz, & Heming, 1994). Adler (1982) views mental health as resulting from a feeling of human connectedness, a willingness to contribute to the welfare of others, and a willingness to develop oneself fully. Again, we see how the concepts used by theorists interested in individual differences map onto the concepts of belonging, doing, and understanding.

In terms of *types or functions of caregiving* (section C), Thoits (1985) has identified three functions of support groups (socioemotional aid, instrumental aid, and informational aid), which also correspond to the three key aspects of professional caregiving outlined by Sheryle Whitcher-Alagna (1983): treating care recipients with respect and support, encouraging partnership or enabling, and providing information. Recently, Masten (2001) proposed that there is a relatively small set of global factors associated with resilience, which suggests the operation of basic human adaptational systems. These factors or types of resources include connections to competent and caring adults (belonging), motivation to be effective in the environment (doing), and positive views of the self, along with cognitive and self-regulation skills (understanding).

The final section in the table (section D) outlines several theories concerning the *meaning of life events or the determinants of quality of life, health, or well-being*. In his book *Meaning and Void: Inner Experience and the Incentives in People's Lives,* Eric Klinger (1977) seeks to explain meaning in life using motivation as the vehicle. He argues that the key is commitment to three spheres of life, as seen in pursuing the goals of intimacy, identity, and understanding. In his book *What Makes Life Worth Living?: How Japanese and Americans Make Sense of their Worlds,* Gordon Mathews (1996) takes a cultural-anthropological approach and explains meaning in life in terms of the spheres of life to which people make commitments. People make commitments to the family or group, to activities in their daily lives, and/or to self-realization. Gary Kielhofner's (1985) model of occupational behavior refers to the performance components of belonging, doing, and understanding. John Clausen (1993) categorizes prompts to psychological turning points as involving attachment, involvement, or reflection.

Quality of life, as described by Robert Schalock (1990), refers to a feeling of well-being that results when people have feelings of positive social involvement and opportunities to fulfill their potential. Several quality of life frameworks exist that are highly similar to the three key concepts or aspects of meaning we propose. For example, the quality of life framework by Dennis Raphael and his colleagues at the Centre for Health Promotion at the University of Toronto introduces the notions of belonging, becoming, and being (Raphael, Brown, Renwick, & Rootman, 1996). The notion of *belonging* deals with how people fit in with other people and places. *Becoming* refers to activities that facilitate personal goals, hopes, and wishes (doing). The notion of *being* refers to who you are as a person—physically, psychologically, and socially (understanding).

The various theories and frames of reference in the table therefore convincingly demonstrate the existence of three fundamental concepts, which are related, on various levels of analysis, to the three aspects of meaning in life.

SILENCE OF THE DISCIPLINES

It is interesting that frames of reference generally are silent with respect to their fundamental assumptions. That is, one cannot see the organizing perspective in the categorization of the three concepts unless one backs away from the framework and compares it to the other frames of reference. *Assumptions*, in fact, refer to things that are so obvious that they are not thought of or verbalized. They are things we take for granted. According to John Dewey (1958), disciplines focus on the *found* (what is being sought) rather than the *given* (the context). The context or background assumptions are silent or dormant.

When we adopt a single perspective, we cannot see that there are alternate ways of thinking about the world because we are locked into a frame that is on one level of analysis (focused on individual differences, interpersonal relationships, societal issues, or on broader meaning) and based on certain assumptions about what is primary, fundamental, or causal. For example, Abraham Maslow's (1970) framework of human needs assumes that needs are the main determinants of how we behave and whether we are satisfied with our lives. In contrast, Gordon Mathews's (1996) framework of ways of investing the self in spheres of life assumes that commitments are the primary determinants of behavior and life satisfaction. The authors of the present book designed a study to look at how people experienced turning points in life. We went looking for meaning. Is it any wonder that we found meaning and then developed a framework describing three key paths to meaning in life? How we, the authors, defined the things we were interested in, how we constructed the interview questions, and how we interpreted the information provided by participants was, of course, influenced by our training, our world view, our values, and our experiences.

The observation that frames of reference are silent with respect to fundamental assumptions is similar to the quantum mechanics idea that subatomic particles cannot be measured directly because the measuring tool or point of reference affects the observation. By putting all these ways of viewing the three concepts side by side in a table, however, we can see more clearly the basic assumptions made by each frame of reference.

POPULAR CONCEPTIONS OF MEANING

Let's leave the scientific literature behind and consider the evidence in the nontheoretical literature for the three concepts. People's reports of their own experiences, such as those provided by participants in the present study, provide strong evidence for the three concepts. Many of the examples presented in chapters 2, 3, and 4 about the importance of belonging, or engaging in something with enthusiasm, or developing new understandings of the self came from newspaper articles, magazine articles, books, and songs. One does not need a university degree to know what it is that gives meaning to life. You, the reader, are challenged to watch the newspaper for one week for descriptions of the paths to meaning. You are almost certain to find something.

A relevant framework in the popular literature is that of the soul, body, and mind. The concept of feeling or belonging relates to the soul, doing or experiencing relates to the body, and understanding relates to the mind. Ellyn Kaschak (1992) talks about the fundamental issues of a person's life, which are the meaning of relationships, of events, and of our own actions and those of others. Here again, then, we see the three ways of chunking the world. Blau, in "In Defense of the Jewish Mother" (1969), talks about protective factors that are useful for us all. These protective factors can be grouped according to the three aspects of meaning: a tight family structure, strong bonds of love, legitimacy of emotional expression (belonging); valuing of education and achievement (doing); and clear identity along with the "experience of struggle to become self-reliant" (understanding). As discussed in chapter 4, employment can provide a sense of collegiality (belonging), meaningful activity (doing), and growth or professional development (understanding).

Finally, coping strategies are, not surprisingly, capable of being tied to one or more of the aspects of meaning. An arsenal of coping strategies is a good thing to have. People use various techniques to cope with the stress in their lives—listening to music, meditating, sleeping, working more, seeking out friends, seeing humor in the situation, praying, spending time in nature, exercising, and using positive self-statements. These coping strategies can be grouped according to those that involve belonging, doing, and thinking (understanding).

Despite the differences in preferred explanatory concepts, there is a powerful consensus across many theories and frames of reference, and in our own understandings of experience as reflected in popular thought. They converge in a remarkable way at the same essence—what we have called in this book the three aspects of meaning.

Why do we see these three aspects again and again in descriptions of human experience? According to Ian Hacking of the University of Toronto, author of *The Social Construction of What?* (1999), there is no one reality. We inhabit many worlds, continually shape those worlds to meet our ends, and so each of us experiences reality in a different way. Thus, there are many truths—each to his or her own. The truth described in this book, however, does not deal with *what* is important in life. We are not discussing the content of our reality. Rather, this book deals with *how* reality is constructed—how to lead a rewarding life; the paths to acquire or create meaning in life.

So, why are these three aspects of meaning seen as fundamental? First, the three strands encompass the three life spheres that occur repeatedly in the literature, including Uri Bronfenbrenner's (1979) categorization scheme involving the self, the self in relation to others, and the self in relation to the larger world. Second, the three aspects reflect the basic processes of belonging, engaging in, or understanding the world. Third, they relate to fundamental human needs: to belong, to do or achieve, and to understand. The three aspects therefore reflect the content or structure of the world, the way we interact or engage in these aspects of the world, and our basic human needs. The life experience model therefore has a comprehensive, far-reaching scope, in addition to a solid empirical and theoretical basis as determined through consensus and coherence. If we create meaning by giving value to something, then we value three basic things—belonging, doing, and understanding.

ACKNOWLEDGING OUR PERSPECTIVES: MAKING THE INVISIBLE "VISIBLE"

> The greatest good you can do for another is not just to share your riches, but to reveal to him his own.
> —Benjamin Disraeli, British prime minister
> (in 1868, and from 1874 to 1880)

A connoisseur is someone with encyclopedic knowledge and keen discrimination in a field, especially in the fine arts or in matters of taste. Connoisseurs have a heightened awareness and educated perception of something, such as wine, opera, or painting. They pay attention to details and aspects of these things that the rest of us have no clue about—things that are invisible to most of us.

A gourmet is a connoisseur of food, someone who likes and is a judge of fine food and drink. Gourmets appreciate subtle nuances in the flavor or quality of food and would understand and appreciate the skill of a chef who created a dish such as Roasted Organic Root Vegetables in a Deconstructed Format with Legume Sauces and Quinoa. A gourmet would even know what quinoa was.

Similarly, in the field of music, it is well known that people who learn critical listening skills come to experience the delights and complexities of music much more than they did before. They hear what is inaudible to the rest of us. They discriminate between sounds on a more finely tuned basis. They have smaller, finer boxes for chunking this aspect of the world.

We can have blind spots due to our preferred ways of viewing the world. When we acknowledge our perspectives, however, this makes them visible (at least for a fleeting moment). This is healthy because it can lead to deeper understanding. It also can lead us to integrate different perspectives into new ways of seeing or understanding things. Thus, acknowledging our perspectives can lead to growth, rather than a stagnant state where we stay within our preferred or prescribed boxes or ways of viewing the world. We can all benefit from having bigger, or just different, boxes.

Boxes, therefore, refer to the frames of reference we use to view the world. These boxes differ in size and shape but are a fact of life. Boxes help us order events and experiences. They provide coherence and allow us to make sense of the world. Turning points are one kind of box, a box that defines a type of life experience that is emotionally compelling, has a trigger and a resolution, and leads to a fundamental shift in the direction of our lives. Without turning points, we can go through life in a habitual, unthinking way. Turning points force us to clearly see meaning—and often this transforms our lives.

Boxes also can be confining and limiting because they lead us to think in set ways. For instance, one of the biggest boxes faced by people with disabilities is others' assumption that having a physical impairment also means having a cognitive impairment. Another box is the view that people with disabilities can't possibly be satisfied with their lives.

Myths are widely held, popular stories that are misconceptions or mis-representations of the truth. They are unfounded beliefs. The word *myth* challenges us to put our preconceived ideas behind us. Many difficulties can arise from false beliefs because beliefs affect our expectations and behavior in subtle and not so subtle ways. For instance, the language that we use when talking about individuals with disabilities can impart subtle messages. Saying "he is a hemiplegic" rather than "he has hemiplegia" implies that the person as a whole is disabled and that his disability is his most important, or defining, characteristic. Our assumptions influence what we notice or pay attention to, so that we can come to see problems because we expect them to be there. Our assumptions also affect what we expect from others. Negative assumptions often lead to low expectations, which profoundly affect how young people, in particular, view them-selves. Myths are like stereotyped attitudes. There may be a grain of truth behind the belief, but problems arise when the belief is applied indiscrim-inately to all individuals, lumping them into one group and disregarding their individual characteristics.

When we are aware that boxes exist that may constrain our understand-ing, we can break out of them or *push the envelope* with respect to their limits. We can come to appreciate boxes and use them to build new worlds and understandings. We can refuse to be trapped in one box by consciously choosing to use different frameworks to gain perspective on issues and our experiences. Boxes can constrain us and free us. Boxes can be both good and bad. It depends on the purpose to which they are put—whether they are used to control and limit us or whether we feel we can open them up to see what is inside but then freely discard one for another.

> The meaning of any situation or set of circumstances is found in the frame within which we view it.
> —Sandidge & Ward, 1999, p. 201

The quote above indicates that, without a frame or box, there is no meaning. Here we see the usefulness of the boundary provided by a box. By defining something—giving it a context—boxes serve a fundamental purpose with respect to the generation of meaning. Similarly, Daniel Levinson, author of *The Seasons of a Man's Life* (1978), states that the meaning of a life stage is defined by its part in a sequence. Ellyn Kaschak (1992) says that only by drawing an arbitrary boundary can anything be considered figure or ground, foreground or context. According to Stephen Hawking, author of *A Brief History of Time* (1998), it appears that even the universe has a context—a beginning and an end. Even the universe has its limits. If there were no boxes, no frames of reference, and no points of view, there would be no meaning. Everything is relative. It appears that nothing is certain except death, taxes, and context.

Mihaly Csikszentmihalyi gives an intriguing illustration of the usefulness of pushing against boundaries. In his book *Flow: The Psychology of Optimal Experience* (1990), he states that we enjoy ourselves when we are at the boundary between boredom and anxiety—when we are in an optimal state of arousal: not too much and not too little. *Playing at the boundary* is similar to the notion of *pushing the envelope*. When we are at the boundaries of our skills or understandings, we have the best possible opportunity to challenge ourselves and, thereby, to learn. Inside the security of our envelope, we still feel safe as we push against the sides. This *playing at the boundary* between our personally defined sense of safety and risk can bring a sense of freedom and mastery, culminating in learning and growth. A good example of people who display this *playing at the boundary* are the skippers who sail single-handedly at sea. Derek Lundy, author of *Godforsaken Sea* (1998), says these professional sailors feel acutely alive when in dangerous situations. They appear to adopt a *protective frame of mind,* a psychological fortress that allows them to feel safe from the dangers of sailing alone around the world in turbulent seas.

We change our frame of reference when we come to understand something in a different way. Clinical psychologists and psychotherapists deal on a day-to-day basis with changing fundamental beliefs and reference points. People seek therapy when they feel stuck in unwanted, self-harming ways of thinking about themselves or their relationships, and therapists assist them in changing these belief patterns.

Turning points and other extreme situations involving threats to the self can call for fundamental changes to our belief systems. Even outside these extreme situations, being able to think about an issue in a variety of ways is a useful strategy because it can build a spectrum of understanding. This process is known as reframing—literally, putting a new frame on something, just as professional sailors do by adopting a *protective frame of mind.*

There are two types of reframing strategies: context and content reframing (Sandidge & Ward, 1999). Context reframing occurs when we change the environmental context in which a situation occurs (for example, the intellectual, cultural, or historical filter through which we view an event). We place events into a larger perspective when we do context reframing. For example, people often think their workplace is full of difficulties and problems. Going to another work setting (a new context) often brings a sense of perspective—a realization that their workplace has advantages or isn't as bad as they thought ("the grass isn't always greener").

Content reframing involves changing the meaning of the situation itself, as shown in the following statements: "This isn't failure, it's just delayed success"; "We're not retreating, we're just advancing in another direction"; "I'm not stupid, I would have done better on the test if I'd studied harder." In content reframing, the changed meaning leads to changes in our expectations, the possibilities we see for ourselves, and the choices we feel we have. The attributions that we make for events, especially those that involve success or failure (loss or gain), can have a profound influence on our future behavior.

Reframing is the same thing as changing our perspective or point of view. It is about seeing and understanding things differently. It means stepping outside our typical way of viewing things. It can be very liberating and refreshing to see things in another way. Reframing is akin to transforming because something is made into something else. As we have seen, the change brought about by turning points can involve bringing a new perspective to an issue or aspect of life. It is interesting that turning points can involve an external, environmental change (a stressful event), which leads to a process (reframing or transforming) that involves an inner change (a change in meaning).

Politicians and leaders are adept at reframing. They provide new ways of looking at events or situations—new spins or takes on the meaning of things, such as rising unemployment rates or increasing divorce rates. Reframing therefore is more than a coping skill; it is also an organizational skill. By defining the playing field, the framer defines the focus of attention and channels our actions accordingly.

Robert Sandidge and Anne Ward (1999) talk about two useful frames of reference. One is the *learner* frame in which we see ourselves as perpetual learners. This is an empowering frame of reference that stresses that we learn throughout life from mistakes, experiences, and losses. This way of viewing the world provides us with a sense of hope for our future because what is ahead is always new knowledge—gain rather than loss. Peter Adler, a psychologist (1982), says that competent individuals have positive, optimistic, and proactive views of themselves in relation to the world. An attitude of lifelong learning brings the same things.

The second useful frame of reference discussed by Sandidge and Ward (1999) is an *environmental* frame that involves enlarging people's opportunities and choices. By reducing restrictions and barriers, people have greater opportunity to pursue what is important to them in life.

A third frame of reference, not discussed by Sandidge and Ward (1999), is that of seeing commonalities rather than differences in people (the *similarity* frame). Adding this third way of viewing the world gives us three perspectives that correspond to the three aspects of meaning. An attitude of lifelong learning involves how we view ourselves (*understanding*), a focus on providing greater opportunities and choices for all people relates to the *doing* aspect, and looking for similarities rather than differences in people relates to our interconnectedness or *belonging*. Thus, the three aspects of meaning can be tied to frameworks or points of view that can be used to guide our actions throughout life. These can also be thought of as values or fundamental orientations toward life.

LIVING OUR LIVES: BALANCING THE TIGHTROPE

> Work like you don't need the money, love like you've never been hurt, and dance like no one is watching.
>
> —Anonymous

If there are three fundamental ways of acquiring meaning, then what does this say about how we might best live our lives? As is the case for many things, the answer seems to be to strive for balance and integration. The challenge is to give the proper attention to each aspect of meaning or part of our lives. We can obtain a long-lasting sense of meaning in life—a sense that life is worthwhile, that it has value or worth—by engaging in life experiences of a complex, rich nature that satisfy our fundamental needs, engage us in all aspects of our world, and provide a sense of belonging. When we have these sorts of engrossing life experiences, the chances are that we will develop the personal characteristics and supports around us that give us resiliency. We will be enmeshed and engaged in life, interdependent with family, friends, and other members of society, and have a strong sense of ourselves and our abilities. We will be better able to bounce back from difficulties in areas of our lives, whether it be in our relationships, our workplace, or our self-perception. Quality of life is not something we have but something that we have to actively work to create, along with the support of others.

According to Daniel Levinson (1986), people have a structure to their lives. This underlying pattern or design to a person's life has central components, which are those of greatest significance to the person at that point in time. In *The Seasons of a Woman's Life* (1996), Levinson talks about juggling the spheres of life to give equal priority to the various components of our life structure.

Life definitely is a balancing act and it can be extremely hard to achieve the balance that we crave. Trying to achieve this balance can be a source of much pressure in itself. Lots of minor corrections are required day-to-day to keep our sense of equilibrium. Whether we see ourselves as tightrope walkers or jugglers, the key seems to be to control the different aspects of our lives so that balance is achieved.

Joan Borysenko, author of *A Woman's Book of Life* (1996), points out, however, that complex lives are happy lives. The people who are busily engaged in meaningful activity—whether paid work, volunteer work, homemaking, or recreational activities and hobbies—are among those who are the most satisfied with their lives. According to Gail Sheehy, author of *Pathfinders* (1982), we need to develop more than a single source of identity and self-worth to have a flourishing sense of well-being. Being an accountant or a father or a kayaker is not enough. Being involved in all three roles is better. Sheehy encourages people to find a balance between individual growth (understanding) and caring for others (belonging). In addition, we would say that meaningful activity (doing) also brings meaning to life. People are not fully engaged in what life has to offer when they ignore any of the three aspects or paths to meaning. Multiple roles and identities bring multiple sources of meaning to our lives. Elizabeth Vandewater, Joan Ostrove, and Abigail

Stewart, from the University of Michigan, have found that engaging in multiple roles in early adulthood leads to the development of a strong sense of self (understanding), which leads to a sense of well-being later on in life (1997).

Different roles and identities allow us to connect with others in different ways, to obtain satisfaction through a variety of activities, and to develop a complex understanding of ourselves. When the going gets rough in one area of life, such as troubles at work or at home, there are a variety of people and activities to which we can turn. We can build a safety net for ourselves by ensuring that we have lots of opportunities or ways to reinvest ourselves, and therefore find meaning, in other areas of our lives. It is easier to make new friends or develop new interests if we have been able to live our lives in such as way that these are near at hand. When difficulties are experienced in any one area, focusing on another area can be an effective coping strategy that helps get us through the hard times. John R. Kelly, author of *Leisure Identities and Interactions* (1983), talks about the critical role of leisure activities and family connections at times in life when work roles come to lack meaning. At these times, we can turn to other identities or aspects of ourselves to see us through. Leisure activities can provide us with a sense of continuity about who we are and can also open doors to new opportunities and relationships.

According to Eric Klinger (1977), it is better to have more than one major commitment in life because the more incentives we have, the more meaning our lives have. Aaron Antonovsky (1987) also believes that people need to be engaged in both meaningful activity and love in order to develop a strong sense of coherence and to function optimally.

To Suzanne Kobasa (1979), *hardiness* involves commitment, control, and challenge. Hardy people are committed to the importance of what they do and involve themselves fully in many situations of life (work, family, relationships, etc.). They believe they can influence their experiences. That is, they have a sense of control or self-efficacy and they regard life changes as a stimulus to growth. Commitment, control, and challenge can be seen as overarching values that give meaning to life.

Mihaly Csikszentmihalyi (1997) states that happy people lead vigorous lives, are open to a variety of experiences, have strong ties and commitments to others, and keep learning until they die. He describes happy people as having the same characteristics as those associated with resilience. It seems that happy people are resilient people.

Gail Wagnild and Heather Young, from the School of Nursing at the University of Washington, discuss resilience in terms of personal competence (self-reliance and determination) and acceptance of self and life (adaptability and equanimity) (1993). *Self-reliance* is a belief in yourself and your capabilities, which involves recognizing both strengths and limitations. *Equanimity* refers to having a balanced perspective of your life and experiences, a sort of "going with the flow," or a sense of peace that allows you to remain optimistic about the future.

Thus, to have meaning in life or to be hardy, happy, or resilient involves the pursuit of belonging, meaningful activity, and self-understanding. There is a strong consensus about how to live a life that is full of meaning.

It seems that, in general (individual differences aside), we are happiest when we interact in lots of different ways with lots of different people, when we balance the time and energy we spend in commitments to self, family, and work. But wait a minute. While many authors talk about the importance and benefits of a balanced life, there are undoubtedly times when it makes sense that the scales are tipped toward one area of life rather than another. For instance, it appears that success in any area of endeavor is not achieved through balance. It is difficult to achieve excellence in an area without being out of balance in our lives as a whole (Sheehy, 1982). So, balance may not always be desirable, depending on our goals in life. If our goal is contentment, however, then balance is what everyone says we should strive for.

Some say people aren't happy when their lives are out of balance, but this is debatable. We can be so involved in a sport, hobby, career, or relationship (or writing a book chapter), that there is little room for other aspects of our lives. This can happen because we enjoy the sport or job so much that it has become addictive. We derive great pleasure from the activity. When we are enthusiastic about something, it means that we have an intense or eager interest in that activity. We feel passionate about it. It can put us in a state of flow.

Derek Lundy, author of *Godforsaken Sea* (1998), uses the term *edgeworkers* to describe people who pursue dangerous activities out of choice, particularly extreme sports such as skydiving, mountain climbing, and race-car driving. These extreme experiences are like turning points in that they lead participants to new realizations and ways of seeing the world. Life is transformed by the experience. Mundane aspects of life are appreciated much more. Sailors who cross the globe single-handedly can come to understand themselves much better through the hardship, and they can feel closer to others as a result of being alone for so long.

Wayne Oates, who received a Ph.D. in the field of Psychology of Religion, is the person credited with coining the term *workaholic* to describe a

person who drops out of the human community in a drive for peak performance. In *Confessions of a Workaholic: The Facts about Work Addiction,*
Oates (1971) talks about both the dark and light sides of passionate addiction to work. Work can be so intoxicating and rewarding that people
neglect their partners, families, and friends, as well as their personal well-
being. The dark side of work emerges when work takes over and people no
longer feel in control—they are consumed by their work. The Japanese
secret epidemic of *karoshi* refers to death or disability caused by a rever-
ence for overwork. Many Japanese work long hours on a regular basis, to
the detriment of both their personal health and their family relationships.

Eccentricity is yet another illustration of being out of balance.
Eccentrics are people who overbalance on the *doing* side of things. They
are called whimsical, peculiar, unconventional, or odd. They have an overwhelming passion to which they devote themselves, which results in the
exclusion of other things, usually relationships with people. Eccentrics
derive a true sense of meaning from their commitment to an activity or
endeavor, whether it is running, building model railways, growing
orchids, or saving hedgehogs. *Eccentric* literally means "out of the center"
or "off center," which means lacking in balance.

History has shown a number of flower crazes, among them the Dutch
tulip mania of the 1630s and the Victorian *orchidelirium.* Susan Orlean, a
writer for the *New Yorker* magazine, chronicles the life of John Laroche, a
true eccentric, in her book on orchid obsession, *The Orchid Thief* (1998).
John Laroche's obsession with orchids was just his latest obsession in a
series ranging from turtles to Ice Age fossils to precious stones, old mir-
rors, and tropical fish.

We were introduced in chapter 2 to Charles Fipke, the brilliant and
eccentric discoverer of Canada's first diamond mine. Like many
eccentrics, he was devoted to his work, with consequences for other
aspects of his life. In 2000, his bitter divorce battle with his former high
school sweetheart made the national newspapers (Partridge & Stueck,
2000). At $120 million, his divorce settlement was touted as the largest
Canadian divorce settlement ever to be made public.

Apart from those of us who are superachievers, workaholics, or
eccentrics, why do most of us crave balance in our lives? Our world has
become so fast-paced that we are more conscious than ever before of the
need to slow down. Many people now question why they speed through
their days at such a fast pace, trying to meet all demands and seldom having the time to be alone and do nothing—just sit and think. German environmental thinker Wolfgang Sachs (1999) believes that people crave a

balanced life in which there are periods of high-tempo activity and periods of restful tranquility. It is hard to achieve both because it is hard to change from one state to another.

Both balance and imbalance, therefore, have their time and place in our lives. We grow from times of imbalance, such as turning points. We also grow from periods in which we choose to invest in one thing over another, such as in work, school, or a new relationship. At certain times, it makes sense to invest heavily in things that contribute to our personal growth by helping us acquire new skills or see ourselves in new ways. Imbalance is living on the edge and taking a risk, but the payoff can be significant. Perhaps living on the edge is alright for the short term, but imbalance over the long term can lead to problems with our physical or mental health, or our relationships. Over the long haul, we need to stay in balance to get all life has to offer, but the teetering can be kind of fun and the wobbles can help us learn that we can stay upright regardless of the circumstances.

TYING IT ALL TOGETHER: THE IMPORTANCE OF COMMITMENT

The opposite of life is not death, it's indifference.

—Elie Wiesel

The meaning of life is meaning: whatever it is, wherever it comes from, a unified purpose is what gives meaning to life.

—Mihaly Csikszentmihalyi

I guess I mean that nature hates a vacuum. If there are no things which are important, then things are assigned importance arbitrarily and defended at great risk. Because the risk validates the importance.

— Robert B. Parker, *Double Deuce*

We can't leave you with three aspects or ways of creating meaning in life. Pursuit of a unifying theory drives us to consider whether there is an even more fundamental commonality to the three aspects of meaning we have been considering. Despite the fact that we know that there are three strands in our model of life experience, we are also aware that our visual model—the Möbius strip—is a whole thing in and of itself. What can tie everything together?

The answer seems to be the act of trying, of pursuing, of being committed to something, of having a goal, of being motivated to understand, achieve, or belong to something or with someone. So many of the frames of reference we considered earlier in this chapter gave a nod toward the importance of commitment or motivation.

Daniel Levinson (1986) says that the components of life that have the greatest significance for us provide us with a source of motivation and a unifying plot. At transitions, such as turning points, we make choices about our lives and give these choices meaning and commitment.

Gordon Mathews (1996) talks about people finding lives worth living through their commitments to what they value most in their lives—their families, work, dreams, creative endeavors, and/or religious beliefs. In this way, he focuses on the object or *raison d'être* of life, the *ikigai,* rather than on the process. Similarly, John R. Kelly (1983) believes that we derive meaning from investment in our roles in life. Jean Watson (1985), a nurse, shows us that caring for others is the act of valuing them. By caring for others, we give them the message that they are worth caring for. Here again we see the importance of *value*. We value things that we are committed to, things like love, service to others, and peace of mind. Values are very similar to aspects of meaning or pathways to meaning. Values are things we esteem that lead us or direct us to live our lives in certain ways. Viktor Frankl, in *The Unheard Cry for Meaning* (1978), states that people find meaning in activities done for things they value—for the sake of a cause, a loved one, or a higher being.

In his thought-provoking book on meaning and void in life, Eric Klinger (1977) defines *meaningfulness* as summarizing the way in which people are related to their individual world. According to Klinger, people need to be absorbed. We structure our lives around pursuing and enjoying things that are emotionally compelling to us—the idea of incentives. Personal relationships, immediate pleasures, and future goals all are incentives that provide purposes for acting—something to do, someone to love, and something to look forward to. What makes life meaningful is pursuing and enjoying incentives. In this view, then, meaning comes from having a purpose, from having an aim, even if it is simply to get up in the morning and enjoy a cup of coffee and a moment of peace looking out at your garden. Meaning comes from the act of valuing or caring about something and acting on that belief.

Eric Klinger (1975) believes that depression results from failure to reach goals, which involves a loss of incentives. To him, depression is a normal and even adaptive process accompanying disengagement from an incentive. A feeling of loss occurs when any aspect of a person's self, real or imaginary, is no longer available; that is, when a person feels deprived of a source of value or reward. Klinger explains recovery from depression in terms of detachment. When people detach themselves from the previously important thing, they recover. Depression therefore is a useful emotional state in that it helps a person disengage from what has proved to be a hopeless effort or goal. This is the "I don't care about that anymore" way of coping. Jean Watson (1985) takes this a bit further by stating that the resolution to the grief arising from loss is reinvestment in something else. In her view, then, it is not enough to disengage, one also has to reinvest. Similarly, John R. Kelly (1983) talks about the idea of disenchantment with work and how meaning and satisfaction with our roles in life come from the enactment of the role (the doing).

Life is a process of repeated engaging and disengaging. John Laroche, the "hero" of *The Orchid Thief,* was able to do this exceedingly well. Susan Orlean writes:

> As much as I marveled at Laroche's devotion to the things he was devoted to, I marveled even more at his capacity for detachment.... I suppose that is exactly what I was doing in Florida, figuring out how people found order and contentment and a sense of purpose in the universe by fixing their sights on one single thing or one belief or one desire. Now I was also trying to understand how someone could end such intense desire without leaving a trace. (1998, pp. 244–245)

Mihaly Csikszentmihalyi (1990) also gives predominance to goals and intentions. The state of flow integrates the self because thoughts, intentions, and feelings are all focused on the same goal. Goals allow all psychological processes to be in line and this feels harmonious or coherent to us—we feel together with ourselves, other people, and the world in general.

Leonard Pearlin and Carmi Schooler (1982) have considered how people's coping strategies reflect the importance of commitments to goals. A successful and frequently used coping strategy is to manipulate goals and values in order to distance oneself from a problem. This has been found to be the most effective form of coping for impersonal sorts of problems, such as financial or job-related worries (Pearlin & Schooler, 1982). Detaching or disengaging is not an effective coping mechanism, however, for more personal problems involving partners or children, where a person needs to remain engaged and committed to the relationship.

The literature on post-traumatic growth also indicates the importance of commitment and detachment. Persons experiencing trauma need to disengage from beliefs, goals, and activities that no longer make sense (Calhoun & Tedeschi, 1998). The ability to appropriately engage and disengage is thought to be a key life skill (Carver & Scheier, 1998).

Gail Sheehy, in *Pathfinders* (1982), also talks about involvement, commitment, or purpose in life. She believes that we find meaning in involvement in something beyond ourselves, such as our work, an idea or quest, or other people. Commitment is what gives our life meaning. A sense of purpose may come from many things—from our children, our work, or giving to others. Our interconnectedness to others can be thought of as a stone thrown into the water that has the potential to affect generations to come through the ripples that are created. The value of our life can be seen in terms of the relationships we have had with others—those people who have affected us and those we have influenced and touched in various ways. Our commitments to work, a sport, a recreational activity, or a cause also can provide this strong sense of value to our lives.

The idea of commitment or motivation therefore can explain many things: why people come to find different things meaningful in life and how these things come to be meaningful, the experiences of loss and depression, and how turning points are resolved. The idea of commitment also provides the answer to the questions posed at the beginning of this chapter. There are other possible answers to some of the questions. The notion of commitment, however, provides the most reasonable and parsimonious answer to the group of questions as a whole.

- *Why does absence make the heart grow fonder?* Absence can make the heart grow fonder when we care about the person who is absent. This is because being deprived of someone we value (an incentive) makes us value them more. Physical proximity—the opposite of absence—is crucial in the formation of relationships (Festinger, Schachter, & Back, 1950), but physical absence increases attraction to someone we already care about.

- *Why do we often come to love the things we suffer for?* Philosopher Fredrick Nietzsche long ago recognized that people must accept pain as a necessary stage on the road to anything valuable. The most satisfying endeavors in life often entail pain, change, and even torment. Struggle and joy are closely aligned. According to Bem's (1972) theory of self-perception, we need to bring our beliefs in line with our behavior. When we see ourselves suffering for something, we must justify this—and one way to do this is to decide that what we suffered for was truly worth it. Cognitive dissonance theory also proposes that people are motivated to have consistency among their thoughts about the world (Festinger, 1957).

- *Why does saying "I don't care" help distance you from something bothering you?* Saying "I don't care" helps you detach from the situation. It gives you the illusion of being disinterested in what has happened and allows you to move on to something else.

- *Why is having a pet often a wonderful thing?* Pets give us something to care for and commit to. Pets help us feel a sense of belonging, which is one of the fundamental ways in which we create or acquire meaning in our lives. Pets also are nonjudgmental and accept us for who we are, which increases our sense of commitment to them.

- *Why does winning the lottery not lead to happiness?* The road to happiness is in the trying, in the process of life, rather than the outcome. Money and other "things" can be nice but they do not provide happiness.

- *Why are "love and understanding the best answers we've heard yet?"* Love and understanding (and doing) are the best answers we've heard yet because they provide meaning in life.

- *Why is it better to have loved and lost than never to have loved at all?* It is better to have loved and lost than never to have loved at all because the process of committing yourself to a relationship provides understanding and learning about the self. Being in love also provides a sense of belonging, even if it is only temporary. According to John Dewey (1958), the things that are most precious in life turn out to be the things that change. These things are precious precisely because they are transitory and ephemeral.

- *Does a reevaluation of life necessarily involve pain and disruption?* Yes, emotional pain and disruption are a normal part of growth. They cause us to stop and reflect and reevaluate. Without them we would continue on as we always have. Conflicts and crises are necessary for the healthy development of the personality (Erikson, 1963) and strong negative emotions are implicated in many theories of adaptation to traumatic events (O'Leary, Alday, & Ickovics, 1998). The more stable a person's life situation, the more difficult it may be to experience personal change (Tennen & Affleck, 1998).

Now, the chicken or the egg question flaps into view. Do we get meaning from having incentives in our lives, the causal direction that Klinger (1977) seems to prefer, or does the need to have meaning make us seek things to which we can commit ourselves? We are not talking about the *meaning of life,* which is an existential question (why are we here?), but rather about how we derive and establish meaning in our day-to-day lives. Is life worth living because there are incentives in our lives or does our need to establish meaning cause us to invest in the pursuit of belonging, achievement, and/or knowledge? Or are both part of the answer?

Let's go back to the braided Möbius strip. As a totality, as a single thing, it represents *trying*. It represents the process of life itself rather than any outcome. We have seen that experiencing turning points in life reveals a basic truth about how we make meaning. We do this by committing ourselves to important relationships with others, pursuing meaningful activities, and investing ourselves and our energies in understanding ourselves. The process is the key, not the outcome. As Eric Klinger (1977) says, happiness cannot be pursued directly. Rather, happiness is the offshoot of intense involvement with some activity, relationship, or goal in our lives. Mihaly Csikszentmihalyi (1990) makes a similar point when he says that happiness is a condition that must be cultivated and prepared for. John R. Kelly (1983) says the same thing. He states that fulfillment in our roles in life is a process rather than a prize that is gained once and for all.

> It is by being fully involved with every detail of our lives, whether good or bad, that we find happiness, not by trying to look for it directly. (Mihaly Csikszentmihalyi, 1990, p. 2)

> Meaning transfigures all. Once what you are living and what you are doing has meaning for you, it is irrelevant whether you are happy or unhappy. You're content. You're not alone in your spirit. You belong. (Sir Laurens van der Post, author of *The Lost World of the Kalahari* and survivor of a World War II Japanese prison camp, cited by Lemle, 1997)

It seems that the key thing then, is to have a goal. Any goal can give meaning to our lives. Susan Orlean captures this idea when she writes in *The Orchid Thief:*

> The great Victorian-era orchid hunter William Arnold drowned on a collecting expedition on the Orinoco River....Orchid hunting is a mortal occupation. That has always been part of its charm. Laroche loved orchids, but I came to believe he loved the difficulty and fatality of getting them almost as much as the flowers themselves. The worse a time he had in the swamp the more enthusiastic he would be about the plants he'd come out with. (Orlean, 1998, pp. 55–56)

John Laroche himself acknowledged the importance of pursuing a goal: "It's not really about collecting the thing itself," Laroche went on. "It's about getting immersed in something, and learning about it, and having it become part of your life. It's a kind of direction" (Orlean, 1998, p. 279).

Oscar Wilde encapsulates the importance of goals in the following quote: "In this world there are only two tragedies. One is not getting what one wants, and the other is getting it. The last is the real tragedy" (Foreman, 1966, p. 417). When final goals are successfully attained, there is literally "nothing to look forward to." This explains "the apparently paradoxical situation where positively motivated and relatively successful individuals, who would be expected to be satisfied and 'fulfilled' as a function of their success, are in fact restless, bored, uninterested, and 'lost' at the pinnacle of their careers" (Raynor, 1982).

If goals are what is important in life, then what we need are opportunities both to discover goals and to follow the goals we choose to pursue. What we need are opportunities to participate in all the aspects of life that we desire.

Taking part in different activities, enterprises, and endeavors enables us to develop self-confidence and self-efficacy, to learn both what we are good at and what we are not so good at, and to understand what it is we enjoy doing. Participating in various social groups allows us to form relationships, to gain a sense that we belong to a group or something bigger than ourselves, and to gain a sense that our skills are valued and needed by others. In our North American culture, we participate in work environments to enhance our skills, set goals for development, and experience a sense of flow—as well as to make money. We also participate through sports, leisure, and recreational activities. It is no misnomer that *recreation* refers to "re-creation"—the opportunity to recreate ourselves.

As discussed in chapter 4, participation in activities is the context in which people form friendships, develop skills and competencies, express creativity, achieve mental and physical health, and determine meaning and purpose in life (Brown, Brown, & Bayer, 1994; Fidler & Fidler, 1978). Participation is a vital part of children's development because it enables children to understand the expectations that others have of them and it helps them to develop the physical and social skills required to be able to function in their communities. When people are satisfied with their activities, they express greater satisfaction with their lives as a whole and report greater well-being (Kinney & Coyle, 1992). Participation is also linked to resilience: children who participate more display greater resilience.

Participation allows us to learn in action, through experience. For example, through play, children learn the rules for interacting with others and with objects. They gain skill and competency in various activities, a sense of belonging through playing with others, and a sense of their abilities. Adults also need opportunities and challenges to expand their abilities and sense of themselves. According to Mihaly Csikszentmihalyi (1990), when we participate we gain many things: enjoyment, a sense of control or mastery, and a sense of our abilities and ourselves. Happiness arises when we pursue the things of value to us and have a positive outlook on our prospects.

By *participation* we don't mean recreation. We mean opportunities for people to engage in life in the ways they desire, which includes social connections (with whomever they desire), meaningful activities (whatever they may be), and pursuits that entail self-understanding. Therefore we believe that what has been said about the paths to meaning in life will be applicable across cultures. There are, however, historical, socioeconomic, cultural, and attitudinal barriers to what has been said about optimal participation. Some of us cannot participate in the scope of activities that we may like due to limited finances, limited mental or physical energy or skills, competing priorities, our own and other people's views about whether we can or should participate in certain activities, and the limited availability of appropriate activities. People with disabilities can face barriers as they attempt, as everyone does, to find meaning in life through pursuing goals that can only be fulfilled through participation in life.

SWEET MYSTERY OF LIFE

> The more the universe seems comprehensible, the more it also seems pointless.
>
> —Physicist Steven Weinberg

Understanding how we experience *meaning in life* is not at all the same as understanding the *meaning of life*. There is still ample mystery in life in terms of higher purpose. We have considered what it takes to live life in a way that makes it feel worthwhile—how we construct meaning through commitments to others, to activities, and to understanding ourselves and our world. The *meaning of life* refers to bigger, metaphysical questions about the nature of being or reality.

When we lack *meaning in life,* anomie and alienation are the result. Purpose is needed for life to feel worth living. Purpose develops and commitments are made through opportunities to interact with others; to take part in leisure, work, and other types of activities; and to understand ourselves—the three ways of engaging or participating in life.

We are fully aware that our qualitative methodology and the questions we posed to study participants have led us to see process rather than outcome—to see life in terms of the experiencing rather than the experienced, the how rather than the what. According to Wolf Wolfensberger (1994), who has written extensively on disability-related issues, virtually all so-called outcomes are really processes; one can conceive of just about anything as a process. In John Dewey's view, process and outcome really are the same essence (1958). Metaphysically, process and outcome are on the same level. Each can only be known or understood in contrast to or in relation to one another. John Dewey also says that if you break things into categories, then you need some device to bring them together again. The Möbius strip model of life experience provides such a device.

We've come on a long journey toward understanding turning points, resilience, and meaning in life. Along the way, we've considered how people have fundamental commonalities but are uniquely different, how turning points and change are more the status quo than are continuities in life, how turning points often reflect the dynamic interplay between loss and gain, and how personal qualities, social support, and spiritual beliefs can lead to resiliency. We've seen how frames of reference both provide structure to our world and limit our perspectives, how adversity can lead to meaning in life, and how meaning in life is created and maintained.

The key to meaning and resilience in life is the opportunity for us to participate in life as fully as we desire and in the ways we desire. People share a common need to make valued contributions to others and to their communities. According to Mihaly Csikszentmihalyi (1990), good communities offer people the opportunity to enjoy as many aspects of their lives as possible. Meaning in life comes through equilibrium (a state of balance in our life commitments), by attaining a state of equanimity (well-being or peace of mind), and through equality (freedom to do what we want to do).

> I have had three personal ideals.... And the third has been to cultivate such a measure of equanimity as would enable me to bear success with humility, the affection of my friends without pride, and to be ready when the day of sorrow and grief came to meet it with the courage befitting a man. (Sir William Osler, Canadian physician and humanist, cited in Bliss, 1999, p. 330)

> [I would like to see] a more humanistic and cooperative society in which every individual participates, first as a human being, and, second, where differences are incorporated or celebrated as the norm. (Study participant)

190   RESILIENCE

REFERENCES

Abreu, B.C., Peloquin, S.M., & Ottenbacher, K.O. (1998). Competence in scientific inquiry and research. *American Journal of Occupational Therapy, 52*(9), 751–759.

Adler, P.T. (1982). An analysis of the concept of competence in individuals and social systems. *Community Mental Health Journal, 18*(2), 34–45.

Allardt, E. (1975). *Dimensions of welfare in a comparative Scandinavian study.* Research Group for Comparative Sociology. University of Helsinki: Research Reports, No. 9.

Antonovsky, A. (1987). *Unraveling the mystery of health: How people manage stress and stay well.* San Francisco: Jossey-Bass.

Arendt, H. (1978). *The life of the mind.* New York: Harcourt, Brace, Jovanovich.

Bem, D.J. (1972). *Self-perception theory.* In L. Berkowitz (Ed.), *Advances in experimental social psychology* (Vol. 6). New York: Academic Press.

Blau, Z.S. (1969). In defense of the Jewish mother. In Peter I. Rose (Ed.), *The ghetto and beyond.* New York: Quadrangle/New York Times Book Co.

Bliss, M. (1999). *William Osler: A life in medicine.* Toronto: University of Toronto Press.

Borysenko, J. (1996). *A woman's book of life: The biology, psychology, and spirituality of the feminine life cycle.* New York: Riverhead Books.

Breathnach, S.B. (1998). *Something more: Excavating your authentic self.* New York: Warner Books.

Bronfenbrenner, U. (1979). *The ecology of human development: Experiments by nature and design.* Cambridge, MA: Harvard University Press.

Brown, R.I., Brown P.M., & Bayer, M.B. (1994). A quality of life model: New challenges arising from a six year study. In D. Goode (Ed.), *Quality of life for persons with disabilities* (pp. 39–56). Cambridge, MA: Brookline.

Calhoun, L.G., & Tedeschi, R.G. (1998). Posttraumatic growth: Future directions. In R.G. Tedeschi, C.L. Park, & L.G. Calhoun (Eds.), *Posttraumatic growth: Positive changes in the aftermath of crisis* (pp. 215–238). Mahwah, NJ: Erlbaum.

Campbell, A., Converse, P.E., & Rodgers, W.L. (1976). *The quality of American life: Perceptions, evaluations, and satisfactions.* New York: Russell Sage Foundation.

Carver, C.S., & Scheier, M.F. (1998). *On the self-regulation of behavior.* New York: Cambridge University Press.

Clausen, J.A. (1993). *American lives: Looking back at the children of the great depression.* New York: Free Press.

Connell, J.P., & Wellborn, J.G. (1990). Competence, autonomy, and relatedness: A motivational analysis of self-system processes. In M. Gunnar & L.A. Sroufe (Eds.), *Minnesota symposium on child psychology* (Vol. 22, pp. 43–77). Minneapolis: University of Minnesota Press.

Cowan, P. A., Cowan, C. P., Schulz, M., & Heming, G. (1994). Prebirth to preschool factors in children's adaptation to kindergarten. In R. D. Parke & S. G. Kellam (Eds.), *Exploring family relationships with other social contexts* (pp. 75–114). Hillsdale, NJ: Erlbaum.

Crawford, D., & Godbey, G. (1987). Reconceptualizing barriers to family leisure. *Leisure Sciences, 9,* 119–127.

Csikszentmihalyi, M. (1990). *Flow: The psychology of optimal experience.* New York: Harper & Row.

Csikszentmihalyi, M. (1997). *Finding flow: The psychology of engagement with everyday life.* New York: Basic Books.

Deci, E. L., & Ryan, R. M. (1985). *Intrinsic motivation and self-determination in human behavior.* New York: Plenum.

Dewey, J. (1958). *Experience and nature.* New York: Dover Publications.

Dunst, C. J., Trivette, C. M., Davis, M., & Cornwell, J. (1988). Enabling and empowering families of children with health impairments. *Children's Health Care, 17*(2), 71–81.

Erikson, E. (1963). *Childhood and society.* New York: Norton.

Festinger, L. (1957). *A theory of cognitive dissonance.* Stanford, CA: Stanford University Press.

Festinger, L., Schachter, S., & Back, K. (1950). *Social pressures in informal groups: A study of human factors in housing.* Palo Alto, CA: Stanford University Press.

Fidler, G. S., & Fidler, J. W. (1978). Doing and becoming: Purposeful action and self-actualization. *American Journal of Occupational Therapy, 32,* 305–310.

Foreman, G. B. (Ed.). (1966). *The complete works of Oscar Wilde* (2nd ed.). London: Collins

Frankl, V. E. (1978). *The unheard cry for meaning: Psychotherapy and humanism.* New York: Simon & Schuster.

Hacking, I. (1999). *The social construction of what?* Cambridge, MA: Harvard University Press.

Harter, S. (1982). The Perceived Competence Scale for Children. *Child Development, 53,* 87–97.

Harter, S. (1983). Developmental perspectives on the self. In P. H. Mussen (Ed.), *Handbook of child psychology* (pp. 275–385). New York: Wiley.

Hawking, S. (1998). *A brief history of time: Updated and expanded tenth anniversary edition.* New York: Bantam Books.

Jacobson, D. E. (1986). Types and timing of social support. *Journal of Health and Social Behavior, 27,* 250–264.

Kagan, J. (1972). Motives and development. *Journal of Personality and Social Psychology, 22,* 51–66.

Kaschak, E. (1992). Making meaning. In E. Kaschak, *Engendered lives: A new psychology of women's experience* (pp. 9–36). New York: Basic Books.

Kasser, T., & Ryan, R. M. (1993). A dark side of the American dream: Correlates of financial success as a central life aspiration. *Journal of Personality and Social Psychology, 65*(2), 410–422.

Kasser, T., & Ryan, R. M. (1996). Further examining the American dream: Differential correlates of intrinsic and extrinsic goals. *Personality and Social Psychology Bulletin, 22*(3), 280–287.

Keeler, G., & Cuddy, J. (1988, 1989). "Love and understanding." From the CD *Diamond Mine*. Scarborough, ON: Risque Disque Music/Home Cooked music (CAPAC).

Kelly, J. R. (1983). *Leisure identities and interactions*. London: Allen and Unwin.

Kielhofner, G. (1985). *A model of human occupation: Theory and application.* Baltimore: Williams & Wilkins.

King, G. (in press). The meaning of life experiences: Application of a meta-model to rehabilitation sciences and services. *American Journal of Orthopsychiatry, 74*(1).

King, G., King, S., & Rosenbaum, P. (1996). Interpersonal aspects of care-giving and client outcomes: A review of the literature. *Ambulatory Child Health, 2,* 151–160.

Kinney, V. B., & Coyle, C. P. (1992). Predicting life satisfaction among adults with physical disabilities. *Archives of Physical Medicine and Rehabilitation, 73,* 863–869.

Klinger, E. (1975). Consequences of commitment to and disengagement from incentives. *Psychological Review, 82,* 1–25.

Klinger, E. (1977). *Meaning and void: Inner experience and incentives in people's lives.* Minneapolis: University of Minnesota Press.

Kobasa, S. C. (1979). Stressful life events, personality, and health: An inquiry into hardiness. *Journal of Personality and Social Psychology, 37,* 1–11.

Lemle, M. (1997, March–April). Son of the morning star. *New Planet, 20.*

Levinson, D. J. (with Darrow, C. N., Klein, E. B., Levinson, M. H., & McKee, B.) (1978). *The seasons of a man's life.* New York: Knopf.

Levinson, D. J. (1986). A conception of adult development. *American Psychologist, 41,* 3–13.

Levinson, D. J. (1996). *The seasons of a woman's life.* New York: Alfred A. Knopf.

Lincoln, Y., & Guba, E. (1985). *Naturalistic inquiry.* Newbury Park, CA: Sage.

Lundy, D. (1998). *Godforsaken sea: Racing the world's most dangerous waters.* Toronto: Alfred A. Knopf Canada.

Maslow, A. H. (1970). *Motivation and personality* (2nd ed.). New York: Harper & Row.

Masten, A. S. (2001). Ordinary magic: Resilience processes in development. *American Psychologist, 56*(3), 227–238.

Mathews, G. (1996). *What makes life worth living?: How Japanese and Americans make sense of their worlds.* Berkeley: University of California Press.

Naess, S. (1987). *Quality of life research. Concepts, methods, and applications.* Oslo: Institute of Applied Social Research.

O'Leary, V.E., Alday, C.S., & Ickovics, J.R. (1998). Models of life change and posttraumatic growth. In R.G. Tedeschi, C.L. Park, & L.G. Calhoun (Eds.), *Posttraumatic growth: Positive changes in the aftermath of crisis* (pp. 127–152). Mahwah, NJ: Erlbaum.

Oates, W. (1971). *Confessions of a workaholic: The facts about work addiction.* New York: World Publishing Company.

Orlean, S. (1998). *The orchid thief.* New York: Ballantine.

Parker, R.B. (1993). *Double deuce.* New York: Berkley Books.

Partridge, J., & Stueck, W. (2000, February 25). $120 million diamond deal caps Canada's richest divorce. *The Globe and Mail,* pp. A1, A6.

Pearlin, L.I., & Schooler, C. (1982). The structure of coping. In H.I. McCubbin, A.E. Cauble, & J.M. Patterson (Eds.), *Family stress, coping, and social support* (pp. 109–135). Springfield, IL: Charles C. Thomas.

Pender, N.J. (1987). *Health promotion in nursing practice* (2nd ed.). Norwalk, CT: Appleton & Lange, 1987.

Perls, F. (1973). *The gestalt approach and eye witness to therapy.* Palo Alto, CA: Science and Behavior Books.

Rajecki, D.W. (1982). *Attitudes: Themes and advances.* Sunderland, MA: Sinauer Associates.

Raphael, D., Brown, I., Renwick, R., & Rootman, I. (1996). Assessing the quality of life of persons with developmental disabilities: Description of a new model, measuring instruments, and initial findings. *International Journal of Disability, Development and Education, 43,* 25–42.

Raynor, J.O. (1982). A theory of personality functioning and change. In J.O. Raynor & E.E. Entin (Eds.), *Motivation, career striving, and aging* (pp. 249–302). Washington, DC: Hemisphere.

Sachs, W. (1999). Planet dialectics: Explorations in environment and development. New York: Zed Books.

Salebey, D. (1992). *The strengths perspective in social work practice.* White Plains, NY: Longman.

Sandidge, R.L., & Ward, A.C. (1999). Reframing. In J.F. Gardner & S. Nudler (Eds.), *Quality performance in human services: Leadership values, and vision* (pp. 201–221). Baltimore: Paul H. Brookes.

Schalock, R.L. (1990). *Quality of life: Perspectives and issues.* Washington, DC: American Association on Mental Retardation.

Schaefer, J.A., & Moos, R.H. (1992). Life crises and personal growth. In B.N. Carpenter (Ed.), *Personal coping: Theory, research, and application* (pp. 149–170). Westport, CT: Praeger.

Schwandt, T. (1994). Constructivist, interpretivist approaches to human inquiry. In N.K. Denzin & Y.S. Lincoln (Eds.), *Handbook of qualitative research* (pp. 118–137). Thousand Oaks, CA: Sage.

Sheehy, G. (1982). *Pathfinders.* New York: Bantam Books.

Smokowski, P.R., Reynolds, A.J., & Bezruczko, N. (1999). Resilience and protective factors in adolescence: An autobiographical perspective from disadvantaged youth. *Journal of School Psychology, 37,* 25–448.

Stewart, A.J., & Ostrove, J.M. (1998). Women's personality in middle age. Gender, history, and midcourse corrections. *American Psychologist, 53*(11), 1185–1194.

Tennen, H., & Affleck, G. (1998). Personality and transformation in the face of adversity. In R.G. Tedeschi, C.L. Park, & L.G. Calhoun (Eds.), *Posttraumatic growth: Positive changes in the aftermath of crisis* (pp. 65–98). Mahwah, NJ: Erlbaum.

Thoits, P.A. (1985). Social support and psychological well-being: Theoretical possibilities. In I.G. Sarason & B.R. Sarason (Eds.), *Social support: Theory, research and application* (pp. 51–72). Boston: Nijhoff.

Triandis, H. (1971). *Attitude and attitude change.* New York: Wiley.

Vandewater, E.A., Ostrove, J.M., & Stewart, A.J. (1997). Predicting women's well-being in midlife: The importance of personality development and social role involvements. *Journal of Personality and Social Psychology, 72*(5), 1147–1160.

Wagnild, G.M., & Young, H.M. (1993). Development and psychometric evaluation of the Resilience Scale. *Journal of Nursing Measurement, 1*(2), 165–178.

Watson, J. (1985). *Nursing: The philosophy and science of caring.* Boulder: Colorado Associated University Press.

Wax, J. (1972). The inner life: A new dimension of rehabilitation. *Journal of Rehabilitation, 38*(6), 16–18.

Weinberg, S. (1977). *The first three minutes: A modern view of the origin of the universe.* New York: Basic Books.

Whitcher-Alagna, S. (1983). Receiving medical help: A psychosocial perspective on patient reactions. In A. Nadler, J.D. Fisher, & B.M. DePaulo (Eds.), *New directions in helping: Vol. 3. Applied perspectives on help-seeking and receiving.* New York: Academic Press.

Willer, B., Linn, R., & Allen, K. (1996). Community integration and barriers to integration for individuals with brain injury. In M.A.J. Finlayson & S. Garner (Eds.), *Brain injury rehabilitation: Clinical considerations* (pp. 355–375). Baltimore: Williams & Wilkings.

Wolfensberger, W. (1994). Let's hang up "quality of life" as a hopeless term. In D. Goode (Ed.), *Quality of life for persons with disabilities: International perspectives and issues* (pp. 285–321). Cambridge, MA: Brookline.

INDEX

ABOUT THE EDITORS
AND CONTRIBUTORS

Gillian A. King was the primary investigator for the research study on which this book is based. She is also the lead editor of the book. Gillian has a doctorate in social psychology and has had numerous articles published in peer-reviewed journals on an array of topics. Gillian is the director of the Research Program at Thames Valley Children's Centre in London, Ontario, Canada. In addition, she is the director of the Research Alliance for Children with Special Needs, based in London, Ontario, which aims to enhance the participation of children with special needs. From 1989 to 2003, she was a research investigator with *CanChild* Centre for Childhood Disability Research, based at McMaster University in Hamilton, Ontario.

Elizabeth G. Brown is one of three editors. Liz is a social worker who has practiced in clinical settings for several years. Interviews with many of the 15 people whose stories you will hear in the book were conducted by Liz in her role as research associate at Thames Valley Children's Centre.

Linda K. Smith is also one of the book editors. In her position as research officer at Thames Valley Children's Centre, Linda is responsible for the creation and dissemination of accessible and practical research publications for therapists, educators, and the broader community.

Tamzin Cathers has an academic background in social and developmental psychology and in social work. As a research associate at Thames Valley Children's Centre for five years, she was involved in many research projects.

Lisa Havens was a mentor at Thames Valley Children's Centre. In this role, Lisa shared her experiences and insights with school-aged children with disabilities. She contributed her intimate understanding of the issues faced by people with disabilities to this book and the research study on which it is based. She has cerebral palsy. Lisa has returned to school to pursue her education in the field of social work.

Elizabeth MacKinnon is a speech-language pathologist in private practice and she manages her own adult rehabilitation services company. Liz has a long history of work in the area of children's rehabilitation services.

Janice Miller Polgar has a doctorate in education and is an occupational therapist and a professor in the School of Occupational Therapy at the University of Western Ontario in London, Ontario. Her commitment to a book on this research study helped us secure a publication grant from the Canadian Occupational Therapy Foundation.

Jacqueline Specht has a doctorate in developmental psychology. She is a professor in the Faculty of Education at the University of Western Ontario. From 1993 to 2003, Jacqueline was a professor in the Psychology Department at Huron University College at the University of Western Ontario.

Colleen Willoughby is an occupational therapist who worked at the Child and Parent Resource Institute in London, Ontario, from 1992 to 2002. This agency provides services to children with emotional and behavioral difficulties and their families. Colleen is now employed by Rehability Occupational Therapy Inc. in London, Ontario.